D1600671

COMING TO THE
EDGE OF
THE CIRCLE

AMERICAN ACADEMY OF RELIGION
ACADEMY SERIES

SERIES EDITOR
Kimberly Rae Connor, University of San Francisco

A Publication Series of
The American Academy of Religion
and
Oxford University Press

CREATIVE DWELLING
Empathy and Clarity in God and Self
Lucinda A. Stark Huffaker

HOSPITALITY TO STRANGERS
Empathy and the Physician-Patient Relationship
Dorothy M. Owens

THE BONDS OF FREEDOM
Feminist Theology and Christian Realism
Rebekah L. Miles

THE SPECTER OF SPECIESISM
Buddhist and Christian Views of Animals
Paul Waldau

INCARNATION AND PHYSICS
Natural Science in the Theology of Thomas F. Torrance
Tapio Luoma

OF BORDERS AND MARGINS
Hispanic Disciples in Texas, 1888–1945
Daisy L. Machado

HSIEH LIANG-TSO AND THE ANALECTS OF CONFUCIUS
Humane Learning as a Religious Quest
Thomas W. Selover

YVES CONGAR'S THEOLOGY OF THE HOLY SPIRIT
Elizabeth Teresa Groppe

GREGORY OF NYSSA AND THE CONCEPT OF DIVINE PERSONS
Lucian Turcescu

GRAHAM GREENE'S CATHOLIC IMAGINATION
Mark Bosco, S.J.

COMING TO THE EDGE OF THE CIRCLE
A Wiccan Initiation Ritual
Nikki Bado-Fralick

AMERICAN ACADEMY OF RELIGION

COMING TO THE EDGE OF THE CIRCLE

A Wiccan Initiation Ritual

NIKKI BADO-FRALICK

OXFORD
UNIVERSITY PRESS

2005

Library
Quest University Canada
3200 University Boulevard
Squamish, BC V8B 0N8

OXFORD
UNIVERSITY PRESS

Oxford University Press, Inc., publishes works that further
Oxford University's objective of excellence
in research, scholarship, and education.

Oxford   New York
Auckland   Cape Town   Dar es Salaam   Hong Kong   Karachi
Kuala Lumpur   Madrid   Melbourne   Mexico City   Nairobi
New Delhi   Shanghai   Taipei   Toronto

With offices in
Argentina   Austria   Brazil   Chile   Czech Republic   France   Greece
Guatemala   Hungary   Italy   Japan   Poland   Portugal   Singapore
South Korea   Switzerland   Thailand   Turkey   Ukraine   Vietnam

Copyright © 2005 by The American Academy of Religion

Published by Oxford University Press, Inc.
198 Madison Avenue, New York, New York 10016

www.oup.com

Oxford is a registered trademark of Oxford University Press

All rights reserved. No part of this publication may be reproduced,
stored in a retrieval system, or transmitted, in any form or by any means,
electronic, mechanical, photocopying, recording, or otherwise,
without the prior permission of Oxford University Press.

Library of Congress Cataloging-in-Publication Data
Bado-Fralick, Nikki.
Coming to the edge of the circle : a Wiccan initiation ritual / Nikki Bado-Fralick.
    p. cm.—(American Academy of Religion academy series)
Includes bibliographical references and index.
ISBN-13 978-0-19-516645-3
ISBN 0-19-516645-0
1. Initiation rites—Religious aspects—Ohio. 2. Rites and ceremonies—Ohio. 3. Witchcraft—Ohio.
I. Title. II. Series.
BL615.B33 2005
299'.94—dc22   2005002176

9 8 7 6 5 4 3 2 1

Printed in the United States of America
on acid-free paper

Dedicated to my husband,
Eric Fralick,
who believed in me before I did

Preface

In this book, I use a detailed description of a particular kind of religious initiation ritual from a specific community in order to challenge our assumptions about rites of passage, questioning a paradigm that has changed little since its creation by Arnold van Gennep in the early 1900s. In particular, I hope to challenge notions of initiation as a tripartite process with sharply defined movements of separation, liminality, and reincorporation. This etically derived tripartite model and its variations usually employ a unidirectional spatiality and a linear understanding of the process of transformation. But when approaching the ceremony from the dual perspectives of a scholar-practitioner, a linear and spatial analysis proves inadequate to describe particular emic aspects of the ceremony.

As a practitioner and an interdisciplinary scholar, my approach to initiation is necessarily reflexive and pluralistic. Within a broad philosophical framework, I draw upon the insights and methods of ethnographic folklore studies, somatic theories, metacommunication theories, feminist critiques, and especially a performance approach, in order to access meaningful aspects of the initiation within both the immediate and larger process of a particular ritual performance.

I explore an initiation ritual performed by a small coven of Witches located in Ohio. Members of this religious community, called either Wiccans or Witches within this book, practice a contemporary nature religion variously called Wicca, Witchcraft, the Old Religion, or the Craft by its practitioners. Wicca is an extremely diverse and decentralized religion with a great deal of local autonomy in membership, practices, and organizational structure.

Although I think a close examination of other forms of initiation ritual might also compel us to reconsider the tripartite paradigm, there are many reasons that this group's ritual works particularly well. Within this specific religious group, initiation is both a ceremony through which an individual becomes a member of the community and a central, significant transformative religious experience that is arrived at through an extensive learning process.

Key to understanding this process is a concept of ritual expertise as a somatic praxis, a repetitive discipline that engages both the body and the mind in learning. Also significant is the emergence through praxis of "intimacy" as a worldview or cultural orientation that is objective but personal, in which relations are interdependent, and in which knowledge has an affective and somatic dimension and is dark or esoteric. An examination of how Wiccans deliberately cultivate somatic praxis and an intimacy orientation may, in turn, give us clues about how ritual performances and praxis function in other religions as well.

My ultimate goal is to employ a perspective as both scholar and practitioner to enable us to capture new information, to weave new and more accurate models and paradigms into our scholarship. I hope to challenge and extend our scholarship on ritual more generally, allowing us to pose questions about rituals in other religious communities, and to think about rituals in some new and profitable way.

Acknowledgments

I have many people to thank in the creation and production of this work. My deepest thanks goes to those scholars who most influenced me: Tom Kasulis, Pat Mullen, Nancy Falk, and Dan Barnes. As my advisors, Tom and Pat were not only willing to take a chance on an unusual project, but also helped me develop my ideas across two very different disciplines— philosophy and folklore. Dan's unfailing support bolstered my confidence during rocky times. And Nancy has inspired and challenged me from the very moment I met her.

I am incredibly lucky to count these fine scholars as mentors and friends.

Deep appreciation also goes to the series editors and my anonymous outside readers, whose comments and criticisms have made this a more compelling work. Thank you, Carol Myscofski, for soliciting this book; Kim Connor, for relentlessly tracking down appropriate readers; and Cynthia Read, for trusting in my book enough to go the extra distance. Special thanks to my production editor, Stacey Hamilton, and copyeditor, Kelly Martin, whose detailed and discerning eye made sure all i's are dotted, t's are crossed, and no participles dangle precipitously.

I must also thank my family: my brother, George, for his cheerful confidence in me, and my husband's parents, Charles B. and the late Mary E. Fralick, for their encouragement and support, and for the Apple laptop computer that made this technologically possible. I have Chuck to thank for the photographs in this book; he patiently took shot after shot in blistering Iowa summer heat.

Tremendous thanks to my husband, Eric Fralick, who, in his guise as first and best editor, has encouraged me to make this a more readable book as I translated the original from academese into something more resembling English. I hope you agree.

Thanks also to the editors of *Folklore Forum*, where some of my ideas have previously appeared in articles: "A Turning on the Wheel of Life: Wiccan Rites of Death," *Folklore Forum* 29.1 (1998): 3–12, and "Mapping the Wiccan Ritual Landscape: Circles of Transformation," *Folklore Forum* 33.1/2 (2002): 45–65. Guidance from *Folklore Forum* editors and readers helped sharpen my thinking on several counts.

I would like to thank two additional sources of information for this book. Thanks to the editors of the *Religious Studies Newsletter* for permission to quote from articles by Nancy Falk and Laurie Patton. These articles are used by permission of the American Academy of Religion and Religious Studies News-AAR Edition. Grateful thanks also to the editors of *Western Folklore*, for permisson to quote from their special issue of "Reflexivity and the Study of Belief."

I must thank those many friends and colleagues with whom I have been blessed over the years. They helped me through this most difficult process with their patience, encouragement, jokes, chocolate, occasional shopping sprees, sympathetic ears, and their willingness to see and hear endless drafts of this work. A special thanks to my dear colleagues of the Midwest Region of the AAR, who have heard many first drafts of my ideas. And thanks to my colleagues at Iowa State who read all or parts of the manuscript—our reading group "Straw Dogs," and especially Eric Northway, who gamely suffered through all chapters.

It should go without saying that this project could not have been done at all without the support of the Merry Circle. I miss you all terribly: Rita, Smike, Brian, Karen, and John. And especially Lauren, Dot, and Sandy— you three will always be true sisters and part of my heart. My thanks and blessings go to all of you, wherever the path may take you in the future.

Finally, let me thank my students in my religious studies classes, who are, ultimately, the reason why I do this at all.

Contents

1 Dancing between Binary Poles: Life as a Scholar-Practitioner, 3

2 Stumbling toward Wisdom, 23

3 The Merry Circle, 43

4 The Path toward the Circle, 63

5 The Rite of Dedication: Getting behind the Wheel, 87

6 Coming to the Edge of the Circle, 113

7 Concluding Remarks, 141

Epilogue: She Changes Everything She Touches, 147

Notes, 149

Selected Bibliography, 161

Index, 177

COMING TO THE
EDGE OF
THE CIRCLE

1

Dancing between Binary Poles

Life as a Scholar-Practitioner

Standing at the Edge of the Circle

Witches say you'll never forget your initiation into the Craft. This may be true; the memory of my own is vividly alive to me, although it happened nearly thirty years ago. I can still feel the hardness of the chair I sat in, my eyes fixed inwardly in reflection while the flame of a candle glowed softly against the darkness, its flickering light setting shadows dancing. I concentrated on my breath, counting slowly, trying with varying degrees of success to breathe myself into a state of deliberate calmness. The cavernous room of the old house had a slight chill to it, even though the time for chill was nearly past.

It was May in Ohio.

Maybe the chill came from the sound of Walter Carlos's[1] synthesized wolves howling to their winter moon, their stark music set to distract me from sounds I could barely make out, coming from the rooms above. Surely the shiver came from the cold and not from hearing the soft tread of footsteps on the stairs, someone coming to bring me to the edge of the Circle,[2] to the place of my own death and rebirth—for that is precisely what initiation into the Craft is.

Now, after so many years, I stand again at the edge of the Circle and wait, reflecting. That many things change is not surprising in nearly thirty cycles of the Solar Wheel. The cavernous room and the old house have long been replaced by a grove of trees and an arc of sky, sprinkled tonight with stars and ominous flashes that we hope are only heat lightning. No electronic wolves serenade the moon tonight with their howls; I hear only the chirp of crickets, the occasional squawk of a night bird, and the ever-present whine of mosquitoes. I am no longer a newcomer to the old ways, but a High Priestess in my lineage, one who is well seasoned in the rites of initiation.

Yet surprisingly, some things seem the same. Shadows still flicker, set dancing now by the bonfire at the center of the Circle, useful tonight more for its light than its heat. I still breathe myself into a state of calm awareness, but now automatically, my body adopting the ritual mode without thinking. The familiar shiver returns, despite the fire and the sticky warmth of the night, as I hear footsteps along the path. The initiate-to-be is brought to the edge of the Circle, where I—hooded and robed as Death—await to deliver the challenge that ultimately transforms. . . .

At Play in a Universe of Lights and Shadows

According to a kind of scholarly thinking once quite common in both ethnography and the academic study of religions, the previous paragraphs label me an "insider," a believer, and that immediately makes my scholarship suspect.

The insider/outsider problem remains one of the most controversial and divisive issues among scholars of religions and belief studies,[3] affecting not only whose voices are heard within the Academy, but the hiring and tenure processes within universities as well.[4] The dichotomy between insider and outsider, or native and nonnative, reserves scientific objectivity only for the outsider. Insider knowledge is perceived as tainted with subjectivity and is therefore useless to the serious scholar.

As both a scholar and a long-term practitioner, I feel compelled to confront head on the dilemmas of the insider/outsider issue before continuing with either description or analysis of Wiccan initiation ritual. (Those of you who instead wish to continue with me on the journey to the Circle's edge may proceed to chapter 2.)

I have encountered several instances of the insider/outsider dichotomy in my career. As an undergraduate studying the philosophy of religion, I was advised early on that it would be best to study a religion that was either "long ago or far away—preferably both." Such ethnographic distance was thought to provide a fortress for scholars, surrounding them with a protective moat of objectivity that insulated them from the potentially messy and sometimes contentious interactions with, or criticisms of, natives who might disagree with their scholarly analysis. In the ethnography of the times, it was perfectly acceptable for a scholar to adopt the stance of participant/observer as long as he was careful not to participate *too* much. "Going native" was an egregious sin tantamount to committing scholarly suicide.

While this situation has changed considerably in the field of ethnography,[5] it can be argued that religious studies has lagged behind. In 1990, a few years after receiving that bit of undergraduate philosophical wisdom, I submitted an abstract for my first paper at the national American Academy of Religion conference. The subject of that paper, which was later accepted and presented at the conference, was the influence of the women's movement on The Old Religion—a topic that makes me an insider in at least two major directions. While my being a woman was curiously ignored as a possibly contaminating influence,[6] I was advised by the section chair not to make my abstract sound too much like it was written by a religious practitioner in order to avoid the appearance of insider pleading or Wiccan apologetics.

With these experiences in mind, I acknowledge that identifying myself as a Wiccan High Priestess can be a risky venture. At the extreme, it may call forth a response similar to the one Donald Sutherland received in the movie remake of *Invasion of the Body Snatchers*: having survived all sorts of harrowing scrapes, he was discovered in the end to be "other" and was encircled by pointing pod people. Is revealing myself as insider tantamount to identifying myself as other to the scholarly enterprise, the equivalent of committing scholarly suicide?

Let's see if we can get beyond the insider/outsider dichotomy into a more useful way of understanding and utilizing the work of scholar-practitioners. Is the insider/outsider distinction even an accurate or useful one? The scholarship that produces the insider/outsider distinction shares some similarities with other forms of dichotomous thinking, producing such binary oppositions as subjective versus objective and practice versus theory. In fact, the poles of these binary oppositions are frequently philosophically aligned: outsider/objective/theory against insider/subjective/practice. These distinctions are often far too easily and quickly made, concealing the underlying assumptions making the distinction problematic.

The insider/outsider distinction assumes that there is only *one* insider voice, or that insider perspectives are uniform or monolithic. It also implies that there is only one correct or objective outsider voice, an assumption rarely entertained seriously by scholars familiar with the diversity of scholarly voices and the competition of scholarly perspectives with one another. Perhaps less familiar to the scholar is the fact that insiders also express varying perspectives and disagree among themselves at least as much as scholars do. Dichotomous thinking almost always essentializes, reducing each end of the binary construction to a uniform monolith not reflected in actual human experience. Rather than a single, unitary voice or perspective, the terms insider and outsider conceal an entire realm of discourse engaged in by a multitude of shifting voices and perspectives in negotiation or even in contestation with one another. Religious practice, like scholarly practice, tends to be a messy affair, with various descriptions, judgments, analyses, and outright opinions contending, and sometimes conflicting, with one another. In religious practice, as in scholarship, there is more than one legitimate point of view.

And dichotomous thinking is problematic in itself. Dichotomies are sets of binary absolutes that function logically as "on/off" switches. No interplay or dynamic shifting tension is implied between the binary pairs. Why is this an important point? A metaphor of light and dark, inspired by the pre-Socratic philosophers,[7] gets at the difference between a dynamic polarity and a dichotomous absolute. In dichotomous thinking, light and dark function as absolutes, very much like the on/off light switch we're familiar with in our homes. In absolute darkness, we are blind. In absolute light, we are also blind. If sight is the point, neither absolute darkness nor absolute light gives us what we want. It is only through the dynamic interplay of light and dark—the shifting of lights and shadows—that sight exists. Furthermore, we are able to see differently according to the degree in which the lights and shadows play with one another. This shifting play of light and dark, the dynamic tension between and movement of lights and shadows, produces the wondrous multitude of sights and perspectives possible in the human experience.

How does this light/dark metaphor help us understand the problem with the insider/outsider dichotomy? And why have I emphasized the word play above? The static binary absolutes produced by dichotomous thinking conceal the extent to which each of the binary pairs actually does play with its opposite in human experience. Objective and outsider, used together to describe the "proper" scholarly stance vis-à-vis religion, conceal the constructed rhetoric of scholarly discourse. All knowledge—including scholarly knowledge—is a mixture of shifting degrees of objectivity and subjectivity, distance and closeness, outsider and insider, theory and practice. Knowing is an activity; it is a doing, a *praxis*[8]—the dynamic participation in and creation of a "discourse of lights and shadows" that constantly shifts and changes to reveal new perspectives or to accommodate new voices. Knowledge, then, is experiential and perspectival. Emphasizing the ludic element draws our attention to the degree of creativity and constructedness, the play and perspective obtained in the human experience of knowing.

Dichotomous thinking is therefore unsatisfactory in several respects. It obscures the range of perspectives, activities, and voices in each end of the binary pair. It misconstrues the relationship of the binary pairs to one another, concealing the extent to which such oppositions as insider/outsider, objective/subjective actually play off of one another dynamically and intertwine in human experience. Dichotomous thinking obscures both the practices of scholars and the theories of practitioners. It obscures the playful, creative, and constructed praxis of knowledge making.

Although many ethnographers today recognize the inadequacy of dichotomous thinking[9] and some fine reflexive and nonreductionistic ethnographies have been produced by folklorists and anthropologists,[10] the insider/outsider dichotomy is nevertheless difficult for some scholars of religions to give up.[11] For these scholars, insider pleading poses a very real problem and remains a threat to scholarly objectivity.[12]

Is insider scholarship or the work of scholar-practitioners *automatically* the same thing as insider pleading or religious advocacy? Does insider knowledge taint my scholarship with bias, making it less worthy of consideration than an outsider's perspective? Is a nonnative or outsider's perspective automatically more trustworthy, more accurate than that of a native informant who is also a scholar?

Such questions are ultimately rooted in a culture of disbelief, or what folklorist David Hufford calls a stance of "methodological atheism."[13] Methodological atheism goes beyond the bracketing of truth claims familiar to us in phenomenology or the suspension of judgment that simple agnosticism or skepticism would entail.[14] Hufford notes a shift in the meaning of rational skepticism from simple methodological doubt or suspension of certainty to a fixed disbelief that warps its usage as a methodology in belief studies.[15]

Skepticism thus moves from the idea of suspended judgment to a determination that certain kinds of traditional religious ideas are false. This "naively advances one culturally loaded belief" (methodological atheism) "as dispassionate neutrality" and fails completely to "grant atheism its due as a *religious* position" (italics mine).[16] While methodological atheism pretends to be a "neutral position" that requires no "reflexive component," it demands that scholars with any other methodological posture "display personal reflexivity *in a social context that guarantees such reflexivity will result in charges of bias unless one's scholarly work discredits one's personal beliefs*" (italics in the original).[17] Within the culture of disbelief, the scholar-practitioner is left with an unappealing choice between religion and scholarship, forcing allegiance to one and betrayal of the other.

Less often considered by the academic community, but often equally important to the religious community, are the parallel questions: Does scholarship taint my religious practice? Can I simultaneously be both a real Witch capable of performing effective and magical rituals and a questioning scholar aware of the constructed nature of ritual performance? Religious practitioners are all too familiar with scholarly treatments of their religions that are rooted in the culture of disbelief. By extending beyond mere suspension of judgment, the culture of disbelief must *necessarily* explain away religious experience as an essential and fundamental "misrecognition" on the part of practitioners. What is *really* going on is either some form of psychological wish-fulfillment or neurosis (Freud), or society worshipping itself (Durkheim), or an outright failure on the part of the religious to realize that they are being duped by an agent of economic oppression (Marx).

That human religious experiences frequently have psychological, sociopolitical, and economic dimensions is not at issue. These dimensions are worthy of nearly endless exploration, and are the driving force behind much of the academic study of religion. What is frequently missed, however, is an appreciation of the quality that remains when a religious experience has been reduced as far as possible by such study, a quality that a practitioner would identify as the essence of religion. Thus the issue becomes what is missed by a reduction of religious experiences to everything *but* something called "religion." Folklorist Diane Goldstein notes that "the centrality of emotional and experiential factors to religious life must be *described* and *understood* before religious scholarship can claim any kind of empirical adequacy."[18] Even when the power of ritual performance is recognized,[19] it is removed from its context in the embodied world of ritual praxis. It is duly cleansed of any reference to the transformative power of magic, prayer, or other discourse of faith. And it is understood by scholars as disembodied text, its power reduced to that of narrative—the power of words to represent or symbolize the possibility of changes that are primarily psychological or political in nature.

While text and narrative undoubtedly have great power, they are not the only things capable of effecting transformation. Nor is the disembodied text of scholarship likely to be recognized by religious practitioners as the agent of change capable of effecting transformation in the *physical* or *objective* world as well as in the psychological or subjective world. Such a reduction misses or fails to address what "feels real"[20] to the religious practitioner. It does not "capture magic."

Confronting the "m-word"—magic—head on, ritual studies scholar Tom Driver, in his book *The Magic of Ritual*, points us to an interesting curiosity:

> Many persons in Western society are skeptical of any transformative powers that may be claimed for ritual, except perhaps the inducement of changes that can be taken as primarily subjective or psychological in nature. This skepticism, being partly a matter of ideology, is strongest in those sectors of society that would have the most to lose were any major social transformation to occur. . . . One way of guarding the status quo against change is to deny the rationality of any expectation that rituals can do much to alter it.[21]

Faced with the actual practice of religious rituals or magic, a scholar working from the methodological stance of cultural disbelief can always simply throw up her hands in bafflement over how seemingly normal, well-educated adults could *possibly* believe this stuff! And when such a scholar obtains her data from religious communities by merely *posing* as a believer or practitioner and subsequently publishes the results, the religious community is likely to interpret her scholarship as an act of betrayal.

The level of mistrust and suspicion can therefore be quite high between the scholarly and the religious communities. Certainly, neither scholars nor religious practitioners have all the right answers, or even all the right questions. Neither group automatically *misrecognizes*, but both scholars and religious practitioners may *differently*, yet also *legitimately*, recognize.

The mere suggestion that religious practitioners may have legitimate insights into religious phenomena calls forth a curious response from some of my colleagues, as if this were the equivalent of saying that religious practitioners have the *only* valid perspective or that scholars must now believe in magic, perform rituals, or deliver emotional and heartfelt testimony as to the power of prayer. Certainly this response is as ludicrous as the idea that the religious always misrecognize. Yet this reaction indicates to what extent our scholarship on religion is rooted in the either/or stance of the culture of disbelief, a stance that ultimately demands an untenable allegiance to a single, monolithic perspective. A more accurate description of the task at hand involves the exploration of a multitude of perspectives—a discourse of lights and shadows—that will yield the most insight into experiences of the sacred.

In the rather unlikely event that relations between scholars and religious practitioners were suddenly to become unproblematic, crucial questions nevertheless remain for the scholar-practitioner. Can a person be *both* a devoted religious practitioner and a serious scholar without compromising the integrity of either? Is it possible to participate competently in multiple discourses, to be simultaneously informed by both scholarly and religious praxis without reducing either one to the other or confusing the two?

Because I am a "self-professed" Witch (as we are so often referred to by the media), it will not come as a shock that I sympathize with religious practitioners when they receive insensitive, arrogant, and even unethical treatment from scholars. I also worry about insider pleading or apologetics, but I think scholars misdiagnose—misrecognize, if you will—the problem. Typically, the issue is framed as a loss of objectivity to the subjectivity of religious practice. Careful examination of the problematic nature of dichotomous thinking reveals that this is not the case. But what can happen is a misunderstanding—a kind of category mistake—that conflates one kind of praxis with another, in this case confusing religious affirmation or advocacy with scholarship. Such a category mistake is often caused by a failure to apprehend the nature of scholarly praxis or a failure to recognize the differences between scholarly and religious forms of praxes.

A metaphor from language philosopher Ludwig Wittgenstein's *Philosophical Investigations* may shed some light on our problem. Wittgenstein conceived of ordinary language as a living game that has its own dynamically evolving set of rules, acceptable moves, and winning strategies. To master the game, the language player must first learn and eventually internalize the rules of the game—what works, what doesn't, what counts as a good move, what is illegal, what becomes a winning play—until the rules and strategies become almost invisible and function on the level of habit. We can also imagine several levels of skill between the level of beginner or learner and that of expert or highly accomplished player.

The image of a person skillfully playing a game now suggests several provocative directions for the comparative study of both religious and scholarly discourses. We can begin by thinking about these discourses as kinds of games, however serious, very much like Wittgenstein's language game. So, like games, let's assume that religious and scholarly discourses have their own sets of rules, acceptable moves, and winning strategies. We can also safely assume that each discourse, or game, has many levels of skill, ranging from beginner to expert, and that it will be possible to evaluate those levels by the criteria appropriate to that particular game.

We might begin by asking questions about the nature of the games themselves: How might the games of religious and scholarly discourse differ from one another? In what ways might they be similar? How do games of scholarly and religious discourse function within our society? As a scholar myself, I suspect that one source of the uneasiness of many scholars with respect to religious praxis may be that scholarly and religious discourses sometimes share common goals or common agendas. Each is often concerned with describing the way the world works, and each may be invested in changing that world to a greater or lesser extent. Religious and scholarly discourses compete and sometimes conflict in the process of worldmaking.

We can extend our questions about the games to questions about the players' expertise and competence. The image of a person skillfully playing a game moves our attention away from allegiance to expertise. It recontextualizes our study at the level of practice. This suggests several lines of inquiry that help us to access the multiple roles and skill levels of the players: What is the process by which a person learns how to play a particular game? How does a person progress from beginner to master of the game? What skills must be acquired to teach the game to others, or to form evaluative judgments about how other players play the game? What happens when the game is played unsuccessfully or unskillfully? Can skills be faked? What skills must be mastered in order to explain the game to a nonplayer?

These questions readily apply to players of different sorts of games. For example, let's apply these questions to a game of chess. We can now set out to discover what skills are involved in learning how to play chess, what it takes to become a chess master, and what skills are necessary to explain or teach the game to a nonplayer. Now change the game to checkers. Or poker. Our attention stays focused on skill and expertise, not allegiance to a particular game. We don't admonish or critique masters of chess because they don't play checkers. We don't evaluate poker players with the rules we discover in checkers. And we don't confuse the games.

Religious practice and scholarly practice fit as readily into our model as chess and checkers. Let's take the papers written by two students in my class on Women and Religion as an illustration. The assignment was to research some aspect of women and religion, broadly defined, and to present the findings in a paper roughly ten to fifteen pages in length. The paper needed to have a central thesis, to develop a coherent argument based on relevant scholarship, and to make some point that illuminated an aspect of women's religious lives. One of the papers was written by a male Catholic, the other by a female Pagan who was interested in Wicca. The Catholic chose the issue of female ordination in the Catholic Church for his topic and agreed with the Church's stance. The Pagan wrote an unfocused paper, its topic ranging from women's esteemed role in religion at the dawn of time, to the creation of patriarchy by invading hordes, and finally to the millions of (women) Witches persecuted during the Inquisition.

Both papers were failures. Why?

At this point, dichotomous thinking might lead us summarily to diagnose the students' failures as due to insider pleading or as examples of religious advocacy. Each paper reflected some aspect of religious practice on the part of the writer. The Catholic wrote a straightforward account of the Pope's statements or the Church's ruling on the issue of women and the priesthood. He presented, without question, justification, or explanation, what many practicing Catholics might reasonably be expected to accept and follow. The Pagan also accepted, without critical reflection or argument, one and only one line of interpretation about the role of women in what appear to be ancient Goddess religions, the rise of patriarchy, and the subsequent persecution during the Inquisition of women as Witches.

Yet a closer look at the two papers reveals that finding them to be insider pleading or religious advocacy is not really an accurate diagnosis. The students' papers were problematic in similar ways, but in ways that had *nothing to do with a loss of objectivity* due to religious practice and *everything to do with an ignorance or misunderstanding of the nature of scholarly practice*. The Catholic's paper was an almost unbroken series of quotes from Web sites that affirmed, or simply listed, the Church's position on women and the priesthood, advocating this position without attempt at argument or presentation of reasoning. The Pagan's paper was an extremely unfocused and very poorly written rehash of some of the most popular and, at the same time, controversial mythic themes in certain Pagan and feminist spirituality circles.[22] Both topics chosen by the students are potentially worthy of scholarly exploration and could have led to fine papers. But in these particular papers, the students presented no analysis, no development of context or rationale for the various statements, no articulation of the issues at stake, no reference to the copious amounts of scholarship (pro and con) on the issues, no central thesis, and no well-developed argument—actually no argument at all.

Both students failed not because of religious praxis, but because they failed to understand the requirements of scholarly praxis. The students' scholarly objectivity was not clouded or compromised by a contaminating allegiance to a religious practice. Instead, *like many students*, they simply failed to understand what kinds of rhetorical strategies are convincing and appropriate within the discourse of scholarly praxis. Neither student understood what constituted an acceptable piece of academic writing, or, in terms of Wittgenstein's game model, what constituted skillful play or an acceptable move in the game of scholarly discourse.

Closer examination of the two papers has effectively moved the locus of our discussion from questions of allegiance to ones of expertise. Shifting to an examination of the skills required of participants engaged in a particular discourse removes us from the trap of dichotomous thinking that necessarily lurks in the background of any discussion framed in terms of insider/

outsider. Reframing our analysis in terms of skillful practice gives us a way to compare and evaluate differing modes of discourse about religion more fruitfully. We are now ready to explore the range of discourses produced by players from the most elementary to the most advanced levels and from the most scholarly to the most personal of perspectives. This releases us from having to choose between religion and profession and defuses the emotional reactions incumbent upon such a devastating and unnecessary choice. Freed from the blindness imposed by the on/off switch of dichotomy, we are able to see and begin to explore the discourse of lights and shadows at play in the multitude of perspectives taken by both scholars and religious practitioners.

We can also use the game model to ask broader and more comparative questions about the discourses produced by different kinds of religious practice or different kinds of scholarship: How does one form of religious discourse or game resemble or differ from another? Do different types of scholarship require different discourses with different sets of evaluative criteria? What is the range of evaluative criteria employed within and across particular forms of religious discourse? By what criteria do scholars and religious practitioners judge the success or failure of a play of the game? What strategies do the practitioners of particular religious discourses employ to compete with those of other religious discourses? Do practitioners of scholarly discourse employ similarly competitive strategies?

At some point, we might even be tempted to develop a comprehensive set of evaluative criteria for all discourses about religion, a meta-theory for religious discourse. Here we must be careful to avoid making the same sorts of essentializing, reductionizing, and decontextualizing analyses that typically emerge from the insider/outsider dichotomy. Many of the previous questions focus on the nature of *particular* games being played. Beginning our inquiry at this level reduces the risk of producing categories and criteria totally removed from the communities of players who practice the game, the communities that produce the discourse and for whom the discourse is meaningful.[23] Attention to the local—the particular—helps us to capture the plurality of perspectives at play within the spectrum of both scholarly and religious communities. Achieving a semblance of accuracy in description and analysis at the local level helps ensure that our larger and more comparative models reflect that accuracy as much as possible.

We can use the language game model to produce still more questions when moving outside a particular game, or moving between games. Like languages, some games or discourses are similar to one another and share many cognates, while others are more distinct. When the games are similar, a competent player may easily and even fluently move between them with little extra effort or skill, as when a person adapts to different dialects of the same language. When games share few similarities—or when the games differ from one another in critical ways—even the most competent player needs to acquire additional or even totally new sets of skills or strategies to commute successfully between games.

In fact, the image of a commuter may be a particularly productive one to apply to the situation of the scholar-practitioner. In the context of Wittgenstein's games, we might reasonably expect a scholar-practitioner to have the skills necessary to be relatively fluent in both scholarly and religious discourses and to be able to commute fluidly between the two. Framing our discussion in terms of fluency in and fluidity across particular and multiple discourses emphasizes the extent to which we are all engaged as commuters across multiple boundaries every day.[24]

As commuters, we can begin to encounter and explore the plurality of perspectives within the diverse spectrum of both scholarly and religious communities. If, like myself, we are commuters who are both scholars and practitioners, it is important to employ a self-conscious critical reflection or *reflexivity* in order to navigate successfully between the multiplicity of perspectives that we both hold ourselves and encounter among others.

Reflexivity in this context is "the inclusion of the actor (scholar, author, observer) in the account of the act and/or its outcomes."[25] Hufford, in fact, emphasizes the need for a pragmatic and realistic form of reflexivity for *all* scholars, not just scholar-practitioners. In the study of religious discourses, this "necessarily introduces the individual: individual scholars including ourselves as scholars, and individual believers *including all scholars, whether their beliefs be positive or negative or agnostic regarding the beliefs in question*" (italics in the original).[26]

A reflexive methodological stance helps us avoid simplistically framing our analysis in terms of any of our favorite dichotomies. Hufford underscores reflexivity as a negotiating strategy between two equally limiting and dogmatic methodological and theoretical extremes of yet another dichotomy—that between *methodolatry*, a position of no reflexivity, which tries to capture the "confidence of positivism," and an extreme kind of *postmodernism*, a position in which reflexivity is all, which abandons reality or objectivity altogether "and treats ethnographic representation as a literary construction that tells about its authors rather than about the world."[27] He summarizes the importance of a responsible reflexivity that is both realistic and pragmatic:

> We *must* learn to tolerate uncertainty and ambiguity, while holding the reduction of uncertainty and ambiguity in our knowledge as primary goals (always sought, never completely achieved). . . . Certainty is a direction, not a goal. . . . Reflexivity and the strong light that it shines on the importance of viewpoint and perspective urges on us a multiplication of perspectives. We can never have a set of observations made from *every*where anymore than we can have a view from nowhere, but the more views we consider, the more reason we have to be hopeful about our conclusions. (italics in the original)[28]

Every reflexive act dismantles the insider/outsider dichotomy by revealing the perspectives otherwise hidden underneath the analysis. Demanding a self-conscious awareness of the scholar's beliefs and perspectives and then including them in the data frees us from the trap of assigning an unassailable purity to a perspective carefully hidden in the guise of "objective outsider." I suspect many religious studies scholars find the reflexive voice somewhat awkward or uncomfortable either to write or read precisely because it is such a stretch from the safe illusion of objective purity with which we have surrounded our actions for years.

Reflexivity keeps us honest.

It is also hard to do.

Speaking from personal experience, finding and using the reflexive voice can be a rather daunting task. It seems to require a peculiar form of consciousness that is at least peripherally aware of self even as it is engaged with other. I find this experience strikingly similar to, and just as difficult as, watching yourself tie your shoe in a mirror—something I suspect few of us routinely do. Your attention is divided, you feel awkward, your body "all thumbs" as you try to be critically and self-consciously aware of something that you do all the time without thinking. Upon reflection, as it were, I find this an apt metaphor for explaining any particular praxis—scholarly or religious—to those who stand apart from that praxis. Reflexivity entails the development of special skills, the cultivation of a special voice, in order to explain to another what has become deeply ingrained, embodied, and embedded in the psychophysical consciousness.

I find that the reflexive voice requires a delicate sense of balance: too much, this becomes my autobiography and risks falling into narcissistic solipsism; too little, and I haven't provided the information needed to make sense of it all. It is easy to be awkward at establishing a pattern of reflexivity, of finding exactly that *rhythm* of voice that distinguishes the Priestess from the scholar—and the multiple dimensions within each—clearly enough so that the audience can follow along.

Reflexivity demands taking a risk, revealing and making accessible the *person* behind both scholarship and religion. Such an act of self-conscious exposure, of intentional vulnerability, demands courage and skill on the part of the *writer*—a willingness to engage, to reveal that mixture of play and seriousness that intertwine in our perspectives on the multiple worlds within which we live. It also demands openness on the part of the *reader*—a willingness to be engaged to both play with and to consider seriously that multitude of perspectives.

Images in a Mirror: Reflections
as a Scholar of Religions

The necessity of tackling reflexivity as a scholar was forcefully revealed to me during my qualifying examinations. I was in my advisor's office one afternoon, planning the schedule for my upcoming exams and discussing my project. After listening to me talk about how to handle fieldwork, my advisor—a philosopher—said to me, "So, what does your background in *philosophy* have to do with the study of religion? Especially since you work with all that *other* stuff." The stuff in question was an interdisciplinary mix of such disparate elements as folklore, performance theory, ritual studies, and women's studies as my areas of concentration.

Caught up short, I was nevertheless ready with an elegant and eloquent reply: "Beats the hell out of me."

Naturally, his question became part of one of my qualifying exams in the philosophy of religions. Far from being a frivolous question, it was quite difficult to answer, in part because the doctoral degree in religious studies at my university is administratively an interdisciplinary one. As such, it is not a degree in folklore, in women's studies, in ritual studies, in philosophy—or even in religion. While obviously not a degree of specialized expertise, I reasoned that perhaps the value of my program lies somewhere in the in-between of these fields, the *inter* of interdisciplinary, or in the weaving of disciplines like threads in a tapestry. In any event, not an altogether promising place to go looking for philosophy.

The other, more daunting task in answering this question was that it actually required something very hard to do: reflexivity, that peculiar form of awareness that consciously engages both self and other, that consciously engages in both acting and capturing that acting. But, I reasoned, perhaps the interdisciplinary nature of my program made such reflection all the more imperative. Taking a deep breath and picking up the mirror of reflexivity, I asked myself, "Ok. So, where *is* the philosophy in what I do?"

My early academic training was not as a specialist in the philosophy of religion. Initially enrolling at the university determined to be a biochemist, I fell in love with philosophy from my very first courses—Plato and Descartes in the first summer term, followed by existentialism in the second. Here were the Great Questions, here were assembled mankind's [*sic*] greatest and most brilliant minds [*sic*] engaged in grappling with the most fundamentally important issues of human life. As a philosopher, I would explore and understand *all* the great mysteries: what it means to be a human being, how we understand our experiences in the world, what is the nature of God, of reality, what the shape of the universe—in short, nothing less than the very meaning of life itself. I was intoxicated with the deep importance of it all.

As a student, I was exposed to much of the usual philosophical fare: introductions to Plato and Aristotle, Descartes's famous "cogito, ergo sum," existentialism, Marx, Nietzsche, arguments for and against the existence of God, theodicy, the dreaded symbolic logic, a smattering of "Eastern religions" done up philosophically, the inscrutable Greek pre-Socratics, medieval philosophers (taught by a self-described ex-Jesuit doing penance), rationalists, empiricists, pragmatists, phenomenology, epistemology, philosophy of language, and so forth.

By the time I left graduate school, I was frustrated with philosophy.

Intoxication had given way to dull hangover. Much of philosophy seemed so detached, so disembodied, its logics cold and remote from the concerns of real people, its arguments endlessly repetitive, its insights obscuring rather than revealing the mysteries of life. I had fallen out of love.

Part of my irritation lay in what I saw as the problem of Western philosophy. It seemed to me then (and to some extent, still does today) that philosophy forged itself into a gigantic coin and sent itself flipping off into space and time, our philosophical arguments revolving around whether the coin lands heads or tails on the particular toss.

Heads—we have rationalism, idealism, the mind.

Tails—we have empiricism, materialism, the body.

I used to entertain myself by musing about who forged the coin and who sent it flipping. Plato, Aristotle, Descartes, Hegel, and Marx, among others, were some of my favorite suspects. Thus were all our dichotomies forged in the minting and the tossing of the Big Giant Coin: Mind/Body, Subject/Object, Theory/Practice, God/Nature, Man/Woman, Objective (public) knowledge/Subjective (private) knowledge, Religion/religion, Insider/Outsider. It seemed to me then that something had gone terribly awry. At the very least, I was convinced that we had to ask new questions, pose new challenges, in order to set that Big Giant Coin spinning on edge.

Ludwig Wittgenstein once said that philosophy was about showing the fly the way out of the fly bottle. And so I flew—released into the real world in ways unexpected and complicated by family and life. In the years following, I have walked along many paths, crossed many boundaries, and woven many threads into the tapestry of my life. But philosophy, constant and sometimes annoying companion, has always walked with me, caught only now and then, in a glimpse out of the corner of one eye, just beside my own reflection in a mirror.

In that magic reflexive mirror, I peered closely at the threads of the tapestry that form my life and thought about the life experiences and areas of study that engage and excite me. I could find many threads that were colored "folklore," and lots of multi-colored threads labeled "ritual," that ranged in color from dull to dynamic, audience to performer, and all shades in between. Here was "performance studies." There was "feminism." I could find threads with "anthropology" on them; others that were stamped "narrative" or "story." Gods and Goddesses were woven throughout the design of my life-tapestry, in shades ranging from black robed priests and Wild Men of the Hunt to silver cloaked Virgins and Dark Goddesses of Magic and Transformation.

And finally, running along the edge of the tapestry like a framing border were the experiences of being a woman from a rural Appalachian, blue-collar industrial, lower working class, Eastern European family.

But where was philosophy? The threads that had formed the stuff of philosophy for me in college had long since faded from my tapestry. I had not meditated on Descartes in a very long time. Thankfully my days were no longer filled with symbolic logic proofs. Arguments for or against the existence of God were nowhere to be found. Threads colored the "nature of God" were twisted and woven into other threads instead, eventually losing their original shade. (*If God is all powerful, can he make a rock so large he cannot pick it up?*) Some threads seem to have abruptly ended in a frayed knot and been woven around. (*If God is both all powerful and all good, how can there be evil?*) The idealist threads were no longer snarling with the materialists.

The Big Giant Coin seemed to have fallen through a hole in my pocket.

I was starting to get worried. How could I answer my exam question? Could it be that I didn't do anything called philosophy at all?

It was then, out of the corner of my eye, that I glimpsed philosophy in the mirror, while my hands were busy following and weaving the threads of my tapestry. At that moment I realized that for me, philosophy is not exactly a particular thing, a discrete disciplinary subject in a course of study at the university. Rather, philosophy is *itself* a *doing*, a practice, a temperament, an engaging of oneself with the world, a way of living in the world, a way of asking questions, a deep curiosity about the ways we are and why. In some important way I had never left philosophy. Its familiar presence runs along all of the threads in my tapestry, and in no particular one. Philosophy was not a thread in the tapestry—*it was the process of weaving itself.*

Methodological Reflections

Glimpsing philosophy in that mirror was an exciting moment of discovery for me. The process of struggling to see my scholarship reflexively brought something out of the depth of my consciousness that I was not usually fully aware of—the extent to which philosophy frames and pushes the limits of the different aspects of my scholarship. That moment of reflexive self-awareness pulled the separate parts of my work together. It gave me insights into myself as a scholar that I value even today, because they are still very much part of who I am.

Upon reflection, I discovered that philosophy was my *metapraxis*,[29] my overarching organizing principle for all of my scholarship. For me, philosophy establishes a stance, lines of questioning, an organizational frame, a window, standards of articulation and reasoning, a mindset—all of which simultaneously enhance and obscure whatever I'm looking at during any given moment. Like all perspectives or filters on the world, philosophy is both my strength and my weakness. My early training in philosophy permeates the *how* of what I do—both how I engage the interdisciplinary process and how I engage my subjects of study. It articulates, evaluates, weighs, organizes, and even at times justifies conflicting practices and understandings of human experience gained from other people. Philosophy weaves together the disparate and sometimes competing threads of my scholarly training and my life experiences into a coherent whole.

How does philosophy weave the threads of folklore into my tapestry? Training in folklore and ethnography provides me with the tools necessary to collect data about religious practices. I happen to think that accurate descriptive information about religious practices—what people do when they *do* religion—is at least as important as information about texts or dogma, maybe more. I suspect that I feel this way precisely because my religious practices do not depend upon texts, here illustrating how my own scholarship and practice are interwoven. In order to collect data about religious practices, it is necessary to do fieldwork, to enter the messy and unpredictable world of human beings and attempt to learn about what they are doing. And my training provides me with all sorts of wonderful models and maps for the fieldwork process.

But the collection of data isn't enough. There needs to be something else. Taking a philosophical stance encourages greater reflection about what the data mean and how they further (or do not further) our understanding of what it is to be people experiencing our worlds. How do data obtained in the encounter with the other enlarge human understanding—stretching and remaking its forms and limits? How does each encounter with the other alter and stretch our image of self? How do our growing encounters with people of different cultures and faiths force us to reflect more courteously and responsibly on both their religious (and scholarly) practices and our own?

How can we better use the data collected about practices, about human experiences as "individuals-practicing,"[30] to help us understand the myriad fascinating and creative ways in which human beings might engage in, encounter, talk about, and experience what we variously call the sacred, Goddess, enlightenment, and so forth? How can we use the data that we uncover to think with, to raise new sets of questions and to pose new challenges to our assumptions?

In this book, I use a description of a particular kind of Wiccan initiation ritual from a specific religious community in order to challenge our assumptions about rites of passage, a paradigm that has changed little since its creation by Arnold van Gennep in the early 1900s. My goal is to employ my perspective as both scholar and practitioner to enable us to capture new information, to weave new and more accurate models and paradigms into our scholarship. I hope to challenge and extend our scholarship on ritual more generally, to enable us to pose questions about religious rituals in other religious communities, to allow us to think about rituals in some new and profitable way.

Ethnographic description plays a large role in my work, requiring the use of both framing and performance theory to construct a rich description of one kind of Wiccan initiation ritual. These two strategies work particularly well in the analysis of ritual and are ones that I find particularly useful within the context of a philosophical metapraxis.

For example, Erving Goffman's notion of framing, which itself draws on ideas from phenomenological sociology and meta-communication theory, provides a device for understanding ritual performance as marking off actions that are special or different from the ordinary everyday. Folklorist Mary Hufford reinforces a framing strategy, pointing out that "the term *performance* suggests 'staged' behavior, that is, *events framed as being of a different expressive order than behaviors outside the frames.* We create such events through contextualizing or framing practices that draw attention to the *double grounding of an extraordinary world opened up within the ordinary*" (italics mine).[31] Barbara Babcock's "metanarrative markers" and William A. "Bert" Wilson's "markers of belief" also suggest special framing strategies for mapping religious ritual.

Unfortunately, scholars applying performance theory to religious ritual tend to secularize ritual and evaluate it as an act of artistry, a moment of religious theater. Diane Goldstein suggests that scholars secularize religious performances in order to make them "safe."[32] Folklorist Jeff Titon notes that performance theory exchanges one set of metaphors belonging to reading and writing for another belonging to theater. A "more holistic enterprise," the possibility of doing justice to "living process," and an emphasis on "persons instead of things" is gained. However, Titon finds the theater metaphor especially troubling for understanding religious rituals because "folklorists cannot escape the inauthenticity implied by the staging" of performances.[33]

As a practitioner as well as a scholar, I suggest that religious communities have their own criteria in determining when a religious performance is inauthentic, staged or faked in some way. Rather than simply despairing over the connections between the term *performance* and *inauthentic event*, it might be more productive to take a move from Wittgenstein's language game and examine the criteria by which a religious community determines the authenticity or inauthenticity of its religious performances. This avoids any tendency to simply impose what we as scholars consider valuable criteria, without taking into consideration what the evaluative criteria of the performers themselves might be.

Folklorists Jose Limon and Jane Young provide a critique of the performance approach that I find useful in support of my argument for the legitimacy of the scholar-practitioner role. They note that the performance approach depends on the need for the "observer's sufficient fluency in the varieties and registers of the linguistic and metalinguistic codes in which emergent folkloric acts are performed,"[34] since analysis of performance implies a close face-to-face knowledge of the speaker and the performative act. This illustrates one instance in which a scholar who is also a religious practitioner may be uniquely positioned to describe and interpret those "linguistic and metalinguistic codes" in which folkloric acts are performed.

Performance theory ties us to what Edward M. Bruner and Victor W. Turner term the "anthropology of experience." This concept ultimately traces back to philosophers such as Wilhelm Dilthey, William James, James Dewey, and—through folklorist Deborah Kapchan's 1995 invocation of a "phenomenology of performances"—to philosopher Maurice Merleau-Ponty. An examination of experience, practice, and performance enables us to challenge our philosophical assumptions about mind and body. It provides us with material to think with, to raise provocative philosophical questions about the nature of religious ritual as an *embodied* process—as well as a *gendered* one—and to reflect on their implications throughout our scholarship.

Gender poses additional problems for the performance scholar. Complex constructions of complementarity, what Barbara Babcock terms "differential access to the sacred,"[35] are especially poorly understood, if not overlooked entirely, with an androcentric or male-centered methodology. In cultures where primarily men perform the "important" rituals (read this as large, public, or flamboyant rituals), the religious performances of women are often missed. In an attempt to go after the best performances or the star performers, we may overlook others—often women—who are equally involved in their religions and equally important to their religious communities. Feminist theory reveals that androcentrism clouds our perception of the processes and activities of women in the construction of religious traditions and rituals.[36]

Philosophy weaves feminist theory into my tapestry by pushing me to raise further questions about the significance of recovering women's religious lives. How does the integration of women's experiences change our understanding of the human experience? Is there an intrinsically gendered perspective? Does worship of a Goddess challenge or alter a symbolic understanding of God by either replacing that symbol system or at least understanding it as polysemous? What does it say about our notions of gender and sex when a *male* religious practitioner identifies with the *female* body of a Goddess and is transformed by Her symbolic journey through death?

Pushing my reflection beyond description of a performance or ritual, philosophy elicits similarly fruitful questions from ritual and performance studies and weaves them into the tapestry: How does the study of performance, rituals, and practices change or perhaps even threaten scholarly understanding of what religion is? How do we evaluate our understanding of religion when confronted with the universe of discourses and practices that comprise even a single religion? Is there such a thing as religion, or are there only religious persons? Must we become more cautious about the removal of religious doctrine from the complex web of its religious praxis? How does an inquiry into religious practices help us explore the experiential dimension of human knowledge? How does information about the ways of the body in ritual practice, in performance, challenge our traditional philosophical understanding of the mind-body duality or our understanding of magic and divine presence? Does a newly discovered (for some) practical relation between mind and body challenge us to ask different questions of religion: not what and why religion is, but how and why does one become religious?

Certainly, some of the questions that engage me now are similar to those that captured my attention when I initially encountered philosophy all those years ago. Others are a bit more modest, if not just as complex—

asking about the nature of our *experience* of reality, rather than the nature of reality itself. I have discovered upon reflection that philosophy is still the driving force throughout all it is that I do, provoking me to grapple with the most fundamentally important issues of human life by using the best techniques and devices at hand. As a scholar-practitioner commuting across multiple boundaries and encountering multiple worlds, each method that I draw upon both enlarges and limits my field of vision, both increases and decreases my ability to engage with the multiple others with whom I come into contact.

I gather the threads for my tapestry in the living of my own life and from the lives of others. Folklore, performance, ritual studies, and the feminist critique of androcentrism are some of the tools I use to spin the fibers, give them colors, plot their thickness and heft. And philosophy weaves them into a pattern that is ideally more coherent, more articulate, more elegant, maybe even more beautiful, than can be woven by any single tool, than can be achieved by the weaving of any single grouping of threads alone. Finding my reflection on my scholarly practice productive, I turn again to the looking glass of reflexivity for similar insights into my religious practice.

2

Stumbling toward Wisdom

Images in a Mirror: Reflections as a
Practitioner of Religions

You're probably wondering why it reads practitioner of *religions*. I was not born into a family that practiced Wicca. My introduction to the Craft was actually quite unexpected, even serendipitous, and occurred the summer before my senior year in high school. I do not consider myself as having converted to Wicca, but rather understand the experience of finding the Craft as being rooted in the practices and experiences of my childhood.

My hard-working family emigrated from Eastern Europe to the coal mines, mills, and railroad yards of the Ohio River valley. Their formal religious practices were mixed with centuries-old folk beliefs and traditions. Born in Steubenville, Ohio, I spent the first six or so years of my life growing up in nearby Mingo Junction. These two cities, and others in the Ohio Valley, were heavily populated with Slavs who formed loose communities of shared languages, religions, music, foods, and traditions. Many of these Slavs practiced some form of the Eastern Orthodox religion, and the area supported several ornate Orthodox churches, including Russian, Serbian, and Greek, their Byzantine domes like shiny gold beacons drawing the faithful scattered throughout the Valley.

My mother was a Serbian Orthodox whose religious practice was anything but. As I was the only daughter, she passed on to me the practical traditions of her religion as she understood them. I learned how to prevent and cure the evil eye (wear *lots* of jewelry, a teaching I try to follow to this day), how to light candles specially blessed by the Priest, how to make offerings to the dead, how to burn incense to drive out illness and misfortune, and that menstrual blood will kill plants (this doesn't work; in a fit of pique, I tried it once on her African violets). After my seventh birthday, during the night of a full moon, she also taught me that the Virgin Mary was the Lady of the Moon, Our Mother, and showed me how to blow Her a kiss in tribute and thanks when we pray to Her.

By this time, my family had moved a short distance from the Valley to Rayland, a very small country town populated mostly by ethnic Germans, Scots, and English. Our Orthodox traditions must have seemed quite exotic to our Lutheran and Methodist neighbors, beginning with our strange insistence on celebrating major holidays like Christmas on the "wrong" day. Serbians follow the old Julian calendar, in which Christmas is celebrated on January 7, rather than December 25. Of course, we were all too willing to accommodate our neighbors, and celebrated Christmas with them on the 25th, and then we celebrated again on the 7th, an arrangement my little brother and I thought was wonderful.

My mother maintained her connection to her Serbian roots as best she could and took my brother and me to church whenever she could persuade my father to drive us the twenty-five miles or so to Steubenville. My earliest recollections of going to church with my mother swirl in my memory like some confused kaleidoscope of competing images, sounds, and smells. There were, of course, the larger-than-life paintings of all the holy people: God, Jesus, the Virgin Mary, and saints and heroes my non-Orthodox friends have surely never heard of. Candles burned at every direction, their light and heat a spiritual and physical comfort in winter, but oppressive in summer. They flickered in the haze produced by the heavy smoke of the incense. The walls of the old church rang with singing, the call and response of Priest and Cantor with the voices of the Choir in their loft upstairs. The fact that the entire liturgy was sung in Serbian—a language in which I was not then and am not now fluent—certainly never lessened its potency for me.

The Priest, mysterious in robes of black and sometimes of gold thread, disappeared occasionally behind the rich and ornate decorations of the altar doors. I was sure those doors held the key to some mysterious power because of the way in which the Priest later emerged, transformed and triumphant to the rising voice of the Choir. Obviously *something* had happened behind those doors, but what?

I suspect that this was my first theological question.

As a woman, Eastern Orthodox tradition denied me passage through those particular ornate doors, and so my theological investigations eventually took me through others.

My father was a proud Hungarian agnostic who was convinced that organized religions "only wanted your wallet." He was nevertheless an enthusiastic teacher of what some call folk belief. He taught my little brother and me how to look for healing herbs (there's a reason they call them *stinging* nettles), how to plant by the signs of the moon, how to tell which mushrooms were good, and which others poisonous. As a kid in coal-mining Appalachia, my father had wanted to be a doctor. Family circumstance and poverty had other ideas in mind. But healing was always a big part of what he taught us—from making soothing teas (where my tradition of terrible tasting herb teas started) to ways to cure a cold (homemade grape or elderberry wine usually figured into this), soothe a sore throat (honey and whiskey), and stop an earache (don't ask). I learned from him how to remove fever from a child by placing a raw potato slice on his forehead to absorb the heat (or cold steel if the fever were particularly stubborn). For some reason it always helped when you wrapped the potato in a red bandana. . . .

Although he didn't practice the Orthodox religion with my mother, my father gamely consented each year to being thrown out of the house on Christmas morning, trudging three times around the house in the snow with my little brother tagging along. On the third time around, they would finally get to say the magic words (in Serbian) and give the secret knock that would allow them to enter, symbolically bringing in the light of the newly born Christ child and good luck for the year. Traditionally, this good luck took the form of walnuts that were supposed to be tossed into the corners of the house to bless it, but we always wound up eating them instead.

Thus my mother and father introduced me to the rich and sensuous worlds of ritual, of folk magic, of healing and herbalism, of religious practices, and simultaneously introduced me to the hermeneutics of suspicion. This odd combination no doubt helped to make me some of what I am today: an experienced Priestess who practices and creates rituals, a folklorist, a magician, a healer, and an extremely skeptical individual. Whatever I have been and whatever I have become over the years, some part of me remains both a skeptical Hungarian and a pagan Serb blowing kisses at the Moon.

My husband Eric is responsible for helping me to make the connections between who I was and who I am. It happened at my father's funeral. Although my father was a devout agnostic, my brother and I had the services in the Serbian Church in Steubenville, where my mother's funeral services had been held only a few years before. Afterward, when my husband and I were driving back home to Columbus, Eric commented that he was struck by how similar the Serbian Orthodox rituals were to the ones I performed as a Witch.

"What are you talking about? Are you kidding?" I asked, astonished that he would seriously make such an observation.

"They wear black robes," he said. "You wear black robes. They light candles. You light candles. They use *lots* of incense. You smoke up the entire house. They have singing. You guys—well, you *try* to sing."

I laughed, but he had something there. The connections were probably more noticeable to him because he comes from a Protestant religious background in which there are few elaborate rituals—in fact, by my standards, few rituals at all. His observations started me thinking about all the little rituals, the everyday acts of magic, all the customs and teachings that we usually call folklore; about the way that the body is always present in rituals—the spirit engaged and enlivened through the actions of the body and the response of the physical senses; and, of course, about the way that the Moon became for me an important figure in both practical acts of planting and theological acts of reflection as the embodiment of Our Mother.

He was right.

Stumbling onto the Craft

When I first encountered Wicca, I recall that I wasn't looking for a *religion* so much as a few good books on how to do astrology. It was the summer of 1971, and I was a high school junior visiting college in a special program for "promising but poor" students. Totally lost for the first time in what seemed to me to be a vast college library, I asked a friendly-looking man at the information counter where I could find books on astrology. While I didn't get any help with the books, I did get an introduction to "some people you might like to meet if you're interested in *those* sorts of things." This was my first time away from home, and although I didn't really know exactly what *those* sorts of things were, I was game for meeting new and interesting people.

A few days later, I first met Sam—the man I would eventually come to know as my High Priest. As I recall, Sam and I got off to a rather rocky start, which no doubt continued, in some fashion, to color our relationship. Brimming with the arrogant overconfidence of the obviously-away-from-home-for-the-first-time, I tried not to act absolutely dumbfounded when Sam and his sweet fiancée, Beth, revealed that they were both *Witches*, followers of what they called The Old Religion, Wicca, or just the Craft.[1] I'm certain he thought the Craft was why I came to visit, and when I stammered something about Taoism and Laozi (I was a precocious reader) being more *advanced*, I'm sure he was puzzled, if not outright offended.

Although I no doubt made a thorough fool of myself, Sam kindly loaned me some books and agreed to meet with me again to talk about Wicca. Over the course of several meetings, I learned that the Craft is a pre-Christian nature religion rooted in the myths and rituals of Europe and Britain. Organized in small groups called covens, Witches worship both Gods and Goddesses and include both men and women as part of the priesthood. Initiation or formal acceptance into a coven may occur after a period of study and training.

Sam introduced me to some members of his coven, including Lauren, who had either just been or was about to be initiated. They were all working on a video about the Craft for a local TV station, complete with taped portions of rituals, long walks in the woods discussing Wiccan philosophy, and a model of Stonehenge used as a stage prop.

I got to help paint Stonehenge.

What mere mortal could resist The Old Religion after that?

The video stands out in my memory as one of the highlights of that eventful summer, not only because it was connected to my first time away from home, but because it was my introduction to the Craft. It was also a darn good video, one of the very best I have ever seen on the Craft, and I dearly wish I had a copy of it for teaching purposes, as well as for personal reasons.

Somewhere in between watching that video, painting Stonehenge, talking with Sam, and reading some of the few books then published on the Craft, I discovered a world both new to me and yet quite familiar. Certainly there were similarities to the religion of my childhood: the chanting of black robed Priests, the heady incense and brightly burning candles, the mysterious rituals of magic and transformation.

But in the Craft, there were no ornate doors through which I—a woman—could not pass. Instead, doors opened wide upon a world filled with magic and mystery, where the Gods and Goddesses of ancient myth walked the woods with Their Children again, where the Virgin Mary rode high in the star-filled sky as the Lady of the Moon. I had not found a *new religion*; I found the spiritual path that I had always walked, but never knew had a name.

I had come home.

Through Briars and Brambles

My journey to initiation would take a little more than three years. Just as I would later fall in love with philosophy, I determined that very first summer to study the Craft seriously and to ask for initiation, but there was one problem. I was still in high school and would be returning home at the end of summer for my senior year. Sam told me that only after a thorough period of study, and after I had turned eighteen (which had both practical and legal implications), should I make the decision to formally study the Craft and ask for initiation. This was study for the priesthood, after all, and such a decision needed to be made out of mature reflection, rather than youthful enthusiasm. And, reflecting back to that time, I see now that I had a long way to go to reach maturity!

You may be wondering about that legal part. Thirty years ago the climate surrounding the Craft was a lot colder than it is today, especially in the conservative parts of the Midwest and the South. People I met who practiced the Craft were usually low key about it, if not downright secretive. They had to be, in order to protect their jobs and families. Pentacles, if worn at all, were tucked under shirts, not worn openly. This was a time when guys could be beat up just for having long hair; add a few pentagrams to that, and you had *real* trouble. In fact, we had a joke that if you met someone who was flamboyantly "out" as a Witch, you could bet he probably wasn't one. It would take many years for the climate to change and for more Witches to come out from underground. Some of us still haven't. One of the first things I learned from study with Sam's group was to keep the identities of its members in confidence. I still do.

This wasn't hard, especially at first, because I didn't actually know who many of Sam's fellow Witches were. Sam arranged for me to meet Kevin, who—unbelievably—actually lived near my hometown and was working there to earn money to come back to school. I began studying with Kevin, meeting him at the library or at a restaurant, borrowing books, and asking questions, slowly gaining an idea of what the practice of the Craft was all about. So began my period of screening and being screened for initiation. I was sure that my family wouldn't understand any of this, and so I met with Kevin under cover of "going to the library" more often than not.

Kevin *was* the library, in a way, since none of the local bookstores or libraries carried many books on the Craft. He introduced me to all the classics of Craft writing. In the early seventies, books by Gerald Gardner, Margaret Murray, Janet and Stewart Farrar, Sybil Leek, T. C. Lethbridge, Charles Leland, and Justine Glass were practically mandatory reading for those interested in initiation. Some of the readings were a bit dry, especially the books on comparative mythology or anthropology. I think this was part of the screening process; if you made it through the more serious books, you were probably interested in the Craft as a religion, rather than as some "cool and freaky spell thing."

Many of these books were some of the first to talk about Wicca as an old religion of nature that survived but was driven underground during Christian times. Gerald Gardner, whose books either brought Wicca out from underground or helped create it outright, is regarded by some as the Father of Modern Witchcraft. Margaret Murray was an anthropologist who dared to suggest that Witchcraft was an older religion that secretly survived into Christian times. Although her works have since been pretty thoroughly criticized for faulty scholarship, I thought she provided a fairly plausible suggestion about the changing nature of religious practices. Given the unorthodox customs of my mother's nominally Serbian Orthodox religious practice, I didn't see anything strange at all in the idea that older religious practices become retooled as the next generation's folk religion or set of quaint and curious customs.

Like walnuts tossed into the corners of a room at Christmas. . . .

My desire to become a member of Sam's coven definitely influenced my choice of a college. When I arrived at school that next summer, I was looking forward to seeing Sam, Beth, Lauren, and some of the other members of the coven I had met while painting Stonehenge. I did see a lot of Sam and Beth, who had married by then, and sometimes Lauren, who was a student like me. But the rest of Sam's group remained largely a mystery to me. Some of them I met only once or twice and knew only by their first names. I had a vague sense that many of them were older, either no longer in college or not connected with the college at all, and working somewhere in the community or the local countryside. I assumed that I would be introduced to all the members of Sam's coven at the appropriate time. That time never came.

Over the next three years, I continued learning about the Craft in general and about Sam's tradition in particular. According to Sam, at that time the Craft was divided into four major groupings: Hereditary, Traditional, Gardnerian, and Alexandrian. Hereditary Witches were thought to have the oldest traditions and to have passed the Craft down through their families from generation to generation. British Traditional groups, like Sam's, were "the next best thing," but passed their teachings on to initiates who were not necessarily members of the family. Gardnerian groups traced their origins to Gerald Gardner, and Alexandrian groups to Alex Sanders. These last two were taught to me as the more recent traditions of Witchcraft.

In keeping with the tradition of secrecy that seemed so prevalent at that time, I must admit that I know next to nothing about those who initiated Sam or, in turn, where they were initiated and by whom. I vaguely remember that Sam had learned or been told that our particular tradition of the Craft traced itself back to parts of southwest Britain near Wales, but what evidence he had for this quite frankly escapes me. This was an incentive, for a brief period of time, to try to learn Welsh, which could have been more difficult only if it were written in Cyrillic.

The Craft was very slowly coming out from underground, at least around campus. Sometimes, in the dorms or student union, Sam would give lectures or mini classes on Witchcraft. He was a very good speaker and would always get a few folks who were interested in learning more. In this way, I had a chance to meet others who were interested in becoming initiates. We started studying with Sam in small groups as well as individually.

Studying with Sam didn't just mean reading books, although there was plenty of reading. We also learned how to identify and properly collect herbs to make healing teas. While they didn't taste any better than my father's herb teas, we found them fairly effective for minor aches and pains and colds. Eventually, a large part of our study involved learning different kinds of meditation and visualization techniques, including how energy flows through the body with control of the breath. We would keep track of our daily progress in journals that Sam would review once a week or so. Each person was also expected to begin mastering at least one form of divination. I was a pretty good astrologer by then, and I also worked on tarot cards and, later, runes.

Our study sessions included a lot of fun, and we had several crazy adventures together as well. The summer I arrived at school, a few of us hitchhiked partway to New York (something I now can't believe I ever did). Once in New York, we went to Samuel Weiser's bookstore, a paradise for occult books; Aphrodisia, a store with herbs and incense of every kind; and Ray Buckland's Long Island museum of Gerald Gardner's Craft relics. Amazingly, I actually met Buckland at the museum, although at the time I wasn't really sure exactly who he was. All I remember is that he wore an earring in one ear (pretty tame by today's standards), had a cool British-sounding accent, and was well dressed. The forty dollars I had with me quickly burned a hole in my pocket, as I decided which books, herbs, incenses, and other souvenirs to take back home with me.

We also spent a lot of time together in more low-key activities. I fondly remember many evenings sitting around Sam's house eating popcorn or ordering pizza, watching old black and white horror movies, and laughing uproariously. Why is it that the hero *always* waits until dark to go into the haunted house with the dying flashlight? You'd think he'd try noon, maybe. Italian vampire movies were very popular on a local station at that time and became some of our favorite films. We especially enjoyed the mandatory chase through the woods at midnight by lesbian vampires wearing diaphanous gowns. And, of course, we would *always* critique the Witch movies for their accuracy and rate them on atmosphere and costume design.

More seriously, we also helped each other through the bad times that come along with growing up, and there was a lot of growing up to do in our college years. This is a time when a lot of life's lessons are learned, and we learned them together. We became a pretty solid group of friends, although there were still the occasional misunderstandings, disagreements, or conflicts typical of close relationships. In short, we were slowly becoming a community.

A few of us went through the Dedication ceremony, an important step in Sam's tradition that formalized one's intention of becoming a Witch. Later, some of the Dedicants would take over Sam's public classes, and the group would develop several layers of students at different levels of instruction. At this point, the Dedicants had been studying with Sam and working with one another for a couple of years. It seemed we talked about initiation all the time. By almost any standards that we could figure out—seriousness of intent, diligence in study, group harmony, basic maturity—we were past due for consideration. When we finally got up enough nerve to ask Sam for initiation, the coven that figured as a secret and silent presence in the background for so long finally spoke.

Sam's group had decided to cap its membership.

Although Sam explained the decision in ways designed not to hurt our feelings, many of us were confused and hurt. I know I was. It seemed that I had overcome many obstacles to walk this path, only to find it blocked with an impenetrable wall of brambles and thistles at the end. What was going on? What had I done to offend these people, some of whom I didn't even know? In this case, the secrecy valued for its protective power also had the power to hurt and cause suspicion or mistrust, albeit perhaps unintentionally. In the hands of less ethical people, secrecy has the power to manipulate others, to erode self-confidence, and even to produce paranoia. Welcome to the dark side of discretion.

The Dedicants continued to study, in limbo for a time, while things played out behind the scenes. Eventually I learned that Sam had started a new coven in order to initiate us. Some of the members of the first coven, including Beth, Lauren, and Kevin, also crossed over to the new one. Since I knew little about the members of the previous coven beyond a few first names, I have scant knowledge of what processes or group dynamics were at work or what happened to those members of the previous coven who had decided not to transfer to the second one.

At long last, the day of my initiation had finally come, and I stood nervously at the edge of the Circle, waiting for the robed and hooded figure before me to deliver the challenge that would bring change and transformation.

It was May in Ohio.

Over the course of the next ten years, change came gradually to the Witches in Sam's coven and to the Craft itself. Although we learned a lot under Sam, most, if not all, of the Witches in Sam's coven eventually left the group. Our reasons were complex and varied. A few of us were college students who simply graduated and left the area. While some of us continued in the Craft, others discovered and pursued different religious paths. Family and work responsibilities took a few of us away from active religious practice.

But there were other reasons that we left—reasons that had to do with the changing nature of the Craft itself and our own inability as a group to grow in response. The Craft was exploding aboveground with public Pagan festivals. Pagans and Witches of all sorts were coming out of the broom closet, even in the Midwest. The old, secretive ways were passing.

Pagans and Witches from an amazing number of traditions started networking with one another, comparing group structures and sharing rituals. We Witches in Sam's group were learning about the existence of other covens, covens that functioned quite differently than our own and presented other leadership styles. The Pagan and Wiccan communities that were starting to emerge would eventually provide us with alternative models of practice that enabled some of us to continue in the Craft without Sam: other traditions, other covens, and other people to practice with.

By this point, we were terribly unhappy with Sam. Over the years, unhealthy patterns had emerged in his leadership of the group, such as the tendency to be three or more hours late for a class or a ritual that he had scheduled. On the one hand, his attention was increasingly drawn away from the Craft and the coven to lighter activities: a "Wicca Lite" Pagan Grove, and eventually role playing games such as Dungeons and Dragons or playing at wizard in Renaissance Fairs. On the other hand, Sam was unwilling to pass on the tradition to others or to share power or authority with anyone else in the group. In all of the years we worked with him, he never formally elevated any of us to second degree,[2] the rank at which a Witch may start her own coven. We were increasingly worried that the tradition would die with Sam.

Our coven slowly ceased to function. Perfect love and perfect trust had given way to perfect frustration. One by one, the Witches who I knew as my lifelong friends and community picked up whatever threads of our tradition we had been able to gather, and started to leave.

I left, too.

Mapping an Ever-Changing Landscape

Ironically, the festival movement that liberated the Witches in our group makes it both easier and harder to talk about The Old Religion, beginning with what to call it. When I was studying to be initiated, The Old Religion, Wicca, Witchcraft, and the Craft were all used interchangeably, with little or no distinction made between Wiccan and Witch. Back then, it seemed more important to distinguish what we did from Satanism. All of the Witches I met during the course of my study stressed that the Craft was the practice of a pre-Christian religion that had nothing to do with the worship of Satan, understood as a figure in the *Christian* pantheon. It also had nothing to do with the unfortunate and widespread usage of the word "witchcraft" by anthropologists when they mean negative magic or sorcery, something I still argue about with my colleagues in anthropology.

Today there is some discussion within the larger contemporary Pagan[3] community about whether Wicca and Witchcraft even refer to the same kinds of religious practices. Some practitioners identify themselves as Witches, but not Wiccans, and vice versa. The distinction seems to be variously understood as referring to differences between the two in terms of origin, organization, formal training, and use of magic, among other things. Old habits being hard to break, I continue to use the terms Witch and Wiccan interchangeably for what I am, although I am quite happy with other practitioners' definitions for themselves.

If naming the Craft is difficult, describing it is even harder. There are at least two major reasons for this. First, although the Craft has a growing and influential number of national spokespersons,[4] there is no centralized church hierarchy or central group of Wiccan elders who establish religious dogma or enforce a regimen of standard ritual practices. Witches emphasize personal experiences of the sacred and ritual creativity, which reinforce an emphasis on local praxis over universal dogma among most Wiccan groups.

Second, the Pagan festival movement not only exposed us to an amazing variety of Pagans and Witches, but likely created new forms of Pagan religious practice as well. Unlike the four neat and tidy categories of Hereditary, Traditional, Gardnerian, and Alexandrian Craft traditions that Sam taught us, there are today an enormous and ever-growing number of ways to type or organize the Craft. There are probably also groups and individuals who simply defy categorization. Looking back, I suspect that those four original categories were never themselves as neatly drawn as we were taught.

Today, the diversity of Craft practices makes it difficult to generalize, so why bother?

If I say "Christianity," you probably have some notion of what I mean. If confronted with the terms "Catholic mass" or "Protestant minister's sermon," you are likely to have some image, accurate or not, of what I'm talking about. Invoking Wittgenstein, these terms signal more-or-less familiar moves in our game. But if I say "Wicca," or "Wiccan initiation ritual," I am likely introducing new and unfamiliar moves that can throw off our game completely.

Or to put it another way, before we explore unknown territory, it's a good idea to have a map—however sketchy.

Fortunately, there is a wealth of material available today devoted to Witchcraft in particular and contemporary Paganism in general, especially compared to the few books available when I was reading with Kevin. Some works track the historical development of contemporary Paganism[5] or give a general overview of its major contours.[6] Others address the significance of nature religions in the modern world[7] or categorize various forms of Witchcraft according to their use of power in magical transformation.[8] There are also several interesting and sometimes conflicting studies that explore the demographics of contemporary Paganism and Wicca.[9] Scholars and practitioners, and those who are both, are busy with lively exploration of one of America's most recent, complex, and ever-changing religious phenomena.

All of these resources help us sketch out a map of or a guide to the Wiccan sacred landscape. Of course, any map that I draw will be colored and framed by my own particular experiences with a specific Craft tradition, and is unsuitable for enshrining as *the* definitive Wiccan guide.

Current practitioners of Wicca may characterize their religion as a modern-day revival or re-creation of practices rooted in the shamanic techniques and indigenous religious practices of a pre-Christian Pagan Europe. Some forms of the Craft use shamanic techniques such as drumming or dancing to achieve ecstatic trance or a state of alternate reality. These techniques are not unique to European forms of Wicca, but are used by people in many parts of the world. While my own practice uses some drumming and trance journeying, Sam's group practiced much more ceremonial magic than shamanism; for us, ceremonial magic meant the use of specialized tools, controlled and ritualized action, and silent visualization. The mixture of shamanism and ceremonialism varies from group to group. Covens today may use either form, some combination of both, or create their own techniques and ritual style.

Some practitioners understand Wicca as part of the Western Mystery Tradition[10] because of its emphasis on initiatory processes and its similarity to what we know about Greek initiatory or mystery religions. Echoing this characterization, journalist and Witch Margot Adler writes:

If . . . we define the Craft as "the European heritage of Goddess worship," the connections with the mysteries of Demeter and Kore become clearer. Above and beyond the murky area of historical and geographical connections, the philosophical connections are real. What little we know of the Mysteries seems to indicate that these rites emphasized (as the Craft, at its best, does today) *experience* as opposed to dogma, and *metaphor* and *myth* as opposed to *doctrine*. Both the Mysteries and the Craft emphasize initiatory *processes* that lead to a widening of perceptions. Neither emphasizes theology, belief, or the written word. (italics in the original)[11]

Although her distinctions are perhaps a bit too cleanly drawn, Adler's comparison of Wicca to Western mystery traditions is helpful to both scholars and practitioners in that it gives us other Western religious models that foreground transformational religious experiences and processes over text or dogma.

Witches often describe the Craft as a nature religion, although precisely how this term is to be understood is contested both by scholars and Witches themselves. Does this mean that Witches are necessarily environmental activists? Or is nature used as a theological and symbolic construct? Is there yet another way of understanding nature religion that takes into account the reality of magic—the *presence* of Nature as a member of the spiritual community, something rarely, if ever seriously considered by scholars? Perhaps the most accurate description involves a combination of the above, or others that I haven't thought of.

Wicca is also occasionally described as a fertility religion. Whenever Sam's group—which I tend to think of now as my parent coven—dealt with fertility in any form, it was usually fertility of the food source. There were rituals showing the corn how high it should grow and encouraging fruitful harvest, but little or nothing about human sexuality. Darn.

Witches do draw many insights from the seasonal cycles of nature, which are celebrated in a calendar of eight sabbats, or holy days, called the Wheel of the Year.[12] Each holy day has two dimensions of activities. One occurs in the natural world: celebration of the times of year for planting or harvesting crops, for example. The other dimension reflects what is going on in the natural world, but the natural becomes a metaphor for a field of activity located within the personal lives of Wiccan practitioners. So Witches talk of planting and harvesting as part of the agricultural cycle, but also as an aspect of other human endeavors, such as sowing new ideas and habits and harvesting the seeds that were planted.

In celebrating the sabbats, Witches express and experience the neverending cycle of change, celebrating equally times of planting and harvest, seeing in every ending a new beginning, in every death a rebirth. Given this perspective, it should not be surprising that a belief in reincarnation is often a central teaching of the Craft.

Deities

Generally speaking, Wiccans are polytheistic and worship both Gods and Goddesses. Many covens choose to worship Gods and Goddesses within a particular group or pantheon of related deities, but also feel free to invoke deities outside of those pantheons as required by the circumstances of a particular ritual or need. Goddesses and Gods are generally worshipped within the context of the seasonal cycles of Nature and, through these cycles, are invoked into worshippers' lives as powerfully transformative catalysts for change and growth.

The Gods and Goddesses of the Witches have aspects or dimensions directly connected to the annual seasonal cycles of the Solar Wheel of the Year or the monthly Lunar Cycle. These aspects have a correspondence to cycles within human life as well. Although Witches certainly recognize the existence of Solar Goddesses in many world mythologies, such as those from Scandinavia and Japan, the Lunar Goddess is one of the major theistic images for many contemporary Wiccans. Her ever-changing cycles of new/waxing moon, full moon, and waning/dark moon afford both female and male Witches ample opportunities to ritually celebrate the stages of human experience. The Moon's monthly cycles of waxing and waning provide a visible reminder of the ebb and flow of life's energies.

The stages of the Moon may be easily and directly keyed to chronological stages in female life, usually visualized as the Triple Goddess in her aspects of Maiden, Mother, or Crone. It would be relatively easy for Witches to create rituals celebrating lifecycle changes using the Triple Goddess in a literal way: Maiden Goddesses for young girls and menarche, Mother Goddesses for birth rituals, Crones at menopause, and so forth. In the body of ritual practices inherited from my parent coven, the Triple Goddess was almost never used in this fashion. There were no rites that specifically addressed either female or male events of *literal* biological transformation, which may say something about the invisibility of such events within large portions of Western culture.

In fact, a literal understanding both of the Triple Goddess aspects and their relation to human lifecycle experiences would be far from accurate in terms of how the aspects are generally used by Witches. The Triple Goddess is understood and used symbolically in a very fluid or multivalent fashion by Witches. This enables women *and men* of all ages, sexual orientations, and biological conditions to invoke Her in order to enact powerfully transformative rites that celebrate and shape the changes in their lives.

Any Witch, male or female, of any age, may call upon the power of the Maiden at the new and waxing moon to ask for Her blessings to secure the skill and inspiration to launch a new project, to obtain a fresh start, or to make a new beginning. At the Full Moon, any Witch may turn to the Mother for the strength and vitality needed to sustain his goals, his projects, and himself. During the Waning and Dark Moon, the Crone gives to any Witch, regardless of age or gender, the power to destroy in order to create, to end in order to begin anew.

Male deities, also fully accessible by both male and female Witches, are often connected to the Sun. They are sometimes understood in terms of the dual aspects of summer and winter, balancing cycles of growth and decay, activity and rest, within worshippers' lives. Gods may also be understood as having a tripartite dimension in the form of solar, vegetative, and forest/animal aspects worshipped within the Solar Wheel. Following the solar cycle, Witches celebrate the returning Sun—the spark of life—at Winter Solstice. This is the time of year when the worshipper rests, contemplating the success or failure of last year's activities, and planning what changes she will make in the year to come. As the Sun grows in intensity (until its height at Midsummer), the Witch plans for the coming year, planting seeds of change in the spring, working hard to establish her goals through the summer, and looking forward to fruitful harvest.

Although it is evident that aspects of deities function as important metaphors within worshippers' lives, the Gods are *not* merely metaphors, but *exist as real members of the spiritual community*. A Witch's relationship with her Gods is primarily experiential. For a Witch, the Gods are *present and alive in the world*, not removed from it on either a disembodied non-earthly plane or on a purely symbolic or abstract level as a mental construct. The Gods have Their own agency and do not exist merely as psychological projections for the worshippers' ritual psychodramas.

The Coming of "Jahweh-in-Drag"

The simple observation that Witches worship Gods and Goddesses is complicated by the emergence of feminist or Dianic Wicca. These groups tend to worship the Goddess exclusively and may also exclude men from their covens. Feminist Witchcraft seems to be connected to the discovery of Wicca by feminists in the mid- to late seventies. It does not reflect the Craft as it was introduced to me or as it is practiced by my current coven, which worships both Goddesses and Gods.

Theologically, the creation of a monotheistic Goddess is troubling because it ignores an intrinsically male and female, polytheistic, and pluralistic worldview that is quite unlike the monotheistic religions more familiar to Westerners. Exclusive worship of *The* Goddess was simply the Judeo-Christian god in another sex, or "Jahweh-in-drag"—an observation made in Craft Circles at least as early as 1975.[13] Would the sense of freedom and the wide accessibility of the sacred within the Craft, which are engendered by the pluralistic and polytheistic worldview, be lost to dogma and control every bit as crippling and stifling as any under the patriarchy?

That worry became real as some worshippers of *The* Goddess excluded men from religious practice, a mirror image of the denial of the priesthood to women in patriarchal religions. A monotheistic Goddess the Mother parallel in form and function to God the Father has disturbing ramifications both theologically, as the dual gendered polytheism is lost, and politically, as men are denied access to Wiccan spirituality.

Accusations of appropriation soon surfaced in Wiccan communities. Sacred songs, rituals, and liturgies created and performed by both men and women for the pleasure and celebration of Gods and Goddesses were being rewritten. A religion of women for women in a female-only voice in female-only Circles for the exclusive worship of *The* Goddess was presented as *this* is the religion of Wicca. So much so, that many of my university students today assume that all Witches are women, a rather chilling echo of a similar understanding of women by the medieval church.

The distinction between feminist Goddess-only Wicca and the Craft as practiced among other traditions reminds us that Wiccan practice and theology are not monolithic. Like most religious practitioners, Witches participate in a universe of competing and sometimes conflicting discourses and practices. We must be careful not to conflate feminist Wicca with Witchcraft in its entirety, or to assume that Witchcraft is a religion only of women and Goddesses.

In fact, one of the things that initially attracted me to the Craft was the existence of strong and powerful Goddesses *and* Gods and equal access to the sacred for women *and* men. At least potentially, a dual-gendered polytheistic Craft encourages new models of religious leadership in which both men and women participate fully, sharing equally roles of authority and responsibility. Unlike many other religions, not only do males in the Craft have important religious roles, but—ideally—women also have roles that are both extremely powerful and valuable, not ones of passivity and obedience to male authority.[14] It is small wonder, then, that the Craft has been attractive to women seeking alternatives to androcentric religious forms.

Having said that, I must also point out that Wicca has never been feminist heaven. While Wicca has many wonderful images of female divinity and great roles for women, it can still be pretty sexist in practice. I remember Sam trying to explain to us—quite unsuccessfully, really—why the High Priest of a coven could be an old man, while the High Priestess must always be a lovely young maiden. An aging High Priestess must step down for a younger woman at precisely the time in her life when she has the greatest experience.

I think this attitude toward aging women was consistent with how the Goddess Herself was viewed. When I was initiated in the early seventies, the most popular image of the Goddess was either as a lovely, blond Maiden or as a nurturing and protective Mother. Presented in these ways, these two aspects were hardly challenging to patriarchy, as feminist scholars have pointed out.[15] The third aspect or dimension of the Goddess, the dark Crone, lady of wisdom and death, was vaguely developed and given comparatively little emphasis.

This was brought home to me in Sam's group when I had to choose my Craft name. This name is specially chosen by a person who is about to be initiated and is meant to represent the person's sacred identity, the truest and most authentic expression of the self. I remember well the look of dismay on my High Priest's face when I chose for my Craft name the name of one of the dark Goddesses of our Celtic pantheon—a formidable Goddess of death and wisdom whose magic challenges and transforms.

Although the discovery of Wicca by the Women's Movement brought what I think are some troubling developments, such as the creation of a monotheistic Goddess and the exclusion of men from Circles, it was also slowly bringing new maturity and insights into our understanding of Goddesses, and helping us to challenge the more limited roles for women in our religious practice.[16] This has reinvigorated the Craft, providing new modes of religious discourse and models of ritual expression, new challenges to rigid hierarchical structures, and an increased sense of political activism among Witches.

The fact that a religion with many strong Goddesses is still not free of patriarchy reminds us to look at religious phenomena more carefully. We need to question how female models of deity are used within a particular community. Do they enable women to negotiate for power and authority, or do they reinforce patriarchal models of religious behavior? Such questions allow us to challenge our own hidden presuppositions and better enable us to cover the extensive range of women's religious experiences in any community.[17]

Structure and Organization

The Craft is practiced by individuals called solitaries (whose activities and experiences do not figure in this work) or by groups called covens. Covens have a great deal of autonomy and vary widely in composition, size, and structure. Some covens practice ritual initiation as a form of entry into the group. This initiation typically takes place, as it does in my own coven, after a period of study and mutual screening. In its largest and most inclusive sense, a coven consists of initiates as well as the students who are working toward initiation. But not all covens practice initiation, and some of those that do may not require a course of study.

The Witches in both my parent coven and my coven today understand initiation as an entrance into the clergy. Our members are called Priests or Priestesses after initiation and may or may not function as such within the larger Pagan community. As a Priestess, I have performed nearly a dozen legal marriages, which we call handfasting ceremonies. Witches also have ceremonies for blessing newborns, sometimes called Wiccaning, as well as rites for the dead. As with clergy in other religions, we are also occasionally involved in counseling or at least in referring others to a good counselor for their problems.

Coven organizational and administrative structures range from minimalist to highly structured patterns of training and degree advancement. Some covens have an extensive training program and a hierarchical structure based on levels of expertise and experience. A few groups have a rigid, even authoritarian, hierarchical structure that may or may not be connected to training. Still other covens have no discernable training, disciplined praxis, or structure, preferring a totally spontaneous and creative approach to worship.

Ritual

Wiccan ritual takes on a dizzying variety of forms, from the elementary to the most sophisticated and from the simplest to the most elaborate and ceremonial patterns of ritual behavior and expression. A Wiccan ritual may be as simple as a heartfelt prayer or as complex as a full Circle: Witches robed and purified, the space made sacred, the altar adorned with tools and decorated for the season, and the Gods called to attend. A single coven may itself practice a wide variety of ritual styles, creatively adapting the ritual to fit both the occasion and the place where the ritual must be performed.

But the Wiccan religion does more than simply present us with a nice array of rituals. It actually challenges us to rethink the categories of religion and ritual themselves. For many people, like my students at university, religion is a label—something we are born into that gives us an identity. We tend to allow only one label per forehead; someone who says he is a Hindu Catholic or a Buddhist Pagan makes us nervous. We like to see religions as discreet entities or distinct categories, bounded by tidy little lines, neatly labeled and placed in a box on the shelf. We see ritual as a static and repetitive ordeal ordered by authority and/or tradition and performed for us or on us. Rituals must therefore be *followed*; occasionally they must be *endured*. Religious rituals are prescriptive and even boring, rather than creative and adaptive.

Witches challenge these categories by creating their own religious rituals. Sometimes these rituals are grounded in years of study and practice; at other times they come through sheer inspiration and artistry to fit the moment. Some reoccur, like the seasonal rituals of Yule or Beltane, but they never repeat. (Like I tell my comparative religions students: "You may celebrate Thanksgiving every year, but hopefully you don't eat the *same* turkey!")

By embracing the deliberately constructed nature of their religion, Wiccans provide ample material to think with, and present an opportunity to examine and understand other religions as examples of creative activities and lived processes. When we are presented with people who create their own religious rituals, our attitudes toward both change considerably.[18] It becomes possible to understand religion in general as a creative *activity*, rather than a label, even one that is consciously chosen. Religion itself becomes a lived *process*, not a product. It is a human creation, a living experience, a performed activity—not merely a body of inherited texts. Human beings constantly reconstruct and reweave their understanding of the sacred, and so the search for the ultimate origin or who has the most ancient texts or practices is rendered nonsensical or irrelevant.

Text and Authority

Speaking of inherited texts and ultimate origins, I must admit to my annoyance at one argument that occasionally flares up among Wiccans and scholars of Wicca. Although the point that Witches emphasize experience over text is largely true, debate arose almost immediately within both religious and scholarly communities as to how old *was* The Old Religion. Did the Craft even exist before Gerald Gardner? How much of the *Book of Shadows*—a collection of ritual manuals, folk wisdom, and philosophical writings that might be loosely termed as the religion's sacred text—was an invention of a retired civil servant with a surfeit of leisure time and an overactive imagination?

The resurgence—some might say creation[19]—of modern-day Wicca owes much to the repeal in the 1950s of the last anti-Witchcraft or fortune telling laws in Britain. This freed Gardner, a retired British civil servant and writer of occult fiction, to publish *Witchcraft Today* and to openly proclaim the existence of The Old Religion as an ancient pre-Christian religion that had been forced underground for several hundred years to avoid persecution.

In the early stages of modern revival, Witches placed great emphasis on tradition, on ancient practices traced in unbroken line, in order to legitimize the authority of their religious experience. After all, we were most familiar with Judeo-Christian religions that had sacred texts whose apparent age and historicity in some sense *proved* their validity. I suspect that many of the arguments about the historical validity of the *Book of Shadows* came out of a desire among Wiccans to have their religion seen as equally (or more) valid or authoritative *because it was older than* religions such as Christianity. I suggest that there are better places to look for the authority of religious practice than text.

There are inherent problems with text that affect both worshippers and scholars. Religious people tend to believe that their sacred texts, whatever they might be, go back to the dawn of time. The newer the religion, the more likely it is to have strong narratives about its ancient historical past. My observation not only applies to Wicca, but also to new religious movements as diverse as Goddess Spirituality and the Mormons. This is the way that we routinely argue religious authority. No one wants to say that his religion began last Tuesday at 3:00 p.m., especially if it did. We need our religions to be *old*, because we think that age gives insights and truths more weight and authority.

And we need our sacred texts to be unchanged from the dawn of time, an unbroken tradition of authority that is historically provable. But religious texts are not static things. Both their forms and meanings change through time and they are constantly written, rewritten, interpreted and reinterpreted in the present.

Scholars tend to be more aware of textual change and often have a sophisticated understanding of how texts come into and fall out of the canon.

But, too often, scholars also tend to rely upon decontextualized texts to define religion, conflating religious texts with practice to the extent of believing if it isn't written down, it must not exist. It is a category mistake to confuse religious text with practices; religious practices and written text are not the same thing.

Scholars also fail to recognize the extent to which categories such as religion are constructed and artificially bounded. Certainly the categories "Hindu" or "Christian" conceal as much as they reveal in terms of the variety of their practices. We create them and name them for our convenience. They do not exist as homogenous and neatly drawn categories in practice. As J. Z. Smith puts it: "religion is not an empirical category. It is a second-order abstraction resulting . . . in misplaced concreteness."[20] Our categories conceal the messy world of religions as they are actually lived and practiced by real people—people with a multitude of competing and contesting practices, customs, traditions, beliefs, ideas, and images—all gathered by the scholar into the same neat box.

Scholars of religions have difficulty dealing with *oral* traditions and *practices* handed down within communities through *praxis*, a self-disciplinary process that involves the whole person. Praxis transforms the way humans think about and act in the world. Because praxis is so often emphasized in the Craft over belief, text, or dogma, the Craft becomes a good candidate for exploring what the recovery of praxis does for our understanding of religions generally.

Folklorist Leonard Primiano observes that the recovery of praxis allows us to capture the experiential dimension of religion as it is lived by the people practicing it. Praxis enables us to recontextualize religion at the level of what Primiano calls the vernacular, and what I call the level of individuals-practicing. It also enables us to dismantle one of the prevalent dichotomies in studies of folk belief and religious studies: *Religion* versus *religion* or Organized-and-Institutional Religion-administered-in-an-Official-manner-by-Hierarchical-Elites versus folk religion. The misnaming of religion as official and unofficial suggests that *Religion* is a Platonic form existing as a pure element that is in some way transformed, even contaminated, by its exposure to human communities.[21]

Primiano notes that a focus on religions as they are actually lived by human beings helps us to grasp the idea that official religion does not, in fact, exist. While there are agencies of normative or prescriptive religion, there is "no objective existence of practice" that constitutes official religion. No one "lives an 'officially' religious life in a pure unadulterated form" without some act of "creation, some dissenting impulse, some reflection on lived experience that influences how these individuals direct their religious lives."[22]

Or, as Thomas Kasulis is fond of saying to his religious studies students: "There is no such thing as religion, only religious people."[23]

Asking questions about the age of texts misses the point of praxis. We need to understand religious traditions as *dynamic*, as constantly interpreted and framed within the present moment.[24] Examining religious praxis, looking closely at how religions are actually lived by human beings, enables us to understand religious authority in a more useful way than deciphering the age of a disembodied text.

Both my scholarship and my own experiences as a religious person mutually reinforce an understanding of religious traditions as dynamic and constantly changing. As a Witch, I have no problem simultaneously understanding my own religious practices as both modern or reconstructed *and* rooted in a distant pre-Christian past. My investigations into the religious and folk practices of my own Slavic and Hungarian ethnic heritage have contributed to an understanding of how practices of worship often continue under different religious labels, theological or symbolic frameworks, and even different names for Gods.[25] These religious practices also change as they are inevitably interpreted and creatively performed by people in the present. What we call tradition changes constantly.

Or, to put it another way, the flowing river is both *always* and *never* the same river.

Having situated myself within both my scholarly and religious practices, and having sketched out a rough guide to the Wiccan ritual landscape, my next task is to introduce my coven and to describe its basic ritual patterns. My descriptions are limited by the personal oaths of religious practice and the ethical fieldwork practices of responsible scholarship. I will not disclose people's identities; all of the names in my writings on Wiccan ritual and initiation are made up, and they tend to change from one work to the next. Given my reflections as both scholar and practitioner, it seems somehow fitting that both scholarship and practice limit what I can say.

3

The Merry Circle

Flowing Water

After the breakup of our parent coven, I was feeling pretty much adrift and unsure of what form my religious practice would now take. Our tradition had taught that "you could not be a Witch alone," and I suppose I learned that lesson too well. Some of us who remained in the area kept in touch, even though our lives were changing radically from our college days together. One of my closest friends in the coven married and left the Craft for the religion of her husband. Over time, we eventually lost track of each other. A couple of others started a coven based on the teachings of British Witch and author Doreen Valiente, but I wasn't comfortable with the style of their practice.

Lauren and I also kept in touch, although we lived on opposite sides of the state. She was teaching a course on Witchcraft at a local New Age bookstore near her town and invited me to come and meet some of her students. Two or three of them seemed very interested in the Craft and wanted to study more seriously for initiation. This prompted us to consider starting a group. We discovered that there were a number of theological as well as practical issues to discuss.

Realistically, did we have the time and energy to put into a group? Lauren was married and had two small children. She was taking classes whenever she could to get additional certification in her field and also did some part-time tutoring. I was married, in graduate school, and working full time. Taking on a group of Dedicants would require considerable work, and a disproportionate amount of that would have to come from Lauren initially, since the students lived on her side of the state. For my part, I would need to travel extensively, especially if I were going to get to know the students really well.

While the practical questions were bad enough, the theological questions were much worse. When we finally agreed that we wanted to start our own coven, we immediately ran into several problems related to issues of gender and power that challenged our grasp of Wiccan theology.

First, Lauren's students were women. And so were we. Why would this be a problem for Witches from our tradition? After all, Wicca is a tradition with Goddesses, distinctive role models, and powerful roles for women. But in our parent coven, men initiated women, and women initiated men. Whenever we asked why, we were taught that the power always passed between male and female, never male to male or female to female, with the possible exception of father to son or mother to daughter. This raised two questions about power: *what* power was being passed and *where* did it come from? And it raised the related and immediate question of how two women could initiate other women.

Second, we faced a problem having to do with the way in which the Gods are invoked into the Circle in formal group practice. In our parent coven, the God was ritually invoked into the body of the High Priest— always Sam—and the Goddess into the woman serving as High Priestess— usually, but not always—Lauren. After these ritual invocations, which were called the Calling Down ceremonies, the High Priest and High Priestess became the God and Goddess incarnate.

While no doubt a transformative experience for the High Priest and Priestess, this had an unfortunate effect on group dynamics. In our parent coven, the Calling Down ceremonies meant that the High Priest and Priestess acted like nobility, while the rest of the coven addressed them as Lord and Lady and served them at every opportunity. The problem here was twofold. How could we successfully do the formal invocations without a man to play the role of the High Priest? And did we really think that our Gods wanted us to act like something out of a bad British costume picture?

I guess you can figure out where I came down on this one.

Finally, Sam had never elevated anyone into the second degree. In our tradition, Witches are initiated clergy in various stages of training and expertise. We recognize two basic levels, or degrees, that are celebrated and acknowledged with group ritual. The first, that of Priest or Priestess, is reached upon initiation. The second degree, that of High Priest or High Priestess, is acquired only if the Witch chooses to pursue additional training that would effectively enable her to start and train her own covens. (Within our tradition there had been rumors of a third level, usually reached after several years as a High Priest or Priestess, and after experience leading more than one coven. The third degree is, as far as we know, assumed without ritual fanfare, and considered a private matter between the Witch and the Gods.) Since Sam had elevated neither of us to second degree, were we qualified to start our own coven?

These problems forced us to confront gender roles and power dynamics within our Circle, and challenged our understanding of the nature of Deity and the role gender plays in the successful invocation of Deity into the Circle. Is *God* somehow equivalent to *man* and *Goddess* to *woman*? Or do both God and Goddess manifest or resonate within each person? What is the connection between sex and Deity? Is it merely one's *sex* that calls forth Deity into manifestation in the Circle? Or one's *skill* and *training* as a Witch?

One way of thinking—that God is equivalent to man—takes us right back to the Serbian Orthodox Church (among others), with its holy altar doors tightly shut against the passage of a woman. Woman is, depending on the understanding of the particular tradition, profane, impure, polluting, or simply an unfit representative of or vessel for the divine spirit. God is man, and only man can represent God. This reduces the successful invocation of God to a function of the presence of male genitalia. Put another way, women have the wrong equipment to invoke God.

This way of thinking also seems to imply that God/Goddess and man/woman exist as neatly bound, discreet and distinctive essences or Platonic forms. And once again, this way of thinking about Deity and humans takes us dancing between binary poles and conceals both the rich diversity of human experiences of Deity as well as the wide range of human expressions of gender.

But there is another way of thinking, one that we argued is more representative of a Wiccan theological worldview: that both God and Goddess manifest in every person. Goddess and God flow throughout all of nature, through each and every man and woman, becoming fully present in the world. Both women and men are therefore fully formed in the image and power of God and Goddess. We could think of no characteristic or attribute not shared in some measure by both males and females, not represented by both Gods and Goddesses. Ruthlessness and compassion, wisdom and folly, death and destruction, birth and renewal—all flow in and through both men and women in different proportions at different times in their lives. There are healing and nurturing Goddesses and Goddesses of War and Death. (Curiously, sometimes They are the same Goddess.) In equal measure, there are Gods of War and Destruction and Gods of Love and Compassion.

As we rejected the cleanly bound essence of Platonic forms for both Gods and humans, so we reasoned that it is not *sex* that calls God fully into the Circle, but *skill*. A Priestess may invoke God, and a Priest may invoke Goddess, each to a greater or lesser degree according to that person's trained awareness and level of experience. The more skill and the better the training, the fuller and more complete the invocation. Gender was no barrier to the presence of Deity.

And if the Gods are within us and all around us, then They should be invoked into the Circle as a whole, not just the bodies of the High Priest or High Priestess, thankfully banishing the British nobility from our Circle. When invocations are performed to the entire Circle, everyone in the group has an opportunity to participate fully in the ritual experience of the presence of both God and Goddess—within the Circle, and within themselves.[1] The *power*, represented by the presence of the Gods in the Circle, does not belong exclusively to any one person in the group, but is shared by the whole. Power is not passed by sex, but shared by skill and training.

We further reasoned that if invocations performed by two trained female Witches were successful, then initiations performed by those same women would also be successful. As to our overall qualifications for running a coven, both Lauren and I had worked with our parent coven for far longer and had had more ritual experience than many of the Pagan and Wiccan Elders we met from other traditions. We decided that our years of experience had earned us the right to carry on our practice.

We no longer needed Sam to confirm our expertise.

Welcome to the Merry Circle

Lauren and I finally started our coven, which I will call the Merry Circle, in 1984. Sandy was our first successful initiate,[2] followed several months later by Dot. Over the years, others would also be initiated, bringing the size of the group to nine initiates and three Dedicants at its height. We kept a lot of the traditions of our parent coven, but adapted or changed entirely those that did not work or fit our experiences or circumstances.

Today the Merry Circle no longer exists as a single, coherent, practicing group. The members of the Circle lived in various parts of northern and central Ohio and eventually divided the coven along geographic lines. Witches call this practice hiving off, and it occurs for a number of reasons. When a coven gets too large, becomes too spread out geographically, or develops interpersonal differences that cannot be resolved,[3] it becomes a matter of common sense to divide. A Priest or Priestess of qualified rank assumes leadership of the part of the group that wants to hive off from the larger body. Depending on the reasons the coven divides, the groups may or may not continue to work together on occasion.

I was the one who initiated the hiving off process for people living in the central part of the state. It had become too much to keep traveling between the two areas. The Witches living in the northern part of the state had a hard time getting to know my students, and I had a hard time really getting to know theirs. We performed a very moving ceremony, and we all hoped to stay in touch, continue to learn from each other, and to practice together again on special occasions.

Eventually more changes came to the Merry Circle. The northern group subsequently split in two. One of these groups, led by Dot and Sandy, continues to practice in the Wiccan tradition. The other group, including Lauren, has become deeply involved in American Druidism, which is a similar but distinct contemporary Pagan religious path.[4] But for the purpose of this book, I describe the Merry Circle and its practices before either division.

The Merry Circle is composed of six Priestesses and two Priests (with an additional Priest initiated into the northern group after the first hiving). There are four High Priestesses: Lauren, Sandy, Dot, and me. Until recently, the four of us formed the core of the group because we practiced and worked together the longest.

The members of the Merry Circle come from a range of European ethnic and socio-economic backgrounds ranging from lower middle to working class; all members are white. Ages range from the mid-twenties to the late-forties. Our educational backgrounds vary a great deal, from members who are high school graduates to one with a Ph.D., and others who range in between.

The following list represents just a few of the labels that the Witches of the Merry Circle might use to describe themselves: parent, real estate agent, astrologer, student, secretary, metalsmith, musician, herbalist, farmer, employee of the Clerk of Courts, photographer, professor, and factory worker. The Merry Circle runs the gamut politically, from leftist "Deadheads" to moderate Republicans, a fact that makes conversation around election time *very* interesting.

When I was writing this book, I spent a great deal of time thinking about what draws a group like ours together. I expected to find large areas of agreement or markedly similar lifestyles and attitudes. I did not. We come from dissimilar enough backgrounds and experiences to have very different attitudes toward just about everything—including our religious beliefs. We most come together in agreement around the *practice* of the rituals performed in our Circle.

The Merry Circle's tradition draws heavily from the mythology and folk traditions found in the British Isles, what today might be popularly considered Celtic. The Deities we invoke into the Circle during rituals generally come from Welsh and Irish pantheons, as did those of our parent coven. Although several, but not all, of the Merry Circle members are ethnically from the British Isles, no one has a problem working with a European tradition that is not specifically represented by his or her particular ethnic ancestry.[5]

In terms of the balance of power between male and female, the members of this coven worship both Goddesses and Gods, favoring neither. Both women and men have equal access to the priesthood. There is little, if any, distinction between the roles of Priest and Priestess within the coven; both roles are accorded equal power and value. Each initiate learns how to cast the Circle, or to create the ritual space, and to invoke both Goddesses and Gods. On a technical level, the rituals are conducted equally well with only Priestesses or Priests attending. The Merry Circle expects each initiate to contribute to the rites according to his or her training and years of experience.

Most of the group is involved in one way or another with the training of new students who are in varying stages of learning. A serious student, or Dedicant, has to have a high level of self-discipline and a willingness to undertake a rigorous course of study—typically for one to three years. Like our parent group, we never charge money for instruction. Clergy have jobs or careers outside of their religious responsibilities. Initiation into the coven is both a central religious experience and a crucial mutual screening process for the group. We give a critical amount of attention to the development of group dynamics, and to a sense of mutual commitment, respect, and trust. Perfect love and perfect trust are two requirements for initiation, which is ideally seen as a lifelong commitment to both religious practice and religious community.

Basic Elements of Ritual

The Merry Circle usually performs its group rituals at night and, whenever possible, outdoors in nature. Lauren has a farm with secluded back acreage that we were able to make into a permanent ritual space. Most of our rituals occur here, unless the weather is too bad to be outside for any length of time. Since it is often difficult for those of us living in urban and suburban places to find a suitably private outdoor location, indoor ritual spaces are common, too. These usually take the form of a spare room or part of a room dedicated to that purpose, decorated with an altar, statues or pictures of Gods and Goddesses, flowers, incense, the Witch's personal tools, and

Figure 1. Typical Indoor Altar

other religious objects (figure 1). We've used indoor spaces as varied as a basement, parts of living rooms, an attic, and a spare bedroom.

We hold our formal group rituals in a specially prepared space called the Circle. The space is quite literally round, or, if created indoors, as round as possible given the limitations of the room and the number of people who must be accommodated within the perimeter. The Circle is often marked off from the space around it by a ring of stones (if outdoors), a ring of red yarn (if indoors), or some other distinctive marking determined by the creativity of the individual Witch. The four directions—north, east, south, and west—are plotted as accurately as possible using a compass and then marked by specially blessed and prepared candles that are used in the ceremony.

An important part of Wiccan ritual training is learning how to cast the Circle, or create the sacred space.[6] Casting the Circle seals off the ritual area from the mundane world, usually through the symbolic invocation of the four basic elements—earth, air, fire, water—along with the fifth element, spirit. Understanding and mastery of the elements are essential to casting a ritual Circle and working many forms of magic within our tradition.

All five elements are represented by the pentagram (figure 2). This five-pointed star is a sacred symbol to many Witches, and is often used decoratively on the altar or worn as jewelry, which, in symbolic importance, would be equivalent to a Christian wearing a cross. In its single-point-side-up position, the pentagram represents the cosmos: each point of the star is one of the four elements, with spirit on the top point as the overarching force guiding all. The circle surrounding the five-pointed star encloses the elements and spirit in unity and wholeness.

The pentagram's misuse (sometimes in an upside down position) by media and filmmakers to represent suspicious occult activity, such as Satanism,

Figure 2. The Pentagram, the Five-Pointed Star

Figure 3. The Witch's Athame

is deeply offensive to most Witches. Witchcraft has nothing to do with Satanism, which many of us see as essentially an offshoot of Christianity.

The Circle's directions correspond to elements, seasons, colors, animals, ages of life, and so forth. In our tradition, the direction of east corresponds with the element of air and the rising sun, south with fire and high noon, west with water and twilight, and north with the earth and midnight. Spirit is associated with the center, from which point the Gods are invoked.

The elements are also represented on the altar and in the personal ritual tools of each Witch.[7] The basic ritual tools include the athame (and sometimes the sword), the wand, the chalice, the pentacle, and the white-handled knife. The athame (figure 3) is a sharp, black-handled, double-bladed knife that represents fire. As a tool of fire, it represents life energy, passion, and vitality. The athame is used for cutting out or marking off the space that will become the Circle and for symbolic or spiritual defense, but it is never used to physically cut anything. The sword has similar properties to the athame, and may be used by a High Priestess or High Priest to cut out the Circle space.

The wand (figure 4) may be made from a number of different kinds of wood (mine is oak with a crystal mounted on the end) and is used to represent the element of air. Other air tools may include the incense burner and feathers used to fan the incense around the Circle. As a tool of air, the wand represents the mind, communication, and the intellect. Though similar in some ways to the athame, the wand is milder in temperament and is often used in blessing objects.

Figure 4. The Wand and Tools of Air

The Witch's chalice (figure 5), used to represent the element of water, may be made out of almost any material that can hold liquid, including glass, silver, or clay. It can be highly decorative or plain and simple, according to the taste of the individual Witch. I have two that I generally use in Circle, both of fired clay and made by friends who are Pagan artists. One is black with a lovely Dark Goddess face, and the other is quite a bit larger and decorated with simple pentagrams. As a tool of water, the chalice represents the emotions, love, depth of perception, and insight. The chalice holds the wine for the ceremony.

The pentacle (figure 6) represents the earth and is a disc or small plate on which a five-pointed star, and sometimes other symbols, is engraved or drawn. It may be made from almost any material, including metal, leather, clay, and wood. Mine is leather and incorporates other symbols in addition to the pentagram. As a form of earth, the pentacle represents body, the material world, strength, and determination.

The white-handled knife (figure 7) is used to cut or chop things, such as herbs for incense. I have three that I use for different purposes. One has a large blade with a simple, unpainted wooden handle; another has a smaller blade (good for digging wax out of candlestick holders) with a handle made out of an antler; and the third has a flint blade with a handle carved in the form of a wolf. Witches usually also acquire a suitable incense burner, some nice candleholders, and so forth to round out their altar equipment.

Many Witches feel that such tools are not entirely necessary to ritual, but they help focus our attention and concentration on the task at hand.

The typical altar (figures 8, 9) is a rectangular table about the height of a coffee table and large enough to hold the Witch's tools, candles for fire,

Figure 5. The Chalice

Figure 6. The Pentacle

Figure 7. The Author's White-Handled Knives

Figure 8. Typical Outdoor Altar

Figure 9. Simple Altar Constructed for an Outdoor Wedding

a small bowl of water, incense for the element of air, and a container of salt or earth for the element of earth. In a pinch, almost anything practical can be used for an altar; I've used a simple cloth on the ground, a large flat outcropping of rock, a coffee table, and a cedar chest passed down to me by my grandmother.

The altar in our tradition is always positioned in the north quadrant of the Circle, decorated with statues of Gods and Goddesses or other religious symbols, and usually decorated according to the season, perhaps with spring flowers or autumn harvest arrangements of leaves, dried flowers, corn, gourds, and fruits.

Casting the Circle

The first task for Witches casting the Circle is literally to clean or clear the space to be used for the rite. For an indoor Circle, this may mean shifting furniture, getting out the vacuum, and generally clearing up the clutter. When casting a Circle outdoors, the Witches usually have to pick up sticks, gather firewood, clear brush, or otherwise tidy up the ritual space. Some of this has to be done hours in advance, while there is still plenty of light to see by. As such, it is one of the activities that bring us together as a group to share and build community. Once the space is cleared, all the necessary ritual equipment—candles, wine, cakes, ritual tools, and so forth—is gathered and taken to the site.

The Priestesses and Priests who will be working the rite always make an outline of the ritual, determining in advance who will do what part of the ritual and what chants they will use. Each Witch takes or has already taken a ritual bath or shower, usually in the privacy of his own home and well before the time of the ritual. On those special occasions when purification or rededication is the purpose of the ritual, the ritual bath takes on a special meaning, and the bath water contains specially prepared herbs. The Witches take turns bathing with freshly made batches of the specially prepared water before they robe for the ritual; the robes must also have been cleaned before the rite. While some groups work skyclad or in the nude, ours works in full-length, black cotton robes that are cut from similar patterns. The robes serve multiple purposes: their similarity helps create a sense of group identity, and their color is both symbolic and quite practical for working outdoors in the dark if one wishes not to be seen.

Properly cleansed and robed, the Witches gather at the site to begin the actual process of casting the Circle. All the Witches form a circle as one Priest or Priestess leads the group in a breathing and visualization exercise, designed to accomplish several interconnected purposes and fundamental to any form of magic or ceremonial work done by the Witches in the coven. Through this exercise, the Witch is able to let go of the cares and concerns of the mundane world and assume her Craft personality, a consciously constructed ritual identity whose personality and attributes are revealed by her Craft name. Grounding and centering is the first act of establishing ritual community.

Each Circle is cast, or constructed, in the same manner, and most rituals within the Circle use the following basic structural format.

Circle Construction
    Cut the Circle (Fire)
    Invoke Air
    Invoke Earth and Water
    Consecrate the Circle
    Invoke the Watchtowers
    State the Purpose of the Rite
Invoke the Gods
Conduct Work of Specific Ritual
Share Cakes and Wine
Complete Any Other Ritual Work
Circle Deconstruction
    Bid the Gods Farewell
    Bid the Watchtowers Farewell
    Break the Circle

Circle Construction

Casting the Circle is a skill demanding a competent and demonstrable level of somatic praxis. It requires disciplined training not only of the Witch's mind, but of her body as well. New initiates will spend much time working with each step of Circle casting, honing both mental and physical or somatic sensitivity to all the dimensions of ritual activity that make the Circle "a fit place for the Gods to enter." When fully trained, the Witch's body, mind, and spirit will be completely engaged in the task, so that casting a Circle becomes almost transparent, second nature, a deeply embedded part of her sense of self as Witch and Priestess.

Unless a newly made initiate is specifically casting a practice Circle, the Merry Circle will determine in advance which High Priestess is to be primarily responsible for casting the Circle. This High Priestess literally cuts the space out of "normal space" by walking around the edge of the Circle three times, using the ritual sword or her personal athame to mark the line of the Circle's edge (figure 10). Both sword and athame are tools of the element fire, and so it is fire that marks the initial separation of sacred space from the everyday. While the Priestess is cutting the Circle, the coven sings a chant to help her focus, and visualizes fire flowing out from the sword or the athame.

Cutting the Circle is followed by an invocation of the air element, which may be done by any Witch present. He takes the incense burner from the altar, fanning incense around the edge of the circle, and places the incense burner back on the altar. Earth and water are invoked simultaneously in this Circle; since the water contains salt, a symbol of earth, it has been consecrated and blessed as both elements. Another Witch takes the consecrated water from the altar, sprinkles it around the edge of the Circle, the

Figure 10. Cutting Out the Circle

Witches in the Circle, and the altar, and places it back on the altar. This movement is done at the same time that another High Priestess stands in the center of the Circle with her athame and charges the Circle, essentially commanding it to be a place of love and truth and a fit place for the Gods to enter.

Next, the four Watchtowers—spirit beings who guard each direction—are invoked through physical gesture, prayer, and intonation. These Guardians of the Watchtowers, usually referred to as the Ancient and Mighty Ones, are called upon to witness the activities of the ritual and to guard the participants of the Circle from harm. As official witnesses for such events as initiation, they are important figures in Craft ritual practice. (When there were four High Priestesses at the height of the Merry Circle's membership, each High Priestess would take a direction and invoke the Watchtower of that direction.) Just as the Watchtowers are invoked, so, too, are they released or dismissed at the end of the Circle. Finally, the purpose of the rite is stated, usually (but not always) by the person who cut the Circle.

After the purpose of the ritual has been stated, the Witches meet together in the center of the Circle, hold hands, and chant or sing a song that expresses a sense of community.

Our group experimented with different songs and chants over the years. As few of us are professional singers, it was a challenge finding something that almost anyone could sing. We finally settled on a song heard by someone at a festival or on a tape, which seems to be how we usually find our songs and chants. The group gave it a simple melody, adjusted the range, and developed the following:

> You are my family, and you are healing me
> You are my family, and you are healing me
> You are my people. We are one.
> You are my people. We are one.

This is repeated several times, occasionally with some fancy harmony if anyone is up to it, until all in the Circle know that it is time to move on. This kind of silent communication, sense of timing, or group knowing is a difficult phenomenon to explain, but it is one that asserts itself increasingly as the members work with one another over time. I suspect that this kind of communication comes with the development of community—what Witches sometimes refer to as group mind—and is an essential part of working together successfully within ritual.

After the group chant is finished, it is time to decorate the Circle. We adorn the perimeter of the Circle, the four directions, and the altar with seasonal flowers, leaves, gourds, or other decorative items in order to make it a place of beauty.

In the Presence of the Gods

Now we are ready for the invocation of the Gods (figure 11), which helps establish the ritual's purpose and raises the participants' energy levels within the Circle. Lauren and I are usually involved in invoking the God and Goddess, and the two of us decide in advance which of us will do what invocation. The group also settles on a chant for each invocation, and the Witches invoke the Gods with a combination of prayer, song or chant, and rhythmic drumming or rattling, and sometimes dancing. Everyone within the Circle participates, and there are no non-participatory observers who stand outside. Even guests who are invited as potential members or as visiting religious specialists from another path are briefed on what will happen during the ritual and participate in the Circle's activities to the best of their abilities.

The Merry Circle has a patron Goddess and God who are always invoked and whose names are known only by the initiates, but other Goddesses and Gods may also be invited to the Circle, depending on Their nature and the specific activities of the rite. For example, if the Circle involves healing, Gods and Goddesses particularly known for Their healing powers will be invited. In the summer, the Witches of the Merry Circle invoke the Goddess first, and in the winter the God first.

After the invocation, the Witches begin to carry out the work or purpose of the ritual, such as seed blessing, healing, celebration of a sabbat, or initiation. When we are finished, everyone sits down on the ground or floor and relaxes. We share our experiences of the ritual with one another, teach each other new songs or chants, tell jokes or stories, and may do some special divination to help with a member's problem.

The ceremony of cakes and wine takes place at this time. Served in a communal chalice, the wine is blessed with the athame to symbolize the sacred union of the Goddess and the God (figure 12). As demanded by hallowed tradition, Lauren and I engage in ritual contest to determine who gets to bless the wine, as the one who starts the wine must eventually drain the cup. (Obviously, some traditions are not to be tampered with.) Before the first drink, a bit of the wine is always poured on the ground as an offering to the Gods.

The chalice itself represents the female, and the athame the male. The cakes are crescent-shaped oatmeal cookies specially baked by one of the Witches, whose success or failure with the recipe usually forms the basis for quite a bit of joking during the relaxed and casual atmosphere that follows. The cakes are ritually blessed with the wand and then shared among the Witches present (figure 13). Each Witch leaves part of their first cake as an offering to the Gods. Any additional Craft business or ritual work is done after the ceremony of the cakes and wine is finished.

Figure 11. Invoking the Gods

Figure 12. Blessing the Wine

Figure 13. Author and Toby, Sharing Cakes

Circle Deconstruction

At this point, the Witches begin to shut down the Circle. Jokingly, I like to call this activity Circle deconstruction, which the rest of the Merry Circle tolerate with amusement. They know that the term is a play on words for me, for both the kinds of scholarship I encounter and talk about—construction and deconstruction currently being popular terms in the scholar's dictionary—and for the process of setting up and taking down the Circle.

Circle deconstruction is as important to a successful ritual as the construction of the Circle. All energies raised in the Circle must be released to their proper purpose (i.e., healing) or safely grounded. We bid the Gods, as well as the Guardians of the Watchtowers, a fond farewell. Everything that is called is dismissed; everything that is raised is grounded. The High Priestess in charge of the Circle breaks the Circle by crossing over its boundary and checks the perimeter to see if anything is amiss. Should the High Priestess detect any unusual or harmful energy (something that's never happened in my years as Priestess), she has a responsibility to immediately recast the Circle to protect the members present and to banish the offending energy.

Circle deconstruction not only brings a sense of closure to the event, but also illustrates the degree to which Witches approach ritual as having experiential *reality*—serious and real physical and psychological effects on our lives—rather than merely as metaphorical abstraction.

After the Circle is ended, the ritual gear is packed up, and either cleaned up by the participating members or carted back to the house if the Circle has been outdoors. A celebratory feast commonly follows the ritual. This can be anything from an elaborate and thematic meal prepared in advance, to a simple pot of chicken soup or a potluck assortment of fruits, cheese, and snacks. The Witches frequently stay up until the wee hours of the morning, talking, singing, joking, playing music, watching movies, and generally having an enjoyable time.

Now that you have a brief introduction to the practices of the Merry Circle, it is time to find the path to the Circle's edge.

4

The Path toward the Circle

My ultimate goal in the writing of this book is fairly straightforward: I want to see to what extent the scholarship on ritual initiation fits my own experience as someone who has been initiated and has also initiated others. Since I have walked the path to the Circle many times, I long ago came to an understanding of Wiccan initiation as rather more complex than and perhaps not as sharply defined in its structural or spatial movements as Arnold van Gennep's three-stage process of separation, liminality, and rein-corporation—or any of its subsequent variations[1]—and wondered if an ex-amination of the Wiccan ritual could shed some light on the ritual process in general.

Certainly part of my understanding of Wiccan initiation as more nu-anced and complex than a three-step process comes from being a scholar-practitioner who has been on both sides of the Circle. Having come to the Circle's edge and crossed over its boundaries, I have been both initiate and initiator. From my dual perspective, I can see that the initiation process as an experience looks quite different depending on which side of the bound-ary one stands. This has not been fully explored in our study of initiation rituals due to the scarcity of analyses by people who are both scholars and practitioners.

When I first thought about this project, I imagined starting with the initiation ritual itself—a single, dramatic event set apart from the mundane world and framed by a series of deliberate actions or special activities.[2] Upon deeper reflection, I realized that initiation as an experiential process is more extensive than any *single* event, no matter how nuanced or multifaceted, could adequately encompass, and therefore requires more than a simple structural analysis of a linear transformation.

Initiation is deeply embedded within a total process of finding the Craft, learning about the religion, and becoming a Witch in practice and in community with others. In fact, a more adequate understanding of the *multi*dimensional and *multi*directional stages of both individual and community transformation seems to require a major shift away from Van Gennep's theories. Upon such reflection, I also discovered that the reflexive methodology so essential in my scholarship is also quite necessary for the understanding and appreciation of my own religion.

When I thought about the initiation ritual as a larger learning process, as the acquisition of a set of skills necessary to participate in a certain practice, the very idea of the Circle's edge as a *boundary* became increasingly troublesome. The notion of boundary all too easily becomes spatialized in terms of insider and outsider, which can hide the complexity of the range of experiences to be had on both sides of the Circle. Laurie Patton's insights on gender identities in the religion classroom apply equally well here: categories such as insider and outsider are "less like categories and more like *provisional descriptions of particular moments in the learning process*" (italics mine).[3] Simplistic categories such as insider and outsider do little to illuminate the range and variety of multiple transformative experiences to be had by persons at different stages of learning how to be a Witch—from first encounter, through different stages of study, and finally to initiation and practice. Wiccan initiation ritual encompasses a wider range of movements and experiences, both spatially and structurally, than has been covered by previous scholarship on such rites of passage. This range is not as neatly linear as a simple progression from outsider to insider might suggest, and, in fact, seems instead to depend on whole sets of *relationships* of perspectives and experiences being considered at specific stages in the learning process. There is an enormous wealth of experiences both inside and outside the Circle's edge, as well as a multitude of transformative steps in between.

Clearly, I need to go back before the initiation rite, to the point where a prospective Witch makes first contact with a coven, and to the process where a candidate begins to acquire the skills necessary to the learning of how to be a Witch.

In an earlier chapter, Wittgenstein's language game metaphor proved useful in helping us to think about religious and scholarly discourses as matters of skill and practice, rather than allegiance. His metaphor enabled us to construct sets of evaluative criteria from within the discourses and to uncover how the players of the game—or the practitioners of the discourse—learn its rules and progress through different levels of skill, from beginner to expert. Wittgenstein's metaphor helped us to understand the discourses as *practices* and to gain insights into the process by which a person becomes a skilled practitioner of each discourse.

Perhaps a similar device can help us to unpack the skills involved in learning how to be a Witch.

But a *language* game metaphor doesn't stretch quite far enough to suit my purposes. Religions are seldom, if ever, only about language or discourse. But, like Wicca, they usually include at least some level of somatic learning. It seems to me, especially as a scholar-practitioner, that religion in some fashion engages the whole person—body, mind, and spirit—and so I want a parallel practice that, at the very least, engages both the body and the mind.

Wicca foregrounds the body as an active participant in religious praxis, and so I want to find an analogous or parallel practice that also foregrounds the body as an important learner in the practice. Sports would be a good candidate, but I don't know enough about sports to make appropriate analogies. Typing is another example of both mental and physical engagement, but typing just doesn't seem to have the same kinds of things at stake in success or failure of the practice.

For our parallel practice, I have chosen something that is quite mundane and yet seems to fit all of the criteria: learning how to drive a car. Driving a car is something that many of us do every day—usually without much thought. For those of us who have been driving for several years, it has become second nature. Driving engages a fairly complex set of activities. It has a distinctive learning process, one that engages both the mind (learning the rules of the road) and the body (actually getting behind the wheel of a car). Additionally, the mind and body need to work together harmoniously in order to drive successfully. Driving has a range of skill levels from beginner to expert that we might fruitfully use in analogy. Finally, the success or failure of the practice of driving "matters."

I have decided that the parallel practice of driving a car can help us better understand the practice of becoming a Witch as a learning process—one that involves the acquisition of certain sets of skills that are similarly complex, engages both mind and body, and demonstrates that mind and body must work together harmoniously to be successful. Finally, that success or failure of this learning process also "matters."

Considering initiation in this wider sense as the acquisition of skills or a learning process has significant implications in two equally important and intertwined directions: first, the acquisition of knowledge and the development of skillful practice for the individual who is initiated, and, second, the construction of a community of practice—the creation of the coven as a coherent group of skilled practitioners. Viewed in this larger sense, initiation is a process that simultaneously transforms both individual and community, beginning at the moment of initial contact between prospective student and coven representative(s), and continuing through the initiation rite itself. Each step along the path toward the Circle involves the acquisition of skills and the complex negotiation of community in order to proceed to the next stage.

Of course, the first step along the path is finding it.

Finding the Path

For those who view initiation as a series of ordeals or challenges, the first one may well be finding a coven. It's certainly easier to do now than it was in the early seventies, due in large part to the courage and hard work of countless individuals and the success of several well-organized and national efforts at public education and outreach. Although still very much concerned with religious discrimination, Witches have made great strides in educating the public about Witchcraft as a positive spiritual path and as a legally recognized religion.[4] National organizations such as Circle Sanctuary and the Covenant of the Goddess (CoG) have mounted extensive educational campaigns aimed at increasing public awareness, tolerance, and respect for a wide variety of Pagan spiritual paths.[5]

As a result of organized educational campaigns, growing numbers of Witches can feel more comfortable being out of the closet in their communities. Today, Pagan festivals and public events occur in almost every region of the country. Although often couched in humor and Halloween stereotypes, local media coverage of these events is usually somewhat positive and recognizes Paganism and/or Witchcraft as "alternative religious paths." A wide range of Pagan publications—from glossy professional magazines to in-house or online newsletters—provides information about Pagan paths and ways to contact Pagan groups.[6]

Consequently, contacts between prospective students and coven members can now occur almost anywhere: through notes left on bulletin boards in coffeehouses or health food stores, through lectures given at New Age shops or Pagan-friendly bookstores, through Pagan student organizations on college campuses, at Pagan festivals scattered throughout the country, or through a wealth of Pagan publications and online listings. But because the coven is a fairly small and close community, and because each Witch's development and religious practice is interdependent on the others in the group, finding the *right* people to practice with can still be a daunting task.

For the Merry Circle, embarking on any activity connected to public education and outreach is an occasion for serious reflection on the part of the individual Witch and usually an occasion for discussion on the part of the coven. Does the individual Witch have the expertise to teach others? Does she have the time? Will it interrupt her development and practice? How will the students change the coven's group dynamics? Will public activity endanger the coven's members in any way? Most of the Circle live in somewhat conservative towns or neighborhoods and are very aware of the potential for religious discrimination. Some have children or work with them professionally. A few are employed in occupations or work in companies that don't look kindly upon individual differences or alternative lifestyles.

There are several options for public outreach and education, with varying levels of visibility. Some Wiccans and Pagans are totally open about their identities and serve the larger community as national spokespersons and contacts for persons wishing information about the Craft or other Pagan religions. Others may be known only by Craft names that function rather as noms de plume. A few work quietly within the justice system, aiding local police departments to distinguish alternative religious practices from acts of juvenile vandalism or hate crimes masquerading as "witchcraft." Still another option for some is to be known primarily within the Pagan community itself, by working as lecturers or workshop leaders and organizers throughout the Pagan festival circuit.

After weighing the risks of public visibility, Lauren and I are the only two of the original Merry Circle who have chosen to be active on a public level, which includes teaching introductory classes on Witchcraft at bookstores. Today, Lauren and her husband, a talented ritualist and Pagan performer who was initiated into the Merry Circle after I hived off, are quite active in public education and outreach, especially on the festival circuit. They choose to be active under Craft names; I continue to be active under my mundane name, working primarily with academic organizations and with public education programs about Paganism and Wicca as growing religions. High Priestesses Dot and Sandy work primarily with Dedicants and initiates.

While the Witches of the Merry Circle have never been aggressive in recruiting, the group has employed a variety of strategies in order to help educate the community and to reach out to prospective students over the years. Members have answered ads in Pagan publications, given interviews to newspapers or spoken on radio and television, presented lectures and workshops at bookstores, college campuses, and Pagan festivals, and taught a series of courses at local magical or metaphysical shops. The coven has also relied upon word of mouth and the same sort of happenstance that allowed me to stumble onto the path.

Possible new members are often drawn from those who are not looking for a coven *per se*, but are more generally interested in "alternative spiritualities." The members of the Merry Circle, as a group and also individually, have become affiliated with the national organization CoG, which, among other things, refers seekers to established member groups or solitary practitioners who may be able to help them.

Each method of public education and outreach has advantages and disadvantages. Media interviews can help us reach a large number of people, but there is potential for misquotation, for things to be taken out of context, or even for outright misrepresentation. Although with interviews there is usually no face-to-face interaction with the audience, occasionally someone will call the station or newspaper and try to arrange a meeting with "the Witch." It can be risky to meet a caller sight unseen. No matter how careful the Witch is to describe the Craft as a positive religious path, the caller may not have the same understanding of Witchcraft and may be operating under the negative stereotypes so easily found within popular culture. Lectures bring the Witch into more direct contact with her audience, but their one-time-only format limits both the amount of information that can be conveyed and the quality of audience-speaker interaction.

The members of the Merry Circle have found that, in terms of both delivery of material and contact with prospective students, teaching a series of classes over a period of eight to ten weeks is preferable to either an interview or a lecture. Here, the Witch can organize and present materials in a coherent fashion, starting with basic definitions of terms, historical background, and explanations about what the religion entails in a general sense, and then moving into more detailed study or special areas of interest that may be expressed by the students. Classes also allow both the teaching Witch and her students ample time to interact as individuals, building a foundation of trust for future work. Teaching a class requires hard work as well as a commitment of time on the part of the Witch. It also demands an appropriate level of skillful practice.

Expert Practice: Teaching the Craft to Others

Success or failure at learning how to be a Witch does not depend only on what the student does, it also depends on the skills and qualifications of his instructor(s). Our parallel practice presents a good example: If we enroll in a driving school or hire a private instructor to teach us how to drive, we want to make certain that the school or the instructor is appropriately qualified. We might check with the Better Business Bureau or some other government agency that can tell us if there have been problems with the driving school, or if the instructor has the appropriate certificates or license to teach others.

Unfortunately, it isn't quite that simple to make sure that the Witch and her coven are qualified to teach, and yet the student's success or failure at least partially depends on the qualifications of the Witch and coven as experts. Nearly thirty years ago, when I was initiated into the Craft, secrecy was much more the norm among the Wiccan community. Covens simply did not know much about each other; sometimes coven members didn't even know much about their own group's history (quite true in my own case). Today, many groups are comparatively open, and the student may be able to find out about the reputation of a particular group simply through word of mouth.

There is also a self-policing effort among today's covens, making prospective students aware of groups or individuals who have displayed a serious breach of ethics, such as coercing students into having sex or extorting money or other services from them—actions that would be considered a breach of ethics in any religion. National groups such as CoG connect students with covens and individuals who have been screened by CoG representatives. While hardly an exact science, such screenings help students avoid groups with serious problems while maintaining the religious freedom and local autonomy prized by covens and other kinds of Pagan groups.

Because the role of the teacher is pivotal to the student's success or failure, I want to address her qualifications and examine some of the instructional problems that can lead to an unsuccessful learning experience for both student and teacher.

Most of the coven's discussion about public or educational outreach will center on three things: the qualifications of the teaching Witch, how teaching others will affect the Witch's religious practice, and how new students will change group dynamics (this last discussion will later intensify as a new student becomes a Dedicant and then a potential initiate).

The first two topics of discussion center on whether the Witch is ready to teach a class: Is the Witch sufficiently qualified to present material to people who don't know much, if anything, about Witchcraft? Naturally, the coven wants to ensure that both the religion and the group are represented to the public by its most effective, if not its most eloquent, spokespersons.

Teaching an introductory course or delivering a public lecture can mark a significant step in the individual Witch's own practice. The ability to competently convey information about a religious practice to people who do not participate in that practice means acquiring new sets of skills. The player has to advance to a level of game skill at least equivalent to that of Kasulis's category of expert,[7] whether delivering a public lecture or teaching an introductory class. Such an advanced level of skill necessarily includes a degree of reflexivity that enables the Witch to translate insights about her own religion for someone who does not practice that religion. This includes being aware of the cultural baggage typically connected with the word "Witch" and being able to anticipate some of the questions a person outside the Circle would likely have.

For myself, this level of skill readily comes into play when I lecture in the college classroom as a colleague's guest speaker on Witchcraft or Paganism, something I have done many times. In this regard, I have found that my training as a scholar and a teacher is actually quite helpful because it enables me to more accurately identify my audience and anticipate the sorts of questions the students are likely to raise. The Witch as expert must be intimately and equally connected both to her subject matter and to her audience, fluidly commuting between the two.

The second topic of discussion—how teaching others will affect the Witch's religious practice—examines whether the Witch is grounded enough in her practice that teaching introductory students will not distract her from taking on the more challenging aspects of her own continued training. There is a danger that *too* much concentration on teaching others might prevent the Witch from deepening her work on herself, a case of avoidance rather than insufficient knowledge or lack of expertise. This is the second part of the question of readiness, and it is usually quite a bit trickier than the first. Here, the Witch can actually use her students as an excuse not to work on herself. Because of the interconnectedness of individuals' practice within the coven, this is actually a very important issue, one that caused the Merry Circle concern, and led to a great deal of serious discussion before the split.

Avoidance usually does not present a problem with students at the very earliest learning stage, in which mutual commitment, if it can be said to exist at all, is minimal. An example of activities at this level would include the general public lecture or introductory class on Wicca at a bookstore. At the next stage in the learning process—with student Dedicants—a higher level of commitment is expected from both student and teacher in the study of the Craft. It is here at this second level of teaching expertise that the Witch may be tempted to sacrifice her own personal study and practice time in favor of helping her Dedicants.

Avoidance behavior can be an indication that the Witch has run up against a wall in her own practice and has hit an area of deep-seated psychological resistance to working on a critical aspect of her self. Part of the Witch's own spiritual practice, especially on a more advanced level, is geared toward intensive work on the self. This is extremely difficult and often means confronting those issues that are deeply embedded in some of our most painful life experiences. These are the issues that hold us back, that keep us from accomplishing our goals, and that can destroy our physical, mental, and emotional health.

In this instance, the Witch avoids these painful issues of dealing with herself in order to devote her time and energy toward teaching her students. Often the Witch herself may not realize that she is doing this; she simply seems to be a nurturing person who is so caring of others that she will sacrifice her own needs to help other people. Sometimes the Witch may take on a proprietary attitude or even a kind of parental role toward her students. As this progresses, the mentor may come to see other Witches as being harsh or mean to her students when they call for more intensive Circle practices that are open only to initiates. Those who are in a more advanced leadership position must be able to recognize this for what it is, and must be willing to deal with the unpleasant consequences likely to occur with direct confrontation.

Of course, the most difficult and delicate situation to deal with is if the Witch enters a state of denial about the problem and refuses to seek help for any of the issues confronting her. Hurt feelings and frustrations are bound to come out in the open and need to be dealt with in a firm but balanced way if the coven is to survive.

Sometimes this problem can be mediated, or even avoided, by sharing advanced teaching responsibilities more evenly so that the Witch does not come to think of the Dedicants as her children whom she must protect and nurture. Though the Dedicants may initially feel flattered and respond positively to her treatment, they will eventually come to consider it confining and oppressive, as most of them already have their own parents. Circles tend to disintegrate when initiates fail to maintain a sufficiently challenging level of practice, and Dedicants who are being mothered to death will eventually find a less controlling environment in which to practice.

Serious disagreements over the inclusion of student Dedicants in every ritual, which some Witches may view as an inhibition to advancing initiate ritual practice, as well as disagreement over particular students who have been Dedicated, may lead to a coven's disbanding. Over the course of several years, the Merry Circle spent a great deal of time discussing and occasionally arguing over how best to juggle the demands of student Dedicants versus advancing the practice of initiates. The use of students as a means of avoiding deepening practice was in fact a topic of much discussion before the Circle split, and contributed to the decision of its members, including myself, to hive off into separate groups.

In retrospect, I wonder if avoidance behavior was a factor in the eventual decline of my parent coven. Sam's attention was increasingly directed outward: more and more new students, the establishment of an outer court Pagan Grove, more playful and lighthearted activities such as Renaissance fairs (all of which constituted "Pagan Lite" to us), while the spiritual development of initiates was neglected. Although I have no way of knowing for certain, I suspect this may have been a factor in his original coven deciding to cap new membership; perhaps they felt the need to work on themselves before adding new members.

Leading a coven successfully is itself an enormously challenging task that requires an array of highly specialized skills. For example, the ability to mediate between others, the ability to delegate responsibility or to share power, to work competently with coven members on deeply personal psychological or physical issues that are surfacing as a result of their practice— all are necessary in the effective management of any group. These are also difficult skills to master, involving a high degree of maturity and dedication. There is often much effort for seemingly little reward. Certainly, dealing with an interconnected web of psychophysical problems can be very difficult for the entire coven, and especially difficult for the coven's leaders. They may feel overwhelmed by their responsibilities and frustrated by having to deal with the intricacies of practice, both for themselves and for those in the coven.

Unlike the leaders of most other religious traditions, Witches are usually given very little in the way of explicit professional training in mediation or counseling. This is because, until quite recently, there were no seminaries for Witchcraft or Pagan religions that provided courses in pastoral counseling,[8] training that I think would come in quite handy. Referring coveners who have problems to a specialist, such as a psychologist, marriage counselor, or even a physician, can be rather tricky if membership in the Craft is likely to come up in conversation. If deeply repressed issues are surfacing as a result of meditative practice, it may be difficult to find a psychologist who is unruffled by Witchcraft (to put it mildly) and who has some familiarity with meditation or other bodymind practice.

One of the hardest lessons for a coven leader to learn is that it is impossible to help someone who really doesn't want that help. The problem could be related to physical health, psychological issues, or even something as mundane as helping someone get their living space organized or get into an exercise program. If the individual does not recognize that there is a problem, does not want the problem to be solved, or, more often, does not want help in addressing the problem, there is very little that can be done on the level of magical practice that will take.

Avoidance is sometimes connected with another problem: hypocrisy. Like all religions, Wicca has its share of pretenders, those who reveal the double-edged natures of *performance*, *practice*, and *play*, and their connections to the theater. I distinguish between *play* in the ludic sense, with its invocation of exuberant spontaneity and dynamic creativity, and *playing at* or *pretending*, which I interpret as a kind of surface appearance without center or real power. Ironically, an examination of hypocritical behavior can sometimes point to the values most highly prized in the religious practice, since they are the ones people are most likely to pretend to have.[9] But hypocritical behavior can do great harm to a group. At the extreme, coven leaders may ignore initiates in favor of playing with more exciting and less challenging acquaintances, or even groupies. If such persons lead the coven, the core eventually disintegrates and the members leave—a somewhat drastic example of the negotiation of community. The dilution of practice to playing at or playing around occurred within my parent coven and eventually contributed to its dissolution.

Unskillful Practice: Teaching and the Implications of Failure

Let's step back for a moment to reflect upon the skills and levels of expertise needed by Wiccan practitioners to teach others who are interested in joining a coven or who are already part of the extended coven community of initiates and Dedicants. There are several levels at which the Witch may operate as teacher; each entails the acquisition and employment of a distinctive combination of skills, such as the ability to read an audience and anticipate their questions. The demands of one set of skills may occasionally interfere with or clash with another, bringing teaching into conflict with deepening personal practice, much as when teaching and the demands of students conflict with a scholar's need for time devoted to research and writing. Sometimes a conflict between skills can indicate a problem within the Witch's own practice.

All of the levels are framed within the larger transformative context of the initiation process and affect the development of both individual practice and the coven as a place of community. While skills are not necessarily grouped by hierarchy, the consequences of success or failure seem to rise in importance as the level of expertise rises—in complexity, and in closeness to both practice and the community.

At the introductory level, failures or mistakes are relatively minor in their implications. Becoming flustered while speaking before an audience or while being interviewed by the media might leave some questions unanswered or leave listeners confused; at the worst, this may leave the audience with a slightly different impression of the religious practice than is desired by the coven.

Failure at the next stage of teaching, however, may damage both the practice of the individual Witch and the beginning stages of the practice of the Dedicants, possibly affecting the whole community. At the highest stage of expertise—leading a coven and being responsible for the training and development of its Priests and Priestesses—the consequences of failure are the most devastating to both individuals and community.

Wiccan spiritual practice is intimately intertwined with both the psychological and the physical dimensions of the whole person. The highest and most demanding level of spiritual practice—the most difficult and important magical work—is the Witch transforming herself. Through a combination of meditative and somatic exercises, she eventually attains those qualities that reflect her true or higher self. This true self represents an integration of mind, body, and spirit, the cultivation of a sacred identity whose personality and abilities are often alluded to by the Witch's Craft name. Daily practice—in the form of meditation, ritualized actions involving postures and gestures, and magical practices—brings to the surface those issues that need to be addressed in order to achieve the whole self.

The process of achieving the whole self requires confronting and overcoming negative habits in all dimensions: improving the physical body and physical health, changing negative mental tapes or thought forms to positive affirmations, confronting fear and inhibition, releasing anger, and pushing through those barriers that prevent the Witch from becoming a fully realized person. Healing takes place through a type of spiritual practice that engages both the body and the mind in exercises of concentration and meditative action, a practice that eventually integrates the whole person. This is the ultimate magical transformation—what some Witches and ceremonial magicians call the Great Work.

The emotional and psychological patterns of a lifetime, deeply embedded in the body, are challenged and transformed in the difficult process of spiritual practice, the success or failure of which has far-reaching implications for the individual Witch and those around her. Japanese philosopher Yuasa Yasuo helps us understand what happens when meditative or other body-mind practice is performed successfully: "Meditation brings to the surface the complexes and emotions sunk in the unconscious region, freeing them and ultimately dissolving them by slowing the conscious activities connected with the cerebral functions."[10] But when meditative practice fails, is aborted by the fear and avoidance of what rises to that surface, the Witch is left in a more distressed situation than before she began spiritual practice, a distressed state that may even effect physical health. What was once buried and repressed deeply in the body and the unconscious mind is now brought to the surface, to the conscious mind where it can be dealt with and dissolved. Conscious awareness of these issues may be so frightening that a state of denial or paralysis sets in.

The Witch in these situations may find any and every excuse not to work on herself, including focusing on the needs of her Dedicants in order to avoid the unpleasantness of facing and healing the injured parts of her self. This may mean that she ultimately does not believe herself to be worthy of healing. Such a belief is a truly formidable obstacle to overcome, especially without professional psychological assistance, and it is an obstacle that may last throughout her lifetime, manifesting itself in various physical, emotional, mental, and spiritual problems. Moreover, since practice within a coven is a communal affair, the resistance of one Witch to change and healing winds up affecting the rest of the coven, frustrating and perplexing her fellow coveners and even affecting the success of *their* practices.

In addition to the observation that Wiccan spiritual practice involves working on the entire person, we have also noted that practice *can* be faked—to a point—and that Witches can pretend or play at their practice in a sense much closer to the theatrical than the spiritually ludic. The juxtaposition, however ironic, of these two observations has a point: It is precisely because the stakes are so high in spiritual practice, and the consequences so deeply embedded in the total sense of person, that failure to meet responsibility at the highest levels of communal practice can be devastating. When the coven leader fails to meet responsibilities because of burnout or frustration, lack of experience, or immaturity, the consequences to the leader and to the coven are bad enough. But when the coven leader is only playing at practice, he is an expert in name only and compounds the consequences of his failure with an ethical dimension.

Let's switch gears for a minute and use our parallel practice to think through the implications of failure. What are the consequences of failure for a driver who is an expert in name only? We will use a teen rebel movie as an example, perhaps a classic of the genre such as *Rebel without a Cause* or the truly forgettable *Rebel Warriors*. Such movies usually include one or more James Dean-type characters playing a game of chicken with their souped-up hot rods. The fantasy is that our teen rebel has nerves of steel, owns the hot rod from hell, never loses at drag racing, and always outruns the police. The reality is, of course, not so impressive, and the lesson from the teen rebel movies is that it all must end in tragedy. Using the menu below, we can actually make up our own movie. Choose from the following items:

Our teen rebel

a. loses his nerve
b. overestimates his ability to handle the situation
c. blows his engine

and he loses

a. respect
b. the girl
c. the car
d. all of the above

because he

a. bails out of the car way before the other guy in the game of chicken
b. fails to bail out of the car in time because his leathers get caught in the door
c. gets shot by the police
d. crashes ineptly into a tree

While it's fairly easy to see what the consequences are for our rebel expert driver gone awry, it is a little more difficult to see what the consequences are for our expert Witch playing at the Craft. The consequences are just as real, *and often just as physical*—not only for himself, but also for those closest to him in the community.

In the case of the High Priest or High Priestess who plays at practice in the shallow sense, the negative consequences to the coven as a place of community are readily visible, even to the casual observer. The coven usually disbands, often with varying levels of rancor, animosity, and mistrust. Witches in my lineage believe that such a flawed practice also rebounds with negative consequences for the individual practitioner. On a very mundane level, this can show up in gossip, or in negative word of mouth or reputation within the larger Wiccan or Pagan community. The community warns its members of those individuals who are merely playing at being clergy without the requisite skills necessary to effectively or adequately lead a coven or implement training for their coveners.

On a more spiritual level, not readily visible to the casual observer, failed coven leadership jeopardizes the physical, psychological, and spiritual health of all initiates in the coven. The potential consequences of failed leadership are enormous for the initiates: a sense of alienation, a loss of direction and self-confidence, cynicism or mistrust of others, and even serious depression. Initiates may feel abandoned or betrayed by their High Priest or High Priestess and leave the Craft, or all religious practice, entirely.

The costs of failed leadership are high as well for the leaders of the coven. The consequences of hypocrisy or playing at Witch invoke an ethical dimension that functions as a kind of negative karma affecting the physical and spiritual health of the individual High Priest or High Priestess in this lifetime as well as in lives to come. In fact, it is part of the oath of initiation that the Witch's personal magical tools will turn against him if he transgresses severely against the spirit and practice of the Craft, including its ethical dimensions. In one or more of his future lives, the Witch will be cast into an unfriendly world and reborn among strangers instead of friends and loved ones. He will have difficulty finding the path to the Circle, and may wander adrift and without spiritual practice. If the actions are terribly egregious and harm many, Witches within my tradition believe that the path to the Circle will be lost to that Witch forever.

Becoming a Student: Learning the Rules of the Road

Once the student has successfully made contact with a coven, he begins the process of learning about the religion in general and the specific traditions of the particular group. Over the years, we've found that teaching a series of classes in a neutral space such as a bookstore, shop, or even a room in a library creates the most effective learning environment for the student. The format of an eight- to ten-week course held in a neutral space is effective, both for maximizing the amount of information the teacher is able to present to the student at this stage, as well as for building a sense of trust and respect between teacher and student. The idea of a neutral space is important for a variety of very practical reasons.

One reason is personal safety and confidentiality, not only for the Witch but for the students as well. The vast majority of Witches worship in their homes rather than at public and community supported sites such as churches or temples. Some live in the country and have land that is suitably private for use in outdoor worship, but most—certainly most of the Merry Circle—worship in their living rooms or some other converted indoor space. This means that Witches often have to juggle conflicting space needs between worship and normal home use. At this early stage of initial contact and instruction, a Witch simply doesn't know the student well enough to invite him into her home. The student also doesn't know her well enough to accept such an invitation or to feel comfortable coming to a private home to learn about Witchcraft and magic. While Witches may like to think the best of everyone who signs up for an introductory course on the Craft, it simply isn't sensible or safe to bring total strangers into their homes.

This is related to another issue—consideration for those who share the home space. When worship occurs within the home, Witches must coordinate religious activities with family, coven members, and the extended families or housemates of members—not all of whom may be participants in the religion. For those who are married and/or have families, or even roommates, inviting a group of strangers into the home can totally disrupt the domestic environment, ranging from merely inconveniencing others to potentially jeopardizing them. Instruction itself may be disrupted by interruptions from family members or roommates, or by feelings of tension or hostility on the part of housemates who wish to have personal space in which to work, play, or rest rather than to be inconvenienced or chased out by a class in progress.

The size and arrangement of the space itself contributes to the successful learning environment. My introductory Craft classes usually have anywhere from fifteen to twenty-five students. None of the Witches in our coven has a home large enough to accommodate that many people in anything remotely comparable to a classroom setting. Teaching may be more easily arranged at a bookstore or shop that has enough folding chairs for everyone to sit on, some small tables at which to write, perhaps a white board, a copier, or even a spare room that can be dedicated for instruction. This setting maximizes potential learning by providing a space for instruction that is comfortable and free of disruptions.

This stage of initial contact between student and Witch begins the process that potentially leads to initiation—the transformation of both student and coven. Beginning instruction involves the sort of basic education about the Craft that clarifies the misconceptions and cultural baggage that the word *Witch* carries. Most of the student's attention is primarily directed toward very basic and general information about the religion and secondarily toward how this particular coven participates in its practice.

A simple syllabus for the course might include the following topics:

- The historical background of the modern Craft and its roots in ancient nature-based primal religious practices;
- An introduction to some pantheons and mythologies of Gods and Goddesses commonly worshipped by Witches;
- The reciprocity and respect accorded *both* female and male deities;
- The ethics of magickal[11] practice;
- The solar and lunar cycles in daily life;
- The eight sabbats or holy days of Wiccan worship;
- The nature of the four elements;
- The use of herbs, color, and visualization in healing, and so forth.

Whenever I teach an introductory class, I always include an extensive reading list on each topic in order to help interested students find additional information that cannot be covered in one class period. The class format allows ample room for students to ask questions or pursue special topics of interest.

Using our parallel practice, this stage of the learning process can be favorably compared to that early stage of the drivers' education class in which students must learn the rules of the road. Similar to this stage in which students are learning *about* driving, most of the instruction in beginning classes on Wicca is geared toward learning *about* the religion, not *practicing* it. Students also begin learning *about* the nature of Wiccan ritual, and how rituals are constructed in a context of a cultivated practice. Very little attention is paid to somatic practice at first. In fact, students in the first few classes of the introductory Wicca class are practicing rituals about as much as drivers' education students are driving cars on their first day of class.

Shifting Paradigms: Gearing Up to Practice

Although the primary mode of instruction at this point is deliberately book oriented or informative and intellectual in nature, this does not mean that classes are designed to be entirely intellectual or stuck in the abstract. At this stage, a Witch may have her students do some creative hands-on projects working with herbs or candles in order to keep the class enjoyable and allow them to participate in some of the things that Witches do. For example, the class will learn about the element air, its importance and directional position in the Circle, and its correspondence to experiences, herbs, oils, and colors. As a class project, a teacher may have her students design a tool to help them become familiar with this element in a sensory as well as an intellectual capacity. By tying feathers and small bells to sections of dowel rods that they paint or otherwise decorate with colors and designs that symbolize air, students can make a fan that could be used in a Circle to waft incense and invoke the element air. Attaching a small, brightly colored cloth bag filled with herbs associated with the element completes the "air tool" and provides satisfying creative and tangible connection between theory and practice.

This immediate (but controlled) exposure to the sensual, tactile dimension of Wiccan religious experience begins to counteract the idea that religion is *only*—or even *primarily*—about belief systems, sets of abstract concepts, or texts. It marks the beginning of a kind of paradigm shift, moving the students into a frame within which practice (i.e., practice that centrally includes the physical body *as the doer of learning*) emerges as equally important to belief or intellectual knowledge.

In this respect, learning how to drive a car has one immediate and useful advantage over learning how to be a Witch. Driving a car is easily identified as a *practice* that engages both body and mind. Generally speaking, you don't *believe* in cars, you *drive* them. This is counterintuitive to an understanding of religions in which belief is primary and practices are secondary, if noticed at all.

But let's back up for a minute. Maybe my naming of the examples is faulty. Instead of learning how to *drive* a car, perhaps the more parallel construction should be learning how to be a *driver*. But notice that even if the name of the example is changed, the practice—driving—is still strongly and even primarily implied. Let's try it the other way: change the name of the activity from learning how to be a *Witch* to learning how to *practice* Witchcraft. That's somewhat better; at least the word *practice* explicitly enters the picture. We have shifted the focus from noun to verb, from religion as *label*—Witch—to religion as *doing*—practice (or "Witching," if you will).

I still don't think that simply changing the name of the game entirely solves the problem. Religion-as-practice is not as apparent as driving-as-practice; the Witch practitioner is not as easily perceived as the doer of an activity as is the driver. If the students in my academic courses on world religions are any indication, religion is typically understood as a system or set of *beliefs*. The problem with this is in the way the term belief is frequently construed. Belief is something that goes on in the head. It involves a strictly mental process resulting in a choice or decision that is itself markedly removed from bodily practice or engagement. The idea that religion might be rooted in *somatic* experiences, that it might be about *practices*, about things done with the *body* as well as the mind, is often a difficult and apparently troubling concept for my students. For most of them, religion clearly functions as an identifying *label* rather than as a *doing*.

But perhaps there is a way to return belief to the body. In everything from simple prayer and acts of kindness to complicated ceremony and intensive ritual training, people *do* their religions. By emphasizing the Craft as a *practice*—especially a practice that engages both the mind *and the body* as active doers of knowing—the teaching Witch may bring about a paradigm shift in her students' understanding of religion as embodied practice.

This paradigm shift begins with small hands-on projects and progresses to very limited somatic practices. At this point, the teaching Witch will begin to introduce some very simple relaxation techniques, visualizations, or guided meditations as the class gets more comfortable with one another and with the teacher. One of the relaxation techniques is likely to include practice with breath control—the gateway to all other embodied ritual practices within my lineage of Wicca, and a technique we will return to in other sections of the initiation process. Proper breathing must be thoroughly mastered by the practitioner in order to successfully accomplish the visualization and concentration needed for all other ritual work, including invocation, divination, and healing. The first step may be simply to notice the pattern of breathing in order to further accustom the student to the idea that the Craft is about practices, and ones involving the body.

Depending on how that goes, the Witch may then decide to introduce trying to control or regulate the pattern of breathing—for example, having students breathe in for a count of four, hold the breath in for the same count, breathe out for a count of four, and hold the breath out for the same count. Students learn that controlling the breath is much more difficult than simply noticing the breath, and they also learn that even beginning Wiccan practices take some work.

These few simple somatic exercises, which are not simple at all in practice, are not only the beginnings of the paradigmatic change to *practice* but are also often the beginnings of counteracting a lifetime of ignoring knowledge that is rooted in the body itself. Many of us seem to be shut out of, or alienated from, our own bodies. From the time we are children, we are taught to ignore or repress the basic needs of our bodies—for rest and sleep, for sex, for exercise, for play—and its warning signals of pain and discomfort. We are taught that bodily timetables and schedules must conform to the timetables and schedules of schools and employers. In fact, employers often reward their employees for overworking their bodies even to the point of exhaustion. When the unnoticed signals and unmet needs of those bodies erupt into illness, some employers even punish their employees for falling down on the job or for seeking compensation for medical bills.

Religion may also teach us to ignore our bodies, considering them unworthy of attention and respect. Some religions reward denigration and punishment of the flesh, casting such practices as spiritual. The foregrounding of the body in Wiccan religious practice teaches the students that their bodies deserve respect and are as much a part of the spiritual endeavor as their minds. Students begin to learn that their bodies are not merely containers for spirit, unimportant in themselves, but are active participants in the religious process. This is the beginning of the paradigm shift to religion as embodied practice.

I want to linger for a moment on the phrase *embodied practice* because it is one of pivotal meaning in the understanding of Wiccan religious practice. The phrase itself consists of two words of equal importance: *embodied* immediately foregrounds the body; *practice* suggests training, repetition until you get it right, disciplined and conscious doing, and cultivation. Although Yuasa is writing about Eastern bodymind practices, he illuminates what is at stake here. He writes that "personal cultivation in the East takes on the meaning of a practical project aiming at the enhancement of the personality and the training of the spirit *by means of* the body" (italics mine).[12]

In order to emphasize the engagement in the training of spirit by, and through, the body, for the purposes of this work I'm going to make a distinction between simply the body and the *body-in-practice*. The body-in-practice is not a passive receptacle for spirit but is an active agent through which the spirit is transformed. It is a subject, not an object. It is active rather than static. The body-in-practice is an achieved state, not a natural one. In other words, the body-in-practice is the body and mind working together to achieve the whole person. Embodied practice is the process— the magic—through which the Witch transforms herself into her most perfect form. Or, as Kasulis notes, a spiritual practice that engages both body and mind is a "process by which *we can gradually change what we existentially are*" (italics mine).[13]

The Craft enables us to regain the body as a maker of knowing, a doer of knowledge, through the engagement of the body-in-practice. By beginning to cultivate the body-in-practice, those studying the Craft will learn how to notice their bodies, how to listen to their bodies, and how to eventually *trust* their bodies. I can tell you from personal experience that these are difficult lessons to master. The body-in-practice is also a difficult concept to get across to students.

One other distinctive and important dimension of the Craft—the creative and consciously constructed nature of its ritual practice—bears some considerable mention here because it can compound the difficulties at this stage of the learning process.

Students often come to the introductory class with an understanding of religious ritual as a static experience, a repetitive enactment of texts handed down to us by tradition or authority. When studying the Craft, they learn about rituals that are not static and repetitive but are consciously constructed, creative acts of worship and magic that potentially transform the understanding of religious ritual in general. Witches see both religion and ritual as dynamic and creative human enterprises. Rather than a test of endurance, ritual becomes a joyous expression, a form of self-creation, a path toward transformation, a community-building form of sacred play in which participation and performance are key.

Students seem to grasp the creative and constructed nature of Wiccan ritual much more readily than they understand the context in which it occurs—that of embodied practice. One reason, of course, is that the creative dimension is much more immediately rewarding, more fun than the dimension that consists of hard work and daily practice. The creative element is often one that is greatly emphasized by popular books on magic and Witchcraft. Many of these books display a collection of spells in recipe format.[14] You, too, can impress your friends and frighten your enemies with these few simple spells. Follow these easy directions, read two pages, add water, stir, and—poof—instant magic! One book even promises to reveal "for the first time in print, the secrets of gaining your own personal desires. Not through hard, time-consuming, constant exercises and gradual development over many months, but through simple, easy-to-do rituals that are a joy to perform."[15] Apparently no one who buys these books likes to be told that magic is hard work or involves training and practice of any kind. And then there are the books that assure the readers (women only, please) that we have a Goddess-given right to magic and Witchiness by virtue of our ovaries.[16]

The first kind of popular book reduces an entire religious practice to a collection of simple tricks—similar, I suppose, to reducing the training of a Catholic or Orthodox priest to successfully learning how to light candles and burn incense. The second kind of popular book reduces religious practice to a function of the genitalia, the sort of biological determinism that feminist scholars of religion feel to be a suspicious and generally untenable move because it has so often been used to argue against women's full participation in religion.

Both types of books fail to situate the creative dimension of Wiccan religious ritual within the context of the body-in-practice. In the first type of popular book, little mention is made of the body, and none is made of work or the idea of practice. In the second, the body is highlighted to some extent, but as a natural and simplistically gendered body, as a physical body only, not as a body-in-practice. Both types of books reduce religious practice in a way that would be nearly unthinkable if applied to any other religion— "Men: Now you, too, can transform that wine in your cup with these simple, easy-to-remember chants"—and make the Craft into an exotic object that emphasizes the Witch as unfamiliar other.

More important than any of the above, failure to situate the creative dimension of Wiccan ritual *within the context of the body-in-practice* will result in the students' failure to successfully learn the rules of the road.[17] Our analogy of learning how to drive a car illustrates the importance of a cultivated body, a body-in-practice, rather than the natural body as a context for creative ritualizing. In the introduction to Yuasa's *The Body: Toward an Eastern Mind-Body Theory*, Kasulis provides a wonderful illustration of the body-in-practice that is directly applicable to our driver. He considers the case of a woman who goes into an "unanticipated but controlled swerve to avoid hitting a dog"[18] and unpacks the complicated maneuver of what went into her reaction using Yuasa's distinction of bright and dark consciousness:

> In a sense, the act was an *impulse*, the triggering of a conditioned response. That is, the specific rationale of what had to be done and how to do it was dark; it was not something of which the driver was self-conscious.
>
> . . . Rather, the motorist's impulse is a *learned* response, the result of months of disciplined training and years of practical experience. The driver's response is conditioned, but not passively by external social factors. Rather years ago, the driver self-consciously decided to condition herself. At some earlier point in her life, the driver had to filter through the bright consciousness all the knowledge used spontaneously by the dark consciousness: knowing how animals might behave along country roads, how to find the brake, how much pressure to use in stopping, and how to steer the car in a skid so as not to lose control. . . . In the split second when the evasive maneuver was executed, there was no time to think of alternatives. There was only the purely responsive act. In a significant sense, the *body*, not the mind, decided the action.[19]

Part of the goal of the cultivation of the body-in-practice is to enable "free movement between the bright and dark consciousness," which is accomplished by the creation of a "psychophysical path"[20] that enables an integration of the whole person. The student in drivers' education may be tempted to get behind the wheel and take the car for a spin before receiving the license to do so. After all, he has observed people driving most of his life, and it looks so easy. To counteract this, there is likely to be a portion of the drivers' education class that uses graphic footage of car accidents to illustrate what kinds of things can happen when the driver is unskilled and/ or physically impaired by alcohol and nevertheless decides to drive. For the student driver, the consequences of getting behind the wheel of a car without sufficient intellectual and physical preparation are fairly apparent.

Unfortunately, the consequences of ritualizing without a context of embodied practice are not so readily apparent for some students. To illustrate the point, one of my favorite stories comes from when I taught a class on divination at a local New Age bookstore. I hit it off very well with one student in particular (I'll call her Joan). Joan would stay after class and chat about her desire to become a physical therapist, her understanding of spiritual matters, and life in general. In one of the conversations, she spoke of how much she admired Native American spirituality. "Did you know," she said to me, "that Medicine Men and Women work hard and study to serve their people from a very young age?" Another time the topic was Buddhist monks, for whom Joan had an equally strong admiration—understanding that they spent their whole lives in study and prayer, and that they might study "for *years* before being allowed to do a simple ceremony."

One day Joan asked me if she could start coming to my coven's student Circle. I was delighted. She really was a very nice person and I thought she would fit in well with some of the other students. I started talking to her about how often the class met, how she would begin her training with a daily journal in which she would record her meditations, how she would alternate readings from the book list with practical projects, how she would learn visualization techniques, how—. Then I noticed that her eyes had started to glaze over. "Is something wrong?" I asked.

And she replied, obviously upset, "I thought all I had to do was be a woman and bring a drum!"

This story illustrates all too well the effect of popular books on the Craft. Joan was prepared to grant every other religion in the world a period of training, preparation, a time of intense work on the self. But for *my* religion, all she had to do was be a woman and bring a drum. This is the downside of creative construction of ritual. Many of our students come into classes with the idea that creative ritual practice means that Witchcraft is a religion that you make up as you go along, or a religion that is inherent to female biology. Joan was clearly influenced by the ovarian school of thought.

In training her students, the teaching Witch cannot emphasize often enough that it is a good idea to really *know what you are doing* before attempting any ritual activity. At this point in training, the teaching Witch will constantly emphasize that creative ritual practice takes place in a context of embodied practice. Embodied practice becomes a point that increases in importance as the students are exposed to more somatic techniques of spiritual work.

The End of the Introductory Class:
Coming to the Finish Line

By the end of the introductory class term, the teaching Witch will probably do a full Circle for her students so that they can see what a ritual is actually like. This is not likely to be an intensive Circle in any sense—nor will the students be asked to participate beyond their abilities—but it will be enough of a ritual to give the students an inkling of whether or not they would like to learn more.

One of the simplest spiritual exercises the students can experience with the teaching Witch is one known as grounding and centering. In the coven, this is used as the preliminary or warm-up exercise to more extensive ritual in order to get people in the right frame of mind to do spiritual work. Grounding and centering can also be used as a kind of ritual in itself. It is the first step to building community among ritual participants, especially in a large Circle, or when working with people for the first time, such as at a festival gathering. It is also highly effective in healing, especially when some sort of emotional or mental distress is evident. The grounding and centering exercise always begins with simple breathing and physical relaxation. As a guided meditation, its ritual form may go as follows:

> Standing in a circle, the participants join hands and are instructed to begin a breathing pattern. Initially, the breathing pattern consists of slow and deep breaths. Once the breathing rhythm is established, the participants are encouraged to relax their bodies, releasing all the tension and worries of the day. They are then guided to feel themselves growing roots—like large trees—deep into the earth, connecting with the Mother. While they maintain the rhythm of their breaths, they are guided to feel the earth's energy rising up through those roots and flowing throughout all parts of their bodies.
>
> Once overflowing with earth energy, the participants are told to visualize a glowing ball of light, like the Sun, in the sky above their heads. They are instructed to breathe the energy of that Sun into their bodies, mingling the sparkling light energy of Father Sky with the energy of Mother Earth. The participants are invited to feel this energy flowing throughout the circle and throughout all of Nature. As they maintain the breathing rhythm, the participants are told to gradually open their eyes, to feel refreshed, full of life energy, and at once balanced and centered between Earth and Sky, Mother and Father, Female and Male.

The ending to this exercise is pretty similar each time that I perform it, including once for a group of folklorists at an American Folklore Society meeting. People open their eyes and smile at one another, reluctant to break the Circle. An air of warmth permeates the room. It seems natural to hug the person next to you. The ritual exercise can end here, or go on to a more extensive ritual in which the directions are called, the Gods are invoked, cakes and wine are shared, the Gods are bid farewell, and the Circle is deconstructed—in much the same pattern as described earlier.

Let's step back and take a look at some of the things that are striking about this part of the ritual exercise and what they tell us about the Craft as a religious practice. First, the ritual exercise is totally participatory in nature. You have to *do* in order to *be* in the ritual at all. The body *is immediately and necessarily involved* in the act. Your attention is, in fact, first focused on the body through breathing, then feeling tension in the body and letting go of that tension. Growing roots down deep into the Earth establishes a necessary connection with the Mother, with She who gives all life. It establishes connection with Nature and invokes the female, who provides strength. The analogy of drinking up Her energy like a tree extends the connection established with the Earth to other life forms in Nature. Bringing in the Sun and the Sky invokes the Father, He who gives us energizing light. Neither male nor female is privileged—both are invoked, both are necessary, both provide all beings with strength and life. The human being, along with all other life forms, is thus situated as centered between male and female, Earth and Sky, Mother and Father, connected and part of each end of the polarity.

Without delivering a speech or a sermon, the teaching Witch has enabled her students to *experience* a significant part of Wiccan philosophy and worldview through the performance of and participation in this very simple ritual exercise. At every step of the way throughout the ritual, performance and participation are the key elements—from the very first breath drawn in Circle to the last hug at the end. The participatory and active nature of Wiccan ritual assures that everyone can feel an integral part of the ritual. Each person is active in connecting with Nature, with the Gods, and with the others there. No one is passively redundant; each is essential for the successful performance of the ritual.

The group's ritual will likely be the end of the introductory class. At this point, students may go on to explore another path, or they may ask to study further and become Dedicants. A two-way screening process, one that intensifies as the class progresses, has been taking place between the Witch and her students since the very first day of class. Students examine not only the information they are presented but the presenter as well, demonstrating that the coven is not the only body with the power to accept or reject. The Witch, meanwhile, is examining her students and attempting to discover who among them might be good candidates for the kind of practice in which the coven engages. Throughout the class term, the students and teacher have engaged in a gradual process of building trust and getting to know one another as people. Sometimes other coven members may visit the class to see how things are going and to meet the students.

Students and teacher are now ready for the next step—getting behind the wheel.

5

The Rite of Dedication

Getting behind the Wheel

Within the Merry Circle, the Rite of Dedication is the first formal, ritual-ized step toward initiation into the coven. This ceremony of self-blessing and dedication to study marks a change in the status of the student from the merely curious to the serious seeker. It continues to develop and in-tensify the relationship between student and teacher begun during the in-troductory classes. The rite formally blesses and dedicates the student to a path of self-discovery that may lead to initiation. Dedication marks a sig-nificant step in the acquisition of skills for the student and demands an intensified commitment to the learning process from both the student and the teaching Witch.

Not every coven has a dedication ritual. For that matter, not all Witches practice initiation. Those who do have an initiation rite may not have a formal ceremony of dedication, preferring instead to initiate students di-rectly into the coven. Some Witches may use a ceremony similar to the Rite of Dedication as a form of self-initiation or as their ritual of initiation into the group. Not all covens have a formal training process, either before or after initiation; it's a good idea to keep in mind that things such as training and ritual practices vary widely among individual covens and sep-arate traditions of the Craft.

While the Witches of the Merry Circle are certainly aware of different ideas about training and initiation, the group has never questioned the value of the Dedicant stage within the overall learning process. Although not as much of a mutual commitment as initiation, the Rite of Dedication is an important part of the screening process for both Witches and students and represents a significant movement toward the incorporation of a potential initiate within the coven. The Rite of Dedication functions as an important step within the overall process of constructing an intimate community of practice and carries specific responsibilities for students and teachers, as well as for the coven at large.

Power and the Screening Process

If the teaching Witch is effective, she will have accomplished several goals by the end of the introductory class. A skillful teacher dispels some of the more common misconceptions about the religion, allowing students to come away from the course with the idea that Wicca is a positive religious path. The students should also have received sufficient information about the religion and the coven to make a decision: Do they want to study further with this particular Witch and her coven, or do they want to move on to something else?

At this level of interaction, the screening process works very much in both directions. The Witch and the coven have power to reject or accept a student, and the student also has power to accept or reject the Witch and the coven. The vast majority of students will move on, and the Witch may never see them again or may run into them only on a casual basis.

Students are likely to have many reasons for deciding to go on to something else. Some have satisfied their curiosity, deciding that Wicca—or at least this particular practice—is not for them. A few of these students may explore a different coven or another kind of Pagan practice. Others will return to religions more familiar to them, explore a different alternate religion, or perhaps leave religious practice entirely.

When students leave, reaction varies with the particular Witch. For myself, I haven't invested enough at this introductory stage to have my feelings hurt when students decide to move on. Sometimes I am actually relieved, which has little or nothing to do with the particular students in the course, and everything to do with not being able to imagine teaching fifteen to twenty students at one time as Dedicants. Sure, teaching an introductory class takes time and energy, but they are nothing compared to the time and energy spent on the stage that follows.

Occasionally, when I grow to like a particular student and think he would make a wonderful Witch and a great addition to the coven, I am disappointed when he leaves. I imagine some of my university colleagues have the same response when they spot a particularly bright and adept student in one of their courses and wish that person would go on to major in the field. I usually console myself by imagining that I have given this student a good grounding in the Craft, and that perhaps someday he will return to it.

Usually there are a few students who want to continue along the path. They know from being told in the introductory classes that any step beyond the introductory stage is one they must deliberately pursue. In other words, students must *ask* to become Dedicants. Specifically, students must ask the teaching Witch, who is likely to be the only person from the coven with whom they have regularly interacted.

The teacher's response has immediate implications that place her in a pivotal position, granting her—for the moment—a certain degree of power with respect both to students and to her fellow Witches in the coven. Her decision grants or denies the student further access to the coven and determines whether her fellow Priestesses and Priests will have new members to train.

The power that the teaching Witch exercises over students who ask to be dedicated has to be situated in the context of the increasing degree of intimacy and trust that dedication will require between teacher and student. For instance, the location of study itself will probably move from neutral space into the intimacy of the Witch's own home, and it is quite reasonable for her to exercise control over who enters the home environment. The Witch's power over the students at this moment is perhaps mediated by the fact that few students are turned away for dedication by the Merry Circle.

At this point, the power granted to the teaching Witch over the coven at large is mediated by the each Witch's awareness of the level of commitment that Dedicants will eventually require from the whole group. This is partly because Wicca tends not to be a religion with a distinct, full-time clergy who are paid for their ministry—certainly the case with the Merry Circle, all of whom have jobs and/or family obligations in addition to their religious duties. Training Dedicants is a time-consuming task, and it is one that not every member of the coven relishes or can easily do. Because a student's dedication can affect the whole coven, we've always tried to be considerate of each another by informing the coven about prospective Dedicants, usually far in advance of a ceremony.

The Witches of the Merry Circle have no single, uniform, or homogenous understanding of the Rite of Dedication. This is hardly surprising, considering the range of attitudes and experiences within the group and the multitude of perspectives—that playful discourse of lights and shadows—that are frequently hidden within the realm of insider.

Some members of the Merry Circle are fairly cautious, or even conservative, about dedicating students, understanding the ceremony as a direct line to initiation in the coven. They see students as dedicating to the coven itself. This is consistent with the understanding that seemed to operate within my parent coven.

Others, myself included, interpret the Rite of Dedication more liberally, tending to understand the ceremony as more of a self-blessing, a commitment to a general path of study, rather than a particular coven. Still other Witches in the Merry Circle have become even more conservative about dedicating students because of negative experiences with students who turned out not to be ready to commit to serious study and training.

Unless I see any serious problems working with a particular student, I will usually participate in blessing and dedicating that person to continued study along the path. This being said, I do have to balance my feeling that the ceremony is generally beneficial with knowing the demands that a Dedicant will place on my time and energy. Because of both personal and professional commitments, I don't want to spend my time working with students who will not or cannot acquire the necessary skills. Still, it's pretty hard to predict for certain whether students will be successful or not, so I tend to give them the benefit of the doubt.

Whatever the Witch's personal attitudes about the Rite of Dedication, it is extremely important for her to communicate those attitudes and expectations to the students who ask her to be dedicated. This way there are likely to be fewer misunderstandings, and students won't feel as though initiation is somehow a given because they have been dedicated.

As a teaching Witch, I don't usually have problems with rejecting incompatible students at this stage of the learning curve. I am not reluctant to tell students that I am not the right teacher for them; it's better to let them know this as soon as I know. It is not only more honest, but also a better use of everyone's time, to send students to someone who would more adequately address their needs. I tell these students as clearly and as gently as possible that it would be best for them to find another teacher and another group if they want to continue to pursue the Craft. Keeping them hanging on with no hope of initiation is cruel.

Has this issue has ever caused friction in the Merry Circle? It has. In fact, this issue has generated intense and sometimes pretty heated discussion. We take the rejection of students at any point in the course of their study—especially after they have been dedicated for a period of time—as a very serious issue.

Each Witch has his or her own way of handling students who must be told that they will not be initiated, relating more often to differences in personal style than theology. Some of my fellow Witches hope that Dedicants who are not making any progress and have little or no chance of being initiated will eventually figure it out and simply go away. I think dismissing them the direct way is the kindest, and the sooner the better, so that the student can go on to something more productive. Now that access to Wiccan groups has become significantly easier through Pagan festivals, the internet, and a variety of publications, it's unrealistic at best, and arrogant at worst, to think that the Merry Circle is the only, or even the best, path to the Circle for aspiring students.

When there is disagreement among coven members over how to handle a particular student, the final decision is usually left to the Witch who has worked most closely with that person. This process of constant negotiation through discussion is an important feature of the construction of the coven as a place of community, one that gets revisited several times over the course of the initiation process.

Even though members of the Merry Circle have different attitudes and expectations about the Rite of Dedication, all agree that the ceremony stands in a pivotal place in the initiatory process. It is a rite that has immediate implications for the individual student's practice and growing implications for the coven as a whole. Because the student must *ask* to be dedicated, the ceremony represents a deliberate decision to seriously pursue the Craft as a spiritual path. It therefore signals a formal intention on the part of the student.

The Witches in the Merry Circle feel that students must never be pressured into taking this step. In fact, Witches have a number of somewhat popular sayings that emphasize our feeling that religion should be a freely chosen path that presents itself at just the right time: "The Craft is not a proselytizing religion." "If the Craft is the right path for an individual, then he will find it regardless of the difficulty involved." "The teacher will appear when the student is ready." "The students will appear when the teacher is ready."

As far as the first saying is concerned, it's true that Witches don't proselytize in a missionary or evangelical sense. But we're not entirely passive about acquiring members, either. Unless a coven has decided to close itself to new members, there is likely to be some way of identifying and screening potential members. A few Witches may even be fairly aggressive in their search for new members, building somewhat larger-than-average covens or becoming involved simultaneously with more than one group, as my own High Priest did early in my acquaintance with him. On the whole, it is probably more accurate to say that the organizational structure of the Craft into small, autonomous groups does not lend itself well to large-scale missionary efforts that produce a great many converts at one time.

The other three of these sayings are no doubt meant to be vaguely reassuring—either to the student or the Witch—that opportunities to find the Craft or to find the students will come at the precise moment we are ready. Of course, we also like to reassure ourselves that our students are responsible persons who are ready to follow the path to the Circle; learning to practice the Craft will require lots of hard work as well as a certain degree of maturity.[1]

The time a student spends as a Dedicant is a make-or-break period in terms of acquiring skills that will eventually make his practice successful. Unless a student is truly willing to expend the effort, nothing is going to make that person into a competent practitioner. As a formal declaration of intention, the request for dedication is a signal that the student understands the responsibilities and is willing to take on the specialized training required to become clergy.

Building an Intimate Community

There's a peculiar sort of dance that begins between teacher and student the moment the student asks for dedication. This dance illustrates a deepening ability to read one another's intentions, a skill that will become increasingly important as their relationship continues. The chances are excellent that the Witch knows which students, if any, will "pop the question." In fact, she has probably already shared her assessment of these students with her coven mates and received their feedback before the students even ask to be dedicated.

There's an equally good chance that the student knows in advance what the answer to his question will be. He's not likely to ask for the rite if he thinks that the answer will be no.

This ability to read one another's intentions arises out of a complex mixture of intuition, a natural or cultivated ability to read people, and the implicit or subtle forms of communication by which people signal or intimate their intentions to one another. It is part of constructing what I term an "intimate community" and is an important step in transforming a loosely knit group of folks who simply share mutual interests into a close community with strong internal bonds.

The concept of intimacy as a particular way of relating is elaborated in Thomas Kasulis's book *Intimacy or Integrity: Philosophy and Cultural Difference*. Using the Latin roots of both words, he identifies two contrasting kinds of cultural orientation—intimacy and integrity—that determine how we look at the world and think about relationships.[2]

For example, intimacy and integrity describe different ways of knowing. Intimacy stresses the affective dimension and empathic imagination. Integrity is purely intellectual: "rational" knowledge is ideally empty of affect or "feeling." Intimacy is somatic as well as psychological: the body is involved as an active *knower* and *doer*. Integrity is purely conceptual: the intellectual and psychological are distinct from the somatic. Intimacy is dark or esoteric: intimacy's ground is not generally self-conscious, reflective, or self-illuminating. Integrity is bright and open: knowledge is reflective and self-conscious of its own grounds.[3] The activities leading up to the Rite of Dedication, as well as the training that students subsequently receive as Dedicants, begin to stress the acquisition of intimate forms of knowledge and are instrumental in essentially moving from an integrity orientation to one of intimacy.

In terms of relationships, intimacy emphasizes a deep sense of "belonging with," a feeling of interdependence. In intimate relations, "self and other belong together in a way that does not sharply distinguish the two."[4] According to Kasulis, "Intimate relations are more than connections I have to other people; they are actually a part of what I am or who I have become."[5] In contrast, integrity suggests "belonging to," independence and autonomy, an emphasis of "external over internal relations."[6] The interactions between the student and teaching Witch that occur before the Rite of Dedication are designed to establish the groundwork for the personal and interdependent relations that mark the coven as an intimate community.

Neither the Rite of Dedication nor the initiation itself is an abrupt rending or separation of the student from the intimate context of community. This is contrary to the classic tripartite model of initiation ritual as separation, liminality, and reincorporation that we inherited from Van Gennep. In the tradition of the Merry Circle, both dedication and initiation ceremonies are framed within a larger process of learning, and embedded within a context of community. Their focus is the establishment of increasingly more intimate relationships with the coven members, the Gods, and Nature as a kind of person. This both foregrounds the concept of intimacy as an important way of relating or form of communication, and extends the concept of community beyond simply the Priests and Priestesses of the coven.

Taking Dedication: Getting behind the Wheel

When a student is accepted, he takes on a set of new activities with his teacher and any other students who are on the same level of instruction. While many of these activities—such as obtaining materials necessary for the rite—have a practical purpose, they also begin to slowly build between members the bonds of trust and mutual commitment that are necessary for working together as a coven. If more than one student is preparing for dedication, their mutual activities also begin to lay a foundation for a new kind of relationship with one another.

One of the first things the student must do in preparation for the Rite of Dedication is to make or obtain a proper robe. The Witches in the Merry Circle used to make students sew their robes by hand—a wonderful way to build anticipation and make a student concentrate on the ceremony he is about to undergo, but a horrible way to get a decent robe. Over the years, the Witches in the Merry Circle have sewn their robes by hand, used a sewing machine, and had students who simply went to a costume or Pagan specialty store and purchased a ready-made robe.

I think that I prefer the process of sewing by hand, or at the least using a sewing machine, to that of purchasing a ready-made robe. Although it is a great deal more trouble, and robes made by hand may be less than perfectly constructed (mine was pretty weird looking, being several inches too short from having been measured incorrectly) some valuable experiences come out of sharing the ordeal of making a ritual garment.

Some of my fondest memories about being dedicated into my parent coven come from making my first robe: shopping for fabric with other students, trying to decipher the pattern (What exactly *is* a gusset, anyway?), and the many mild oaths that escaped my lips every time I pricked my finger with the needle. We would meet at Sam's house to work on our robes for hours at a time. Sometimes we would sew and listen to Sam lecture on death and reincarnation or the laws of magic. Like many of our gatherings, not every sewing session was filled with work or study. Equally precious, maybe more so, to the process of establishing a feeling of closeness, of community, were those times we sat around together into the wee hours watching really bad old movies and eating popcorn.

Laughing and eating, sewing and swearing, mixing drops of blood and butter into the fabric of our robes—all of this made the robe a truly magical garment, and made the connections we students felt to one another and to our High Priest ones built on warmth and laughter as well as serious study. A robe made in this fashion is a truly magical garment. This is much more than a metaphorical expression. The act of making the robe invests its very fabric with power and sacred meaning. This meaning becomes present, is made manifest, is *evoked* in the very fabric of the robe itself.

Even though the Merry Circle no longer requires its students to sew their robes by hand, the students and teaching Witch do other things together that are conducive to the production of intimacy. The Witch and her students visit bookstores together, shop for crystals or stones at rock and mineral shows, plant an herb garden, or get together just for fun in order to establish and deepen the relationship that will eventually become community. These shared experiences are the foundation for the construction of community and form the context within which the ritual experiences of dedication and initiation occur.

The activities in preparation for the Rite of Dedication can have the effect of producing feelings of excitement or anticipation on the one hand, and feelings of anxiety on the other. In terms of learning to drive a car, these feelings are similar to those students have at earning their learner's permit after passing the written portion of drivers' education—anticipation and nervousness at the thought of finally getting behind the wheel. For the student who is about to be dedicated, these emotions will continue building and playing off of one another until they are released during the ceremony.

The Witches in the Merry Circle use techniques of tension and release, anticipation and anxiety on a larger and more deliberate scale during the initiation ceremony, and so we will return to these emotions in greater detail during the initiation ritual.

Right now, it's time to get behind the wheel.

The Ritual

The Rite of Dedication is typically performed at night and during the full moon, although the new/waxing moon would be equally appropriate. The ceremony is conducted in a fully cast and consecrated Circle and in a quiet, secure place—outdoors if possible. This is a rite performed for a single individual. Only the initiates and the person to be dedicated are permitted to be present. The teaching Witch usually conducts the rite alone, although other Witches, if already introduced to the student, may be present. The student who is being dedicated must bring a white candle, a robe, and a bottle of wine for the ceremony. It is also customary for the student to bring an offering of flowers to the Circle to decorate the altar.

The Witch who is conducting the ceremony sets up the altar in the usual manner and casts the Circle out of view of the student to be dedicated. Once the Circle is cast and the Gods have been invoked, the Witch blesses and consecrates the student's robe and candle, and pours some of the wine into the chalice. The Witch places the cakes—small, crescent-shaped oatmeal cookies that she has baked—on the altar near the chalice of wine. She places a small bowl on the altar into which the student will pour some water.

Now ready, the Witch calls the student to the Circle and asks him to remove his clothes. The Rite of Dedication is the only ritual practiced by the Merry Circle in which anyone—here, the Dedicant—is skyclad, or nude, during the rite. The student disrobes at the outside of the Circle, enters the Circle, and stands before the altar, facing the north. His teacher gives him the following instructions.

Light the candle. This is the fire element.

Spread the salt on the floor or ground and stand on it. This is the earth element.

Light the incense. This is the air element.

Pour the water. This is the water element.

The student is now shown the gesture of blessing. With the fingers of the dominant hand in the sign of blessing, the Witch instructs him to anoint with the water the parts of the body that will be mentioned, while repeating the following phrases after her.

Bless me, Mother, for I am Your child.

Blessed be my eyes that I may see Your path.

Blessed be my nose that I may breathe Your essence.

Blessed be my mouth that I may speak of You and utter Your sacred names.

Blessed be my breasts, formed in beauty and in strength.

Blessed be my loins/womb that bring(s) forth life even as You have brought forth all life.

Blessed be my knees that I may kneel before Your sacred altar.

Blessed be my feet that I may walk Your sacred path.

The Witch instructs the student to kneel before the altar and meditate in the posture called the position of enfoldment for as long as he feels necessary. He stands when finished and learns how to make a gesture called the invoking pentagram. The student makes the sign of the pentagram and says, "Blessed Be!"—a phrase that is always echoed by everyone present in the Circle.

At this point, the student is ready to take the Oath of Dedication. He kneels again before the altar, grasps the blade of the Witch's sword or athame while it is held by the Witch, and repeats the oath. Essentially, the Oath of Dedication asks permission of the Gods to walk Their path, affirms the Dedicant's connection with all of Nature, and promises to hold in respect and confidence anything entrusted to him by the coven. The Rite of Enrobement is performed immediately after the oath. Here the Dedicant puts on his blessed and consecrated robe, repeating the words of the rite after the Witch. He will remember these words (or at least the gist of them) each time he dons his robe—reminding him that the robe has been blessed and consecrated, and reminding him of the responsibilities inherent in the path he has chosen to pursue.

The ceremony of cakes and wine now follows, as both the Witch and newly made Dedicant sit and relax in the Circle, relating whatever thoughts or experiences about the rite they may wish to share. During this time, the Dedicant learns additional postures and gestures, the names of the Gods used among Dedicants, and other appropriate teachings.

After the Witch and the new Dedicant have finished the cakes and wine, it is time to take down the Circle. As the Dedicant will learn is the usual pattern, the Gods are thanked and bid a fond farewell. Then the spirits of the four directions are thanked for their participation in the rite and bid farewell. Any energy that was raised is grounded or otherwise dispersed in a positive way. Finally, the Witch crosses the Circle's boundary, opening the Circle so that all may leave.

As a Dedicant, the student is now not only able to witness these activities, but is also fully expected to begin to participate in them to the best of his abilities. Part of his ongoing training will hereafter consist of learning how to perform effectively within the Circle.

Analysis

Using the above description as a working example of the ceremony, let's step back and take a closer look at key elements in the performance of the rite. How does the ceremony affect the student's sense of ritual practice and his understanding of the coven as a community?

Timing

When to hold rituals has both theological and practical implications for Wiccan praxis. The Merry Circle tries to hold dedications at either the nearest full moon or the nearest new/waxing moon after the student has requested the rite, provided the student has gathered the necessary materials, such as the robe. Why is the moon's phase important here?

The student has already learned from the introductory classes that the Moon is an important symbol in Wiccan theology and is often identified as female and Goddess. The Witches' Lunar Goddess is a tripartite deity whose aspects of Maiden, Mother, and Crone are theologically configured to activities, to biological stages of life, and to the ever-changing cycles of the moon. The new/waxing moon is the Maiden and marks new beginnings. The full moon is the Mother, who sustains us with her strength and determination. And the waning/dark moon is the Crone, who fearlessly brings an end to things so that new beginnings can take root.

Perhaps more than any other single image, the Moon functions in Wiccan ritual to mark times of change and transformation. Her emphasis in the timing of the ritual is especially appropriate for the dedication ceremony, which marks the transformation of the student from the merely curious to the dedicated.

What messages or teachings are being imparted to the student by having him wait for the right time—the right cycle of the moon—in order to do the ritual? In addition to chronological stages of life, the student learns that the Triple Aspects of Maiden, Mother, and Crone represent cycles or stages in the progress of projects and events. He learns first-hand that timing rituals to the cycles of the moon can be a significant factor in their successful performance. The Moon as deity is not merely a metaphor, a way to think about things, but a time to *do* things. The Lunar Goddess is important not only on a theological or symbolic level, but on a practical level as well. These symbolic dimensions have immediate implications on the practical level, and this is the first of many ritual occasions when that will become evident to the student.

Location

The location of the rite can be equally important to its successful performance. The members of the Merry Circle usually attempt to hold this ritual outdoors in nature, as they do most of their Circles. When the ceremony is held outside, the Witch uses the natural environment to set the stage for the performance of the ritual. Beyond framing the ceremonial event, however, setting the ritual outdoors foregrounds Nature as an active player—a *person*—in the rite itself.[7]

Although a more usual wording of the phenomenon might be something along the lines of "Nature is personified," I feel that this is inadequate and is even sometimes dismissively used to capture the level of interaction between Witch, student, and Nature. Nature-as-person responds to the ritual through the chill of the night air, the wind sighing through the leaves, the light of the full moon peeking through tree branches, the twinkle of stars— even thunder and roiling clouds. Nature-as-person seems to comment on the ritual activities, or at least to punctuate them, through a perception of being alive and present in some special way to the members in the Circle. In a very real sense, Nature-as-person becomes a member of the community with whom the initiates and the student to be dedicated interact in an intimate manner. The Rite of Dedication is likely to be the first ceremony that a student experiences outdoors, and his ability to respond to Nature-as-person is the beginning of yet another facet of the learning process.

What happens when the Rite of Dedication must be held indoors? Although this is not our preference, certainly we have had the ceremony indoors on several occasions. In fact, all of the dedication ceremonies that I have sponsored in my home have necessarily been held indoors, because, at the time I am speaking of, I did not have access to local outdoor areas that were private enough for religious ritual. Indoor dedication ceremonies have a tendency to foreground feelings of privacy and intimacy. Nature-as-person is not as easily perceived as an immediate and felt presence, but the bonds of closeness and intimacy forged between student and teaching Witch are more strongly emphasized in a ceremony within a small, private, and secure space.

Power Dynamics within the Rite

To this point, I have emphasized the development of a closer and more intimate relationship between the teaching Witch and the student about to be dedicated. However, the performance of the Rite of Dedication illustrates that there is a significant power differential between teacher and student. Two things in particular emphasize their difference in power: what the student is not permitted either to participate in or to witness at the beginning of the rite, and ritual nudity in which only the student is nude.

The first indication that there is a difference in power between the student and teacher in the ceremony comes at the very beginning, when the Witch casts the Circle out of sight of the student. The student also does not witness or participate in the consecration and blessing of his robe and candle. These hidden processes represent activities to which he does not yet have access.

Certainly, Circle casting is not exactly a "secret" to the student, who is at least somewhat familiar with the Circle from the introductory classes. The teaching Witch will often go out of her way to make sure that potential Dedicants have the opportunity to witness and participate in a Circle before they make up their minds to take the Rite of Dedication. This is an important part of students' knowing what they are getting into before making a commitment.

The Witch is conveying a message to the student by deliberately framing this event in terms of a difference in power between them. His exclusion from the casting of the Circle and the consecration and blessing of his robe frames this particular ceremony as *different*, as something outside expectation, and frames the power and status differential between student and teaching Witch as she assumes her role as Priestess of the rite.

The second major indication of the power differential between Witch and student comes immediately upon the approach of the student to the Circle's perimeter. While the Witch is robed, the student is directed to remove his clothes and enter the Circle naked.

The fact that the student to be dedicated is nude while the teaching

Witch is clothed signifies that the two are unequal in power and status. Although some Witches, such as the Gardnerians, regularly perform their rituals skyclad, ritual robes are worn in all formal ceremonial or religious activities of the Merry Circle. The Rite of Dedication is the only ceremony in the Merry Circle's tradition in which anyone is nude—in this case, the student. An occasion of ritual nudity in this context is significant *precisely because it is so rare*. Ritual nudity in the Rite of Dedication has implications in at least two dimensions: what nudity in the Circle implies about power and relationship, and what nudity in the Circle implies about attitudes toward the body.

NUDITY AND POWER   In some respects, the act of baring the body is tantamount to baring the soul, and expresses a condition of vulnerability. The level of trust in the teacher that the student has established over the course of study is immediately challenged and made manifest in the physical act of removing his clothes. To be sure, ritual nudity is not sprung on the student as a surprise test of any sort. The teaching Witch describes the basic pattern of the dedication ceremony and informs the student well in advance of the rite that he will need to be skyclad.

Neither this nor any other part of the dedication ceremony is open to negotiation because it may make someone uncomfortable. In fact, the deliberate discomforting in the act of disrobing jars the relationship between the student and teacher from any complacency or familiarity that may have developed, and challenges the student to at least momentarily question the degree of trust that he has placed in the Witch. To my knowledge, no one has ever refused to take the rite because of ritual nudity, but it is certainly theoretically possible that a student would opt not to become dedicated within the Merry Circle's tradition if this were a critical issue.

As a practitioner and a teaching Witch, I have experienced the ceremony from both sides and can speak reflexively as one who has been dedicated and who has also performed the Rite of Dedication for others. I do remember in my own dedication that this was an uncomfortable moment for me. My experience was very much embedded within a context of laying bare, being exposed, or revealing all. In no way did I at that time, or do I today, possess anything near the ideal female body as represented in American advertising and media. And body acceptance or body celebration was certainly not a commonly heard term growing up in Appalachian Ohio.

I had not experienced ritual nudity of any sort at any time previous to the dedication ceremony—ritual nudity not being a factor in even my mother's Serbian Orthodox religious practice, aside perhaps from infant baptism. Pagan festivals were uncommon at the time that I was dedicated, and so I had not experienced those events at which clothing-optional rituals are a common occurrence.

All this combined to make ritual nudity an alien and uncomfortable concept to me. At the time of my dedication, I was acutely aware of a sense of vulnerability as I removed my clothing. I felt that I was placing a great deal of trust in my teacher, who was also my High Priest, not to ridicule me or take advantage of my vulnerability in any way.

Does the Priest or Priestess who is performing the Rite of Dedication feel uncomfortable because of the student's nudity? This question leads us to consider whether the Witch's power is subtly two-edged or nuanced within a feeling of discomfort or vulnerability. While I would imagine that the answer to this question varies with the Witch, here I can only speak for myself. Although ritual and social nudity don't faze me anymore (after several experiences of both), I must admit to having felt a bit uncomfortable about nudity the first time I dedicated students, particularly male students. I think this is due to a number of reasons.

On one level, I remember my own feelings of discomfort or vulnerability and imagine that the student is feeling the same way. My projection may or may not have any basis in the way the student actually feels, but it serves as a reminder to me to be sensitive. On another level, I'm aware of the possibility that the student will misread ritual nudity as sexual nudity, because nudity is so strongly connected to sexuality within American culture. However, the fact that the nudity is one-sided here construes the activity as something other than sexual and may diminish any feelings of vulnerability or discomfort being felt by the student or teacher.

I wonder if feelings of vulnerability are connected with gender? Maybe it's my being a *woman* that raises this issue. On a related issue, perhaps discomfort is also connected with commodification of the human body— the creation and marketing of the perfectly formed female and (increasingly more common) male bodies. A feminist reading of ritual nudity might easily conclude that women would feel particularly vulnerable or uncomfortable being nude because women's bodies are often judged by idealized images represented and commodified by advertising and media. Male bodies are less often scrutinized in the same way, but this is changing radically.

My totally informal and unscientific query of some of the other Witches in the coven suggests that there is no hard and fast rule about gender, ritual nudity, body shape, and comfort. For example, when I asked her, Sandy simply laughed and said she had no problem either being nude as a Dedicant or seeing nude Dedicant bodies.

OK. Sandy is quite a few years younger than I am and a pretty free spirit at that. I decided to ask Dot, whose age is much closer to my own, and whose shape is zaftig, as is mine. She probably had some feelings of discomfort.

"No," she said. "None at all. I was too worried about getting everything else ready for the ritual to worry about naked bodies."

Sigh. Ok, so maybe it was just me.

Well, as we can see, much depends on the individual experiences of the Witch and Dedicant and their attitudes about their bodies.

I suspect that the issue of ritual nudity is embedded in an intricate web of interconnected theoretical and personal issues: gender, sexuality, commodification of the body, power, and personal or individual attitudes about the body. While exploration of this web is tantalizing, I must defer it for another time, leaving behind my observation that power is perhaps not always held or perceived comfortably by those who hold it.

POWER AND INTIMACY   At this stage in the learning process, the Witch and student Dedicant are engaged in an intricate dance, a delicate balance of power and intimacy. On the one hand, they are forging a deep bond—a closer, more intimate relationship than they had in the introductory class. On the other, they remain very much *teacher* and *student*—a relationship that demands critical distance and a difference in power and authority between the two.

Intimacy clearly does not imply equality.

The Witch and the Dedicant are performing a distinction between the relationship that will obtain within the Circle—within the student's learning process—versus a relationship more similar to our common notion of friendship, which may develop between the teacher and student outside of the learning process. We often have a tendency to conflate intimacy with friendship, but the two are really quite different.

The word friendship ideally implies a kind of egalitarian relationship in which both parties are on the same level of power with respect to one another. The intimacy that exists in the relationship between the Witch and her student is not an egalitarian relationship. The teacher-student relationship is one necessarily built on a hierarchy of experiential practice, mastery, and authority in which the teacher has the expert knowledge that the student is attempting to acquire.

This process of growing closeness and intimacy will continue to develop throughout the successful student's learning process, through and beyond the initiation ceremony. The ongoing relationship between the teacher and student will demand an increasing degree of trust on the part of the student. It is a necessary part of making the coven an intimate community.

If we are left feeling a bit uncomfortable at the notion of an intimate, nonegalitarian relationship that nevertheless demands a great deal of trust, it is probably because we are all too aware of the potential for abuse and the need to be wary or cautious about forming such relationships. Knowing that we create these relationships all the time, and in contexts other than religion, may help place the Wiccan teacher-student relationship into perspective. Perhaps learning how to drive a car can help us perceive a bit more clearly what is at stake, in terms of practice, in the teacher-student relationship, understood as an unequal and yet intimate power relationship.

In the course of learning to drive a car, the student and driver's education instructor may become friendly with one another. However, successfully learning how to drive a car demands that the authority and judgment of the teacher not be compromised by his feelings toward the student. Too much is resting on the successful completion of driving practice for the instructor to overlook the student's mistakes because he is afraid that the student might not like him anymore. Nor should the student expect or be willing to accept that the instructor will cut him some slack because they are pals. The focus must be on a working relationship, one that enables the teacher to effectively impart a practice to the learner.

Several things must come together in order for this to occur. On the one hand, the teacher must be certified to teach others how to drive. He must be competent, an expert, a master. On the other hand, the student must be able and willing to learn. He must embark on a course of instruction that is a mixture of both intellectual and somatic learning. The student must master the material in the intellectual portion of instruction before he is permitted to get behind the wheel and continue his learning experience. He also must trust the authority of the teacher and be able and willing to follow the teacher's instructions, especially once they are engaged in the somatic portion of the instruction.

In the case of learning how to drive, we can readily see that the student's life may well depend on the success of that relationship in teaching and learning the practice. Wiccan initiation is about mastery of a practice as well.[8] Although the stakes are perhaps not as high, nor as dramatic, the student of Wicca must similarly grow to trust the teaching Witch until his own practice has achieved a level of competence and skill.

The Body

The occurrence of ritual nudity at the very beginning of the Rite of Dedication has the effect of immediately foregrounding the body as a significant factor in the ceremony. What might the act of ritual nudity be saying about the *body* itself? Within the Merry Circle's tradition, the Rite of Dedication is distinct from the initiation ritual. It is the only point in the whole initiation process in which ritual nudity occurs. It may therefore be instructive to examine some literature on nudity and initiation to see if we can shed any light on this question.

Interestingly, much of the scholarship on ritual nudity in initiation seems to focus on the symbolism of the *clothing* as an indication of status and tends to ignore the body. For example, Victor Turner, in his book *The Ritual Process: Structure and Anti-Structure*, speaks of the removal of secular clothing and other signs of status as a feature of the liminal state.[9] While this gives us some useful insights into the symbolism of clothing within a process of status reorganization, the body itself is curiously invisible and its significance or importance unknown.

We might make a similar observation of Bruce Lincoln's analysis of women's initiation rituals. In his book *Emerging from the Chrysalis: On the Nature of Women's Initiations*, Lincoln notes an entirely new symbolism of clothing in women's initiation ceremonies:

> The general tendency in women's rites seems to be toward an additive process (clothes put on) rather than a subtractive one (clothes

taken off). This serves to express another contrast with male initiations: whereas men (who have a status) must lose their status in order to assume another, women (who have no status) need not do so.[10]

Again, the focus of analysis here is on the symbolism of the *clothing* and not the *body*.

Unfortunately, Lincoln's intriguing suggestion about the difference between male and female rites vis-à-vis the symbolism of clothing gets us no further into understanding the symbolic dimension of this particular portion of the Rite of Dedication. The dedication ceremony is performed for both males and females, so it is neither a male rite nor a female rite. It is, in Lincoln's terms, both a "subtractive" and an "additive" process. The student (male or female) disrobes upon entry into the Circle and departs robed as a Dedicant. To that extent, clothing subtraction and addition may well be one sign of the change in the student's status from casual student to Dedicant.

I suspect that some things are still lacking in our analysis when we overlook the body itself as the central figure in the rite. What happens to our understanding of this portion of the ceremony when we shift the site of symbolic meaning from the clothing to the body? Ritual nudity may be saying something significant about the importance of the body in its "natural state." Such an observation would be entirely consistent within the framing context of Wicca as a "nature religion."

Returning only briefly to the arena of the symbolism of clothing, we can perceive an additional dimension of meaning—secular clothing as symbols of alienation from the natural world. In other words, to be clothed in mundane clothing is to be apart from Nature-as-person. Such clothing is also a function of controlling or managing the relationship to the elements rather than accepting Nature. In the act of disrobing, the body returns itself to a state of nature, free from the distractions and impositions of the secular world. The brief moment of ceremonial nudity returns the body to its natural state—the body *au naturel*—wherein it ritually blesses itself and then celebrates that blessing with the donning of properly consecrated robes that have (ideally) been made by the Dedicant's own hands.

Another point about the act of disrobing is the extent to which the body becomes an active subject, rather than a passive object, in the act of disrobing. Clothing is not *taken from* the student's body by the teacher. The body *disrobes itself* and enters into the Circle to perform the act of blessing. The body is an active participant in the rite; it is an *actor*, a *doer* of ritual performance. In terms of ritual performance, the body is necessarily foregrounded as an actor in the very act of blessing that comprises the major activity of the ritual. The Priestess does not bless the student. The student asks for blessing from the Goddess and performs that blessing both with and through his body. In this sense, the body is not merely the recipient of blessing, but a doer of blessing as well.

What else is revealed in the dedication ceremony about the body in performance? Already noted is the degree to which the *body* is the *performer* of the rite from the moment it enters the Circle. Also revealed is the extent to which the student's instruction has entered a new phase, one that emphasizes or foregrounds learning on the somatic level. During the performance of the ceremony, the Priestess gives somatic instructions to the student. Sometimes these instructions are delivered verbally, as when she tells the student to light the candle or pour the water. At other times, the instructions must be delivered somatically, as when the Priestess shows the student gestures or postures with her own body that the student must then successfully repeat with his body.

The student's body is not just the actor; in the Rite of Dedication the student's *body* has also become the *learner*. The location of instruction has moved from being primarily intellectual to being equally (or at times primarily) somatic. The body's actions in the dedication ceremony are the first of many patterns of behavior and modes of performance that it will learn throughout the time that the student is a Dedicant.[11] These actions will eventually become second nature to the Dedicant.

One final observation pertains to Wiccan attitudes about the body that are revealed during the ritual act of blessing. The body blesses itself literally from head to toe, including those parts of the body that deal with sexuality and reproduction. While mind and spirit have been privileged in both formal and informal discourse in the West, the body is often perceived as "in fall," "dirty," or "threatening." The nude or semi-nude female body is often both denounced as a symbol of temptation and commodified in advertising and the media. The fully nude male body is frequently considered so taboo or threatening that it must remain "invisible" and is not even available for commodification. I suppose that in a country where governmental officials place sheets over immodest statues, the naked body is sure to be a matter of controversy.

The ritual action of blessing the body emphasizes in a physical and concrete manner, beyond what any merely verbal explanation can impart, the degree to which the body is part of the sacred within the Wiccan worldview. No one part of the body is privileged; no one part of the body is denigrated. With the blessing of the Goddess, all parts of the body are holy; all participate in the sacred dimension.

The Role of the Goddess

Speaking of the Goddess, there is at least one facet of the Rite of Dedication that quite frankly perplexes me: Why is the presence of the Goddess made explicit in the ceremony, while the God is not? The Goddess is very much evident as a presence within the rite. She is actively invoked during the student's blessing, while the God is absent from the actual performance of the blessing. Both the God and Goddess are invoked during the casting of the Circle, which is done by the Priestess outside of the student's view.

However, the God is not made present—especially to the student—in the same manner as is the Goddess. In fact, the God will not be mentioned by name until the Priestess and Dedicant share cakes and wine in the Circle.

I don't remember when it was that this question first surfaced, but it has become an increasingly interesting puzzle to me since embarking on this project. None of my coven mates has any insights about this; they didn't even notice it until I pointed it out to them. I suspect that it is part of a paradigm shift in religious worldview or consciousness that the student's first ritual action invokes the blessings of a *female* deity rather than a male deity. Just as the student is left with little doubt as to the sacrality of his body, he is also left with little doubt as to the importance of the Goddess in Wiccan worship.

Let's explore what else the foregrounding of the Goddess signifies for the student. In the section on ritual timing, the student learns an important lesson about the Moon as a *time* for practice. In the introductory classes on Wicca, the student learned that the stages of the Moon may be easily and directly keyed to chronological stages in female life, visualized as the Triple Goddess in Her aspects of Maiden, Mother, or Crone. He now learns through the performance of the ritual that the Maiden, Mother, and Crone represent cycles of *human* life experience, not just *female* life experience. Although a man, he learns to relate to, and identify with, the Moon's cycles in all Her aspects of transformation. He learns to interpret these life cycles in a fluid and flexible manner instead of a literally biological manner. Everyone, male or female, can participate equally in the Moon's cycles, can share in the life-affirming, transformative powers of the Goddess. No one is left out because she is not a biological mother, or because she is too young to be a Crone or too old to be a Maiden. In fact, no one is left out because the *she* is actually a *he*. The range of feminine symbolic experience surpasses biology. Male Witches invoke the power of the Triple Goddess in our coven just as well as the female Witches. The invocation of the feminine divine by *men* and their subsequent identification with the range of *feminine* experiences in rituals of transformation is something that feminist theologians and scholars of religions may find thought-provoking and worthy of exploration.

The Oath and the Robe

The Oath of Dedication is a simple promise by the Dedicant to respect the practices that he is about to learn through his diligent study and commitment to the path that he has chosen to walk. The new Dedicant also promises to respect the confidences entrusted to him, including the mundane identities of any of the Witches he will meet. Not all of the Witches in the group are necessarily comfortable with public practice.

The oath also functions to reassert the power differential between the Priestess and the Dedicant, and this is embodied in the very postures assumed by each. The Priestess, who is robed, stands while the Dedicant, who is skyclad, kneels. Additionally, the Priestess holds the sword or athame, most definitely a symbol of authority within the Circle. The Dedicant is permitted to touch only the blade of the sword or athame as he repeats the words of the oath.

The robe and the Rite of Enrobement come after the student takes the oath. The robe serves as the symbol of entry into both the group and the mysteries. It is a physical reminder of the student's dedication to a path of study and is the only garment ever to be worn in the Circle.

Cakes, Wine, and Circle Deconstruction

The ceremony of cakes and wine is a time of relaxation and sharing between all who are present within the Circle. The Priestess blesses the cakes and wine by invoking the blessings of the God and Goddess into them. This is done in full view of the Dedicant, who watches but does not participate, alluding subtly to the idea that some things are now accessible to him as a Dedicant, and some things remain inaccessible unless he becomes an initiate. The ceremony of cakes and wine serves to reestablish a more relaxed and perhaps more comfortable sense of community. At the same time, it provides an immediate outlet for those present in the Circle to share whatever religious experiences or insights they may have had. This emphasizes personal experiences of the sacred as an important and natural part of any Wiccan ceremony, and provides a safe and secure venue in which to share them.

After the cakes and wine are finished and casual conversation has started to wind down, the Priestess and Dedicant prepare to deconstruct the Circle. He is now able to witness activities connected with Circle making and unmaking. This is a further indication of his change in status. The Dedicant absorbs an important lesson of practice through the act of Circle deconstruction. Everything that is invoked into a Circle must be dismissed; energy that is raised during a ritual must be grounded at its end. This is the first of many lessons about Circle work that the Dedicant will learn through somatic practice and repeated action.

Taking It to the Highway

My analysis of the initiatory process is primarily situated within two large and overarching perspectives: the development of individual practice and the construction of the coven as an intimate community. Let's take a look at how the Rite of Dedication affects these two dimensions of religious experience.

The dedication ceremony moves the student into a more intense and specialized mode of study that acknowledges his decision to invest serious time and effort into learning what it will take to become an initiate. In terms of the development of the student's religious practice, the ceremony represents a major shift in every interrelated facet of instruction—the what, where, when, and, especially, how of the learning process. In terms of *what* the student is taught, dedication signals a shift in emphasis from general information about the Craft and related Pagan practices to more specific information about what this particular coven practices. For example, students in the introductory classes learn that some Witches worship both Gods and Goddesses and that others worship the Goddess primarily or even exclusively. What Gods and Goddesses do the Merry Circle worship? Dedicants are given special names for the Deities, along with special prayers to say in the morning and at night.

In the Rite of Dedication, students are initially exposed to the idea that the symbolic also has a very practical dimension. This process of exposing and sensitizing the student to both the symbolic and practical dimensions of practice now continues. Dedicants begin to assimilate the vast system of symbolic correspondences underpinning the magical system and connecting such seemingly disparate things as elements, planets, colors, plants, and directions. They must eventually master these correspondences in order to understand what elements must be combined to do a particular ritual work, such as a healing. A practical knowledge of herbs and methods of divination are also added to the Dedicant's curriculum.

The location and frequency of the Dedicant's classes change, along with the substance of the classes. In terms of *where* the student is taught, the instruction now moves from the neutral space preferred by the Merry Circle for introductory classes to the Witch's own home. In part, this move is intended to nurture the sense of community and intimacy between the Witch and Dedicant. There is a second, more practical reason for relocation: the increased amount of ritual work within the Circle that the Dedicant will attempt to learn. The teaching Witch will need to instruct the Dedicant in those behaviors, postures, and gestures used within ritual by casting the Circle within her own home. Circle work also increases the frequency of classes, thereby affecting the *when* of instruction. Along with their regular weekly class sessions, Dedicants now begin to meet with their teacher, and possibly other initiates, at least occasionally for new or full moons and possibly the major sabbats.

The most significant changes occurring in instruction concern *how* the student is taught. The emphasis now gradually shifts to include an ever-increasing dimension of somatic practice along with the book learning. This is consistent with the development of an intimacy orientation in which knowledge has affective and somatic dimensions.

This was prefigured in the dedication ceremony itself, with its emphasis on the *body* as the primarily location of ritual performance and practice. Dedication is the stage at which the body is significantly brought into the learning process, and it is this stage of instruction that often proves to be the make-or-break period for the aspiring initiate.

Learning how to drive a car may provide some insights into why this is the case. In order to learn how to drive a car successfully, it is absolutely essential at some point in the learning process to get behind the wheel physically and take to the highway. Getting behind the wheel and driving the car represents an enormous jump in the acquisition of skills as well as a significant shift in how the student learns. The driver's education class has produced graduates who have learned the preliminary rules of the road, and are now qualified to receive their learner's permits. This means that the students and their instructor are now able to actually drive the car, at first in limited and very controlled situations, and then increasingly in conditions of normal traffic.

This stage of the student driver's learning process necessarily foregrounds learning at the somatic level and is the point at which the body becomes fully engaged as *learner*. Note that it is not the natural body, but the *body-in-practice*—the body and mind working together—that becomes foregrounded as learner in the process of learning how to drive a car. The student has previously and necessarily engaged his mind in the first part of the driver's education course by learning the rules of the road. Both through observation and reading, the student has also started to learn about cars in general: where the gas and brake pedals are located, how the braking system works, what turns the car, how the wheels move when the steering wheel is turned, and so forth. At this point in the learning process, the student will have to engage his body *and* his mind in the actual act of driving the car.

While his mind has sufficiently mastered the theory of driving to warrant the learner's permit, it is his body that must master the practice of driving in order to successfully obtain his driver's license. The body will need to learn how much pressure to put on the gas, how quickly to move the foot from the gas pedal to the brake, how much pressure to apply to the brake and under what circumstances. All of the movements typically associated with driving are engaged by the body-in-practice, the body and mind working together to accomplish a complicated series of tasks. Even a moment of reflection reveals just how wonderfully complex the process of driving is.

At first, the body is "all thumbs" in terms of what to do. In driving a manual transmission, for instance, the right hand has to learn to operate independently of the left hand, which must learn to steer the car. The feet also have to learn how to interact with the car and one another. The right foot must simultaneously exert just enough pressure on the gas while the left is easing up on the clutch. Too little gas, and the car stalls; too much, and the clutch pops. Throw in learning how to move the car forward in traffic from a standing stop on a steeply sloped hill, and you have one of my own personal nightmares about learning to drive a "stick." Yet this kind of complex body-mind learning and maneuvering is something that— if we become successful drivers—we eventually come to learn, to master, and even, perhaps, to enjoy.

In fact, at the levels of mastery and enjoyment, the process that was once so brightly self-conscious, so painfully mind-boggling or even frightening becomes totally invisible to our conscious minds. The complex and multi-layered process of driving has become internalized. In Yuasa's terminology, knowledge that was once so clear in the "bright consciousness" has become "internalized through praxis" into the "dark consciousness."[12] In other words, the process of driving has become part of the dark consciousness. As accomplished drivers, we now cruise down the highway, mentally checking off what we need at the grocery, waving to friends seen along the sidewalk, enjoying the day—all the while not even noticing what our hands and feet, our bodies-in-practice, are now doing quite automatically. This most mundane of examples—driving a car—yields a treasure trove of esoteric knowledge. And it is the body-in-practice that is the key to unlocking its secrets.

The only time we will become consciously attentive toward this process again is if something unusual forces us to "re-cognize" what has become part of the dark consciousness. For example, a hurt wrist or sprained ankle can limit one's ability to drive a manual transmission. The body's "disease" forces us to consciously revisit our psychophysical habits to accommodate the injury. Unusually bad weather or mechanical problems may also call one's full conscious attention back to the process of driving, suggesting that there are additional skills that may need to be acquired in the driving process, such as knowing how to drive in inclement weather.

Finally, we may find ourselves having to function as experts, much as our driver's education instructors were, if and when we teach someone how to drive. This will not only mean recalling from the dark consciousness all those processes of the body-in-practice that have been internalized and assimilated, but also passing the test of having enough of a conscious grasp of these processes to communicate them to another person. In sum, there are several additional levels of skill and expertise to the larger process of driving a car than suggested even by the deceptively simple mastery of normal driving.

Returning to the process of learning how to be a Witch, what does the above analysis do to help us understand where the Dedicant is within the overall initiatory process? In driving terms, our Dedicant has passed his preliminary written test and received his learner's permit. The training that will take place from this point on will be one that engages the body-in-practice to an increasing degree—much in the same way as for our student driver. The Dedicant and the Witch now address the *practice* of the religion itself, at first in limited and very controlled exercises with the body in meditation postures or in simple rituals within the Circle. Eventually, the Dedicant will engage in more challenging and creative expressions of religious practice.

At first this somatic portion of the learning process is painfully awkward, similar to the "all thumbs" stage of our driver's education student who is engaging a manual transmission for the first time. The very first thing that the Dedicant must learn is the most esoteric of all Wiccan ritual practices— how to breathe. After nearly thirty years of practice and several years of teaching others to practice, I have come to the conclusion that mastery of breathing in various postures is the foundation of all Wiccan ritual practice. Witches breathe to relax, to ground and center at the beginning of each ritual. It is through proper breathing that the Witch sheds the mundane personality and engages her spiritual dimension—the Craft personality—which is represented by her Craft name and used primarily within the Circle. It is through the automatic and unconscious mastery of breath that the Witch is able to focus her concentration for divination, magic, healing, and invocation. Mastery of the breath is the foundational somatic practice through which the Witch develops her spiritual being—that total integration of mind, body, and spirit that is the goal of spiritual practice.

Yuasa's terminology of bright and dark consciousness again helps us understand what is going on during this particular somatic practice. Control of the breath is a "direct route by which the bright consciousness can contact the dark."[13] It is one way in which the bodymind fully engages or the body-in-practice is achieved. At first, breathing exercises are geared toward simple relaxation, initially in a prone posture. The student is instructed to breathe in, hold, breathe out, hold, and repeat for, say, an initial count of four. The breathing exercises progress through various postures and various breathing patterns, eventually incorporating complex forms of visualization, concentration, ritual gesture, and other forms of bodymind practices.

The Dedicant's ability to control his breath is one of the most telling signs of whether or not he will be successful in somatic practice. Failure here is akin to the moment of initially getting behind the wheel of a car—and freezing. Some students who have made it through the process of dedication have frozen at the prospect of somatic practice. These students likely will not continue toward initiation. They are the equivalent of the driver's education student who has mastered the rules of the road, but can't bring himself to get behind the wheel of a car in order to learn to drive. Like our student driver, the student Witch will need to successfully engage the body-in-practice in order to graduate from this portion of the learning process to receive his license to practice in the form of the initiation ceremony.

In terms of the dedication's effect on the coven as a place of community, the new Dedicant will increasingly draw on the expertise of other Witches in the coven besides his initial teacher. The presence of a Dedicant in the larger coven community is always an occasion for ongoing conversation among the Witches about the student as a potential initiate, the group dynamics, what new members will do to those dynamics, and so forth. Because of this, the Witches and the new Dedicant will increasingly interact with one another in ritual as well as mundane activities. At first their interaction may take place at new or full moon rituals, often held especially so that this interaction can occur. The Dedicant may also start coming to regular sabbats with the Witches in the coven. Sometimes the Dedicant will have special classes with, or projects assigned by, the other Witches in the coven. It is necessary for the Witches not only to get to know their prospective new members as people, but to know them in practice as well. How the Dedicant is coming along in practice can only be ascertained through first-hand observation, especially during ritual events.

Increased interaction between coven and Dedicant serves a number of purposes. It introduces the student to a wider range of pedagogical approaches and fields of expertise than that found only in the teaching Witch. Having other Witches assist with educating the Dedicant spreads the burden around a bit more evenly through the coven. Increased interaction between the Dedicant and the other Witches highlights and further develops the idea of the coven as a close, intimate community.

The increased interaction between the Dedicant and Witches also is part of the mutual screening process. At any time in the Dedicant's course of study, he may decide to leave the group or the group may ask him to leave. At this point in the initiatory process, both the Dedicant and the coven share power somewhat equally in this respect. In the future, this power will shift to the coven as the Dedicant approaches the Circle's edge and faces the challenge of Death at the point of a sword.

6

Coming to the Edge of the Circle

The Ordeals of Preparation

We come now to the final stage in our journey as we approach the edge of the moonlit Circle that will be cast for the Dedicant's initiation. The intricate dance of intimation that began with the student's request for dedication continues. As with the dedication ceremony, the Dedicant must formally ask to be initiated in order to proceed. Even though he may have been working with the Witches in the group for over a year, the Dedicant nevertheless probably sees this as no small task, but as one of the first of many ordeals of preparation that involves a great mustering of courage. After all, the Dedicant has invested a lot of time and effort working with these Witches, and they could still reject him.

In reality, very few—none, if memory serves me correctly—of those who have asked have been refused, probably simultaneously a reflection of the success of the screening process and the establishment of a framework of intimation between Dedicant and Witch.[1] Those Dedicants who were ill suited to the group or its practices have been either subtly or explicitly encouraged to seek elsewhere, and those who found the Merry Circle unsuitable departed on their own.

After receiving the Dedicant's request to be initiated, all of the Witches meet together to discuss him. They review his progress in practice, discuss what they think his motivations are, and whether or not he will make a good Priest. The Merry Circle also prepares a set of questions to ask the Dedicant and decides who will ask what questions on the list. Even newly initiated members may participate in this activity, especially if they have worked closely with the candidate for initiation.

All of the Witches who can attend then meet with the Dedicant in a semi-formal setting at one of the member's homes. Here they question him about his understanding of the Craft as the Merry Circle practices it. The Witches also ask questions about why the Dedicant wishes to take on the responsibilities of clergy. If the answers are satisfactory and all of the Witches agree that they can work with him, or at least agree that they have no serious problems with him, the Dedicant is accepted for initiation. The actual decision of the coven is made on a more-or-less collective basis, but the words of those who have the most experience in the group—the High Priestesses and the Witches who have worked most closely with the student—carry quite a bit of weight in the decision-making process.

If the decision is a positive one, preparation for the actual rite of initiation now begins in earnest. First, the Dedicant must choose a new name—a Craft name—that will be used only in the Circle and will reflect his sacred identity within the coven. Aside from the actual sewing of a robe by hand for his dedication, choosing a Craft name seems to be one of the most challenging projects a Dedicant must undertake to prepare for a ceremony.[2] I suspect that its difficulty is a result of the dual nature of the task. Finding a name that truly represents one's sacred identity usually means a great deal of intense soul-searching. And unless the Dedicant is gifted with some linguistic imagination, the search for a Craft name is usually coupled with nerve-wracking research into some body of meaningful mythology, trying to decipher complex spelling rules and impossible pronunciation guidelines for names—all to discover the name that will truly fit.

In addition to choosing a Craft name, the candidate for initiation is encouraged to begin looking for personal tools, especially the athame, which will be needed almost immediately in ritual practice. The consecration of ritual tools and their charging with power will be one of the first major tasks the Dedicant will learn to perform after initiation.

Finding a great athame was really hard about thirty years ago. I remember driving with Sam about a hundred miles out of town to the nearest large city in order to find a store with a selection of appropriate knives. The knife has to meet several criteria in order to become an athame: its blade must be double-edged, sharp, and of good steel, and it must have a black haft or handle. The knife has to be the right size, needs to fit the Witch's hand in a certain way, has to have the right feel to the Witch, and must be ceremonially cleansed of any spiritual impurities before it can ever be used in the Circle. Clearly, just any old black-handled knife will not do.

Most of the knives I looked at so long ago were World War II–era military surplus and were made to be used in combat, if not actually used in the war. Since the athame is a knife that never cuts anything in the physical plane (although Witches feel that it has command over both spiritual and physical planes), finding a British or American commando knife that was actually used in war is not a plus. Such a knife would have to be cleansed extensively in order to remove from it energies remaining from actual bloodshed. Sam and I spent hours at the store choosing the knife that was "just right" to become my athame.

Similar care goes into the selection or making of all the other ritual tools as well. The ritual objects connected with Wiccan practice function as more than metaphors; they are created to contain real power and real energy that function across both physical and spiritual planes. Like many things connected with the Craft, finding appropriate ritual tools has become much easier. There are now several supply stores that cater to a Pagan clientele. Ritual items, including athames and ceremonial swords, can be made to order and even crafted according to the desired phases of the moon and planetary hours.

In preparing for the ceremony, the Dedicant and the Witches are engaged in new sets of activities and meeting new challenges together. Each moment brings increased anticipation and heightened levels of excitement and anxiety as the Dedicant approaches the big day. Of course, the Dedicant's excitement and anxiety are shared with the Witches, who offer their strategies and suggestions, their support and encouragement, having themselves been through it all before. In this manner, pre-ritual preparation brings the Dedicant and the initiates together in a new way, as a heightened sense of community begins to be extended to the Dedicant by all of the Witches in the coven.

The Rite of Initiation

Tonight it is Brian's turn to walk the path to the edge of the Circle. Brian is from the last group of students initiated by the Merry Circle when we were all together, and his is an initiation ceremony that is fairly fresh in my own memory and experience.

On the day of Brian's initiation, the Witches gather at Lauren's farm home in the country. The moon is waxing full, and if the weather holds, it will be a beautiful night to have the ritual outdoors. Even if we get a little rain, we'll probably still hold the ritual outside. Lauren's house is entirely too small to comfortably do this ritual indoors. For some reason, initiations always seem to take up a *lot* of space, more space than your average "living-room size" Circle.

Besides space, there's another important reason for holding the initiation ritual outdoors rather than inside Lauren's home. Wiccan theology foregrounds Nature-as-person as a member of the spiritual community whose actual *presence* at the rite is made apparent and engaged by the worshippers through outdoor ritual praxis. Those students who have been dedicated outdoors have already been exposed to this theological and praxological dimension. But it is in the initiation ceremony that the presence of Nature-as-person is ceremonially emphasized.

On the day of the ritual, everyone's anticipation, excitement, and anxiety levels are at a fevered pitch—the Witches' as well as the Dedicant's. Lauren, Dot, Sandy, and I have been preparing for the initiation since very early in the day: checking the site, monitoring the weather, and preparing the materials needed for the altar. Dot has given Brian prior instructions to spend the day in solitude and silence, meditating on the ritual ahead.

Brian arrives—early, much to our amazement. This alone gives us a clue as to the level of his anticipation; Brian is *never* early! We immediately start to rib him about this, amid welcoming hugs. He finds us all in the kitchen waiting for him; we had been dividing up parts for the ritual before he came in. Brian is visibly nervous and excited, desperately trying to maintain his silence—not easy when people are teasing you—and the air fairly crackles with energy around him.

As part of his duties for the ritual, Brian has had to bring the wine and bake the moon-shaped cookies that are shared during the cakes-and-wine part of the ritual. Everybody jokes about his baking, speculating on the weight of the cookies and whether we'll be able to eat them without dunking them in the wine first. We also kid him about the ordeals ahead and begin to drop elaborate hints about *what's in store for you now*. This serves the dual and rather contradictory purpose of both relieving his tension and heightening it, as he starts to wonder just how much is real and how much is exaggeration.

I especially enjoy participating in this part of pre-ritual excitement and anticipation. Since he trained in the northern part of the state, Brian does not know me as well as some of the other Witches, and he is more likely to wonder just how much I am kidding and how much I mean to be taken seriously.

It is now close to sunset. Brian puts on his robe and sprays with mosquito repellent before being taken out back to the pond on the edge of the farm, which is far from the house and also far enough from the ritual site to prevent him from clearly seeing or hearing any of the preparations. Brian is instructed to sit on the ground and meditate on the path he has chosen, with a candle flame as his only light. We leave him in the deepening twilight, watching the stars come out and listening to the sounds of the woods while fireflies dance in the fields. He will be safely out of the way until we are ready for him.

Meanwhile, back at the house, we check all our preparations one more time. The initiation is one of the very few rituals that the Merry Circle have in written form—typeset on a computer in a fancy font, no less. Most of the time, we make only a brief outline on a small scrap of paper as a reminder of who has what parts, and a note as to what chants we have decided to do. And, most of the time, these notes are fairly unnecessary. The initiation, however, is a very long and complex ceremony, so we feel that it is best to have things written down in order not to forget anything at the last moment. We finish deciding parts and begin to put our robes on and gather our ritual equipment to take to the Circle in the woods. Right before we are ready to leave, we do one final divination, drawing the runes to make sure that we are doing the right thing. The runes are positive, and we leave the house quietly and start back into the woods. Along the way, we have to pass near Brian, but we are careful not to make too much noise to disturb his meditation—or to let him see and hear too clearly what we are doing.

At the Circle, which is set back in a far field and surrounded by a grove of thick-standing trees for privacy, the altar is quickly set up in the north with the usual ritual equipment, a vase of flowers, and the wine and the cakes. We check everything over one more time to make sure that nothing is forgotten. We decide not to have a fire because of the oppressive heat that has been building all day, and instead set up candles in the central fire pit and lanterns around the edge of the Circle, in addition to the candles at the quarters, which mark the four directions and represent the elements of earth, air, fire, and water. This will make it easier to see in order to find our way around the circumference of the Circle.

Satisfied that we are ready, we gather in the center of the Circle, around the central fire pit, and do a quick and silent meditation to ground and center ourselves before the ritual. At this point, we begin to change over into our sacred or magical personas, indicated by the usage of our Craft names within the Circle. Each of us puts the mundane world firmly out of mind—all the hassles of the day, whatever worries or concerns we might have about jobs, cars, bills, or homework—concentrating only on the ritual that we are about to perform. In some respects, this grounding and center-ing might be understood as similar to actors getting into character before a production. But unlike actors, who often wear roles that are not attractive or desirable to them, our magical personalities and names reflect what we feel to be the most sacred, authentic, and desirable parts of our beings.

The coven now assembled, we cast the Circle by the symbolic invocation of the elements using the appropriate ritual tools, gestures, and songs or spoken invocations. After the elements have been invoked into the Circle, each of us stands at one of the four quarters and prepares to call the Guard-ians of the Watchtowers to come witness the rite and protect the Circle. The Guardians of the Watchtowers are rulers of the quarters and their elements and are related both to mythology and to ancestors or Ancient and Mighty Ones. The Priestess who has called the final quarter formally states the purpose of the rite. We then meet again in the center of the Circle and hold hands to participate in a group chant, which changes into a song of community and solidarity. At this point, we invoke the Gods into the Circle.

The invocation of the Gods is an important step in the construction of any formal ritual that we do. Because the initiation ceremony is designed to bring a new member into the Circle, it is especially important to formally introduce the initiate to the Gods and spirits, and to invoke the transfor-mative powers of the Gods necessary to make that person into a Priestess and a Witch. As described previously, the invocation of the Gods may be understood structurally as the last formal preliminary step to any work that is to be performed within the Circle. All the steps so far have been leading up to the invocation of the Gods: the creation of the sacred space by the blessing of the Circle with the elements, the sealing and warding of the Guardians of the Watchtowers, and the formal statement of ritual purpose.

Lauren and I invoke the God and Goddess, having already decided on who is to take what part before we get to the Circle. Tonight, Lauren invokes the Goddess, first with a prayer and then with a wonderful chant that she sings while standing in the center of the Circle in the postures associated in our tradition with invocation of the Goddess. Dancing, and rhythmic drumming or rattling accompany the chant, with all of us joining in. The purpose of drumming, dancing, and chanting is to raise the energy level of the participants in the Circle, and to manifest the energy of the Goddess into the Circle itself and into the initiates who are present in the Circle. At Lauren's signal, the invocation stops suddenly and the energy of the Goddess is brought down into the Circle through the appropriate ritual gestures.

Next, I invoke the God, beginning with a prayer performed in the ritual posture associated with His invocation. At some point during my prayer, Lauren leads the other Witches in the chant behind me, knowing how much I like the effect of two chants, or a chant and a prayer, going on at the same time. For me, there is a heightened rush of energy as the chanting creates swirling circles of sounds around me and I focus my will and energy on the calling of the God. At my signal, there is quick silence, and everyone concentrates on grounding the energy of the God within the Circle.

The casting of the Circle is now complete.

At this point, we are ready for the night's purpose—the initiation itself. We suspect (our suspicions are later confirmed) that Brian can overhear parts of the Circle being cast. He tells us afterward that he could hear some of the calls to the quarters, the drumming and rattling, and some of songs and chants, but not clearly enough to make out distinct words. We all like this effect of partial hearing because we feel that it serves both to turn up the level of anticipation and to set the tone for the ritual.

Imagine yourself sitting on the cool damp earth, surrounded by deep night sky and fields full of fireflies, frogs croaking and splashing in the pond behind you. You are anticipating the ritual that you are about to undergo, a squirmy and excited feeling in the pit of your stomach, scared but not scared—and suddenly the breezes come to you with sounds of far-off singing and chanting, drums booming, rattles "snaking," voices raised in harmony.

We call it "Magick."

Our written initiation notes are given one final check. Lauren and I remind everyone—but especially Sandy—that the challenges are to be given in a *very serious and stern* tone of voice. Sandy is very giggly and sweet, and it is hard for her to act stern. Predictably, she giggles and says that she'll do her best to be solemn, and we all joke for a bit about how nice it is to get to be "mean." Our joking around at this point is probably an outlet for relieving our own anxiety and excitement over the ritual we are about to do.

Because Dot has been Brian's closest teacher, she gets to be the guide who goes to the pond to bring Brian back through the woods to the Circle. Although the moon will be high in the sky tonight, the first ordeal is getting back to the Circle without a flashlight, as it is by now quite dark and the path is overgrown. Dot is notoriously night blind, and this situation causes all of us—including Dot—to break into quiet laughter about whether either one will make it back alive. We soon hear the fumbled sounds of someone thrashing around in the brush, and so Lauren goes out to the edge of the path to make sure they will find it all right. When the three of them come back to the Circle together, Lauren hangs back, while Dot moves Brian toward the edge of the Circle.

I, his Death and Challenge, am waiting for him.

The hood of my black robe is pulled down around my face, partially shadowing my eyes, and I stand silent, holding the ritual sword that guards the entrance of the Circle. Death, the Challenger at the Gate, is one of my favorite ritual roles. Unlike Sandy, I have absolutely no problem with appearing to be stern, and I am sure that I present a suitably formidable figure: a large woman hooded in a dark robe and cloak, and holding a large sword. Not only is this a juicy role from a performance standpoint, but it also relates mythically to the Goddess I work with, who I feel claimed me as Hers quite a long time ago. At this moment, I feel Her presence quite strongly within and all about me—made *present* in both my voice and body as the Challenger at the edge of the Circle raises the point of the sword to Brian's breast.

For Brian, there is now no turning back. In a hard and stern voice I deliver the warning to him that unless he comes with two passwords—"perfect love" and "perfect trust"—he may not enter my realm. I tell him that it would be better for him to throw himself on my sword than to make the attempt with fear or doubt in his heart. He replies with the two passwords, and I slowly turn my back toward him, seeming to walk away. Unexpectedly, I swing my sword rapidly around, dealing Brian the symbolic death stroke. He is then immediately blindfolded and loosely bound, in this case by Lauren and Dot, so that his feet can move freely enough to walk without his falling down. Witches call this state "neither bound nor free," and we feel it symbolizes the human condition quite nicely.

At this point, Brian is led (or rather propelled) counterclockwise around the outside of the Circle by Dot, who continues to be his guide. A bonus ordeal is, of course, the challenge of navigating around the outside edge of the Circle, which is quite overgrown with weeds, little trees, and miscellaneous unknown pricker bushes.

At each quarter, Brian is stopped by the Guardian of that Watchtower (played by one of us) and challenged about where he comes from, where he is going, what his intentions are, and so forth. These are all formal questions that have formal answers, whispered in his ear by Dot. Each Guardian denies him entrance to the Circle from that quarter, demanding that he first be purified and consecrated.

To do this, the Guardian asks who vouches for Brian, and Dot replies that, as the Guide of Souls, she does. The Guardian delivers a stern warning that if she finds Brian unworthy, her element will destroy him. For example, if the Guardian of the North finds Brian unworthy, the earth will open up and swallow him. This not happening to Brian, the Guardian administers her elemental purification by engaging the appropriate bodily sense, and passes him to the next quarter. The Guardian of the North may place a piece of rock salt under Brian's tongue, that of the West may make him drink from a cup, the South might pass the heat of a flame under his hand, and the East may present Brian's nose with incense to smell. Each Guardian performs a gesture known to initiates as the banishing pentagram to seal the purification. Brian successfully passes by each challenge around the whole of the Circle until he arrives again at the beginning.

Finally, Brian is given the third password (which he does not know in advance, and which will not be revealed here) and is reborn into the Circle. Dot, as his guide and mentor, is the one who literally pushes Brian over the Circle's edge. Dot and Lauren position Brian, who is still blindfolded, before the altar. Brian stands while Lauren reads him instructions, commanding him, among other things, to love all things in Nature and to allow no one to suffer by his hands or in his mind. Lauren asks him if he agrees to these conditions. Brian replies in the affirmative. At this point, two of us cleanse Brian with incense and the sound of rattles. One of us sounds a drum three times, signaling that the activity should stop.

Lauren tells Brian that he has passed the test and asks him if he has chosen a new name. Brian gives his Craft name and receives the breath of life from Lauren while we remove his blindfold and untie his bonds. Brian swears the Oath of Initiation on the sword, repeating aloud the words said by Sandy. He receives gifts from each of the four elements and from spirit and then kneels at the altar while we sing a naming song in his honor. After the song, two of us help Brian rise and one of us gives him the five-fold blessing, using the wand. The five-fold blessing echoes the blessing ceremony that had been performed by Brian during his Rite of Dedication. While not exact in wording, the five-fold blessing goes something like this:

Blessed are your feet, which have brought you to our ways.

Blessed are your knees, which will kneel at the sacred altar.

Blessed is/are your womb/loins, without which we would not be.

Blessed is your breast, formed in beauty and in strength.

Blessed are your lips, which will utter the sacred names of the Gods.

Dot then leads Brian clockwise to each of the Guardians of the Watchtowers, and proclaims him to be a new Priest and Witch.

After this, the anxiety and tension of the ordeal of the initiation immediately deflate, like air out of a balloon, and all of us cheer and rush to Brian for hugs. Everyone calms down as Lauren and I bless the cakes and wine. Now it is time for us to take a breather from the intensity of the ritual experience. All of us settle on the ground to relax and stretch our muscles, a few of us "old timers" groaning at our aches and pains and wondering aloud which of us *really* had the ordeals.

It is very difficult to gauge the passage of time in the Circle, but the growling noises of our stomachs assure us that several hours—at least—have passed. The cakes-and-wine portion of the ritual affords us an opportunity to really assess the quality of Brian's baking, and this usually leads into much kidding and joking as we all pretend to have to dunk the cookies in the wine to soften them enough to swallow. Actually, the cakes are surprisingly good, and Brian knows that we appreciate his baking skills. In fact—we joke—maybe we'll let him make the cakes from now on. Still very much in the ritual glow, we tell Brian that he will now be read an important story. We instruct him to pay close attention, as the story will reveal important things to him that he will come to understand upon reflection in the future. I stand and read the following story[3] to him, using my best narrative voice:

> *Listen, O Children of Wicca, to the Descent of the Goddess:*
> In Ancient Times, Our Lord was, as He still is, the Guardian, the Protector, and the Bringer of Comfort. But mortals knew Him as Death, the Lord of Shadows and Dark Mysteries. In this world, the Goddess is seen in the Moon, the Light that Shines in Darkness, the Rain Bringer, Mover of the Tides, Mistress of Mysteries. And as the Moon waxes and wanes, and spends some of Her cycle in darkness, so, it is said, the Goddess once walked the darkness of the Kingdom of Death.
> Now our Lady, the Goddess, would solve all Mysteries, even the Mystery of Death. For in love, She ever seeks Her other Self, and once, in the winter of the year, when He had disappeared from the green earth, She followed Him and came at last to the gates beyond which the living do not go. The Guardian of the Gate challenged Her to relinquish Her clothes and jewels, for nothing may be brought into that land. And She stripped Herself of Her clothing and jewels and was bound, as are all who enter the Realms of Death.
> Such was Her beauty that Death Himself knelt upon seeing Her, and laid His sword and crown at Her feet, saying: *"Do not return to the living world, but stay here with Me, and have peace, and rest, and comfort in My kingdom."*
> But She answered: *"Why do You cause all things that I love and delight in to wither away and die?"*
> *"Lady,"* replied Death, *"It is fate that all who are born must die. Everything passes; all fades away. I bring comfort and consolation*

to those who pass the gates, that they may grow young again. But
You are My heart's desire. Return not, stay here with Me."

But She answered: "I feel no love for Your cold comfort."

Then said Death: "Since You will not receive My wisdom in the
spirit of love, You must suffer the purification of all who come to
My kingdom."

"It is better so, to learn what all must learn." And so She received the ordeal of purification—by earth, and water, and fire, and
air—and was made wise in the mysteries of Death. Through Her
ordeal She attained wisdom and knew love for the Lord of Shadows.

And Death welcomed Her and taught Her all His Mysteries. She
took up His crown, which He had laid at Her feet. And it became a
circlet that She placed around Her neck, saying: "Here is the Circle
of Rebirth. Through You all passes out of life, but through Me all
may be born again. Everything passes; everything changes. Even
Death is not eternal. Mine is the mystery of the Womb, which is
the Cauldron of Rebirth. Enter into Me and know Me, and You
will be free of all fear. For as life is but a journey into death, so
death is but a passage back to life, and in Me the circle is ever
turning."

And the Lord of Death and the Great Mother loved and were
one and taught each other all the magics. Yet is He known as Lord
of Shadows, the Comforter and Consoler, the Opener of the Gates,
King of the Land of Youth, the Giver of Peace and Rest. And She
is the Gracious Mother of all Life; from Her all things proceed
and to Her all return again. In Them is the fulfillment of the
great mysteries of death and birth; in Them is the fulfillment of all
love.

During my reading of the narrative, Nature Herself seems to punctuate
my words with flashes of lightning and rumbling thunder in the distance.
While this enhances my performance of the text, it also adds a note of
urgency and immediacy to the Circle, as all of us realize that we must get
on to the rest of the ritual before the loosing of what promises to be a
violent summer storm.

After the reading of the text, we formally present Brian with the ritual
tools of the Craft, explaining the uses of each one, and instruct him in some
of the secrets of the Craft. These may include such things as the names of
the Gods used by initiates in our group, ritual gestures or postures, and
prayers. This revelation of things known only to the initiates—the tools
and the secrets—is a sign to him that he truly is one of us and that we are
pledged to continue to share our knowledge of the Craft with him.

At this point, we all meet again in the center of the Circle, hold hands,
and chant a song of community, which everyone—including Brian—
knows. Love and warmth reflect all around in our faces and in our happy
smiles. The Circle is now unmade, beginning with proper farewell to the

Gods and the spirits of the elements. At the end of the Circle, the Priestess in the last quarter walks purposefully over the boundary, formally breaking the Circle, and announces that the rite is over. Everyone again rushes to give one another hugs, and then we all pack up the ritual gear and hurry to the house through a pelting of raindrops.

Cool-Down Time

Back at the house, everyone cools down and unwinds. Now it is time to party, and we get out the wine and cheese, bread, vegetables, fruit—whatever food that we brought. We all sit crammed in Lauren's kitchen to share food and drink, laughter and thoughts, talking mostly about the ritual we just went through. Although the ceremony is over, we nevertheless consider this period of sharing and eating a necessary and thoroughly enjoyable part of any ritual occasion, but especially so for initiation rituals.

We ask Brian a *lot* of questions: Could you hear us by the pond? What did you think about when you heard us chanting? What were you meditating about? Did you see anything or feel anything while you were meditating? Did any animal spirits appear to you? Was it hard to concentrate? How did you feel when this happened? How about when that happened? What was its effect on you? What did you think about the ordeals? Were you scared? How do you feel now?

Eventually, the conversation leads to stories of other initiations—our own, or maybe someone else's that happened a long time ago. Talk turns to the initiation of a friend of Lauren's and mine: "Now *she* had to walk through a literal wall of fire for one of her ordeals!" Next to that, the pricker bushes weren't so bad, after all. Lauren brings up the old days, stories from the parent coven. Lauren says that she knows of someone who was initiated in a trailer, left bound and blindfolded with headphones on and music playing while the two Witches who initiated him tried to figure out what they were going to do for the rite.

We laugh and agree that this is *definitely* a poor way to do an initiation, and that rituals certainly have *improved* within our tradition! Someone mentions how lucky we were to have been able to have the ceremony outside, in Nature, and asks, "Wasn't the coming storm beautiful?"

Before everyone returns home or crashes at Lauren's for the night, the person who has played Death, the Challenger at the edge of the Circle, gives Brian one final instruction, one final ordeal. I tell him that he must write a paper about his initiation experience for further discussion with either Lauren or me, or both of us. Thus the initiation itself is made the first formal class that Brian will have as a new Witch. This class will lay the groundwork for other assignments that we will all give Brian later on. Brian's training as a Witch does not end with initiation, but, rather, takes on yet another new beginning, as he enters a new cycle of learning within the Craft.

Analysis

Using the above description of Brian's initiation, we can now take a closer look at how the initiation ceremony continues some of theological and practical groundwork begun with the Rite of Dedication, and which, if any, movements of transformation during the ritual follow our tripartite models of rites of passage.

Timing and Location of the Ritual

As in the Rite of Dedication, the timing and location of the initiation ritual has theological and practical implications for Wiccan praxis. Like the dedication, the initiation ceremony occurs during the waxing moon, at any time from new to full. The full moon is ideal for reasons both practical (maximum light at night) and theological (maximum visible presence of the Lunar Goddess). The timing of the rite may also depend on more mundane considerations: whether the Dedicant has completed necessary preparations (e.g., choosing a Craft name, purchasing personal tools, and so forth), and the personal schedules of the Dedicant and the Witches who are performing the initiation.

In the previous chapter, I discussed the practical and theological importance of having Wiccan rituals outdoors in Nature, and the considerations bear brief repetition here. Practically speaking, initiations take up a lot of space, and no one in the group has a house large enough to contain all the necessary activities. Theologically, Wicca is understood by its practitioners to be a nature religion. As such, it makes great sense to hold initiations—the most fundamentally transformative experiences of the religion—outdoors, especially if the student's dedication ceremony was held indoors. The immersion of the Dedicant in the natural world enhances every aspect of the initiatory experience, beginning with his placement at the pond, the first spatial movement of the rite.

Circling through Space: Movement and Metaphor in the Landscape

In addition to timing and location, spatiality and movement through the landscape play prominent roles in the initiation described, offering to us a rich metaphorical landscape that has implications for how community is constructed and understood from different perspectives.[4] Within this landscape, the Merry Circle use space symbolically and deliberately, beginning with the identification of Lauren's house as mundane territory.

FROM KITCHEN Before Brian arrives, the Merry Circle use the kitchen of Lauren's house as a kind of "staging area" to begin preparing for the rite. At the most practical level, this is where the Witches attend to the last-minute details necessary for the successful performance of the ritual. They make a final inventory of the ritual equipment needed as well as double check who is going to play what part in the ceremony that night.

However, on a more symbolic level, the kitchen's cozy and familiar setting reinforces a sense of intimacy and community among the initiates. The initiation of a new Witch is potentially an anxious time for the coven: How will the group change as a result of a new member? Did they make the right decision? Will Brian be happy and successful in his practice with the group? The meeting in the kitchen provides an intimate and comforting space in which to share thoughts, feelings, any possible worries, and usually a great deal of laughter over a cup of coffee or a glass of wine and a few cookies. These reassuring activities help the Witches prepare emotionally and psychologically for the ritual they are about to perform.

When Brian arrives, he also interacts with the Witches in the kitchen. But, like the events leading up to his dedication, he does so to a limited extent—primarily because his silence marks him as not yet officially part of the group. Both his silence and the ritual teasing reinforce a sense of liminality: Brian is not completely an outsider, because he has already undertaken a rigorous learning process, nor is he completely an insider, because he has not yet undergone initiation. The ritual teasing is calculated to reinforce the ambiguity of the event. The Dedicant will presumably wonder just how much joking about the "ordeals of initiation" is real and how much exaggeration. This joking is also designed to make the Dedicant question just how well he knows the Witches who are about to initiate him. This uncertainty frames the moment when the Dedicant meets the challenge of death at the point of a sword.

TO POND   The first spatial action in the initiation ritual is the placement of the Dedicant at the edge of the pond, equally distant from the mundane house and the ritual Circle. His location at the pond is again both practical and symbolically meaningful. Practically, placing him at the pond gets him out of the way as the Witches complete their preparations for the ceremony.

Symbolically, Brian's placement at the pond reveals his own state of liminality—separate and different from those in the mundane world, but not yet an initiate. Distant from the mundane world, he awaits the initiation that will fully incorporate him into the Wiccan religious community. Seen from this perspective, the spatial patterning of the initiation seems to fit with Van Gennep's (1960) and Turner's (1969) descriptions of initiation as separation, liminality, and reincorporation, rather than Lincoln's (1981) model of enclosure, metamorphosis, and emergence.

However, from the perspective of *where* he is placed—in *Nature*—a very different understanding is possible. From the perspective of Nature-as-person, Brian is already united "in community" by the time he is placed out of the way at the pond. He is already in communion or harmony with Nature, although he may not realize it fully. In this sense, initiation will not *bring* Brian into community with Nature so much as it will awaken him through the experiences of his body-in-practice to the community *that is already there.*

The idea of somatic and intimate communion with Nature is an important theological point for this tradition of Witches. For Brian—sitting quietly on the moist, cool ground—every breeze, every star, every firefly, each chirp of a cricket or throaty croak from a bullfrog reinforces the sense of communion between person and Nature, made present in and through the senses of the body, resonating in harmony with the presence of Nature. This is one of the critical lessons of the entire learning process of becoming a Witch. And it is vital that the Dedicant learn this lesson—not just intellectually or emotionally, but somatically, with and through his body.

TO CIRCLE'S EDGE   The ritual itself takes place away from the house, back at the far edge of the farm, and is surrounded by a thicket of woods. This ensures that the ceremony is held away from mundane distractions, and the woods provide the necessary seclusion and privacy for the night's ritual activities. The symbolic placement of the Circle away from the house, on the far edge of the farm and in the "wildness" of the woods, reveals its religious liminality. While not in the middle of the ordinary world and not quite in the realm of the Gods, the woods become a place of magic in between, where the Witches call their Gods to play with prayer and song.

Gathered together under the sheltering trees, the Witches create their sacred space through the ritual casting and consecration of the Circle. The Circle is first deliberately and ritually marked off from the surrounding area, a physical version of Babcock's metanarrative markers, which sets aside particular kinds of speech from surrounding talk. Circle construction may be understood as a form of *metaspatial* marking, setting aside a particular kind of space—here ritual or sacred space—from the surrounding space.

It is important to understand that the area in the woods has no innate or ontological value as a thing in itself. Its location outdoors in Nature gives it a certain theological value for Wiccans, who hold Nature in reverence, but even an outdoor Circle has to be created in order to become the Witches' magic Circle. In this sense, Circle construction would constitute, in folklorist Mary Hufford's terms, "a contextualizing or framing practice that draws attention to the double grounding of an *extraordinary world opened up within the ordinary*" (italics mine).[5] Casting the circle is the literal articulation of a metaphysical realm, the place between the worlds, in which Wiccan religious activity occurs.

In other words, it is the actions of the participants that make the space sacred in the sense that it becomes a place that can be used for religious ritual. In fact, the magic Circle as such is a place that can be arrived at only through a process of deliberate and practiced transformation of space.

This deliberate structuring and transformation of space occurs in much the same way when an initiation cannot be performed outdoors. In this case, areas of the house are marked in much the same manner as are areas of Lauren's farm. My own initiation took place in a very large Victorian house in a small Ohio town. For the pre-ritual meditation, I was placed in an unused room downstairs well away from the ritual area with no mundane distractions and only a candle for light. Music emphasizing sounds of the natural world—the howl of wolves, the shivering whistle of winds— was played to help transport me to a place at least symbolically situated in Nature. I could not hear clearly any of the ritual activities going on in other parts of the house, except for a distant hum and an occasional creaking floorboard. Here, space was used vertically—the downstairs being closer to the mundane world and the upstairs closer to the realm of the Gods.[6]

The concept of the Circle as a place between the worlds deserves further articulation. Witches view the properly cast and consecrated Circle as a place between the ordinary world of human beings and the world of the Gods. For Witches, this is not a metaphorical place; the place between the worlds is not merely some romanticized and literary allusion to or appropriation of the fairy realms of popular childhood and adult fantasy literature. Specially trained individuals who cast the Circle in the way that I have described are literally constructing a field of interaction—not entirely in either world—in which the Gods manifest, and both Gods and humans meet and interact through ritual praxis.

In this particular tradition, neither the Gods nor Nature-as-person are merely metaphorical or symbolic constructs. They exist. They are real. They have their own agency. The Circle so cast becomes an intersubjective field in which the Gods and those persons who have developed the body-in-practice may actually *engage one another* in *shared* subjectivity or "consubjectivity."[7] The place between the worlds is the place wherein human beings and Gods mutually interact and affect change in one another. The properly cast and consecrated magic Circle—the place between the worlds— is therefore particularly significant in initiation as a rite of transformation.

The circular shape of the sacred space is itself symbolic during Brian's journey of transformation. Every action in the Circle that has a direction has a meaning attached to it, from the counterclockwise direction traveled by the Dedicant at the beginning of his journey to the clockwise direction traveled at the end when he is blessed and named Priest and Witch. The Dedicant is unmade and remade through the challenge and purification of death. All actions tend to come full circle, including the ordeals of the Dedicant in his journey around the perimeter of the Circle. This stresses the idea of the completeness of ritual action, which in turn implies the completeness of the process of transformation.

The circle shape forms an enclosure, a community, into which the Dedicant is petitioning entrance through his ordeals. Interestingly, it is the body of the *initiates* who seem to display Lincoln's model of enclosure, metamorphosis, and emergence. The Circle encloses the coven, the bringing of Brian into the Circle is the metamorphosis, and, after this point, the initiates of the coven all emerge changed through the addition of a new Priest. On the other hand, from Brian's perspective, enclosure or community *within the Circle* is a goal rather than a starting point.

With the correspondences of the directions of the Circle factored in— not only the elements, but also the mythological realms and ages of life— Brian's trek around the Circle takes on added meaning as a journey through space and time. Circle time is both historical, in the sense that directions are attached to stages of life, and ahistorical, in that directions are attached to mythic realms, which exist in all historical directions and none. This again calls attention to the Circle's state of liminality, of being again between the worlds.

Circular movements are prominent within the ritual; I can find no clear overarching linear flow within the rite that begins with separation, leaves separation and enters liminality, then leaves liminality and enters reincorporation. Focusing only on Brian's experiences, it might be said that there is a kind of linear flow to parts of it, but I think that misses other interesting facets of the ritual performance—for Brian as well as for the initiates.

To start with, I don't believe that sitting by the pond constitutes a true separation in the classic sense—a rending of the "known"—for Brian. From the perspective of Nature-as-person, Brian already begins with a kind of unknown or unrealized community or intimacy during his meditation by the pond. He will end with a fully realized intimacy with Nature only when his body-in-practice is sufficiently developed, most likely long after the initiation ritual is over.

There is actually a great deal of liminality of various sorts within the ritual: Brian's silence in the kitchen, his placement at the pond in between the house and the woods, the Circle itself, and so forth. Some forms of liminality will, in fact, repeat throughout Brian's association with the coven. For instance, both he and the other Witches in the coven will create and experience liminal space each time they cast the sacred Circle. Finally, to question a simple linear progression further, even when all the initiates are together in the Circle holding hands and singing at the end of the ceremony, they are all still, in a sense, separate from the mundane world.

Perhaps it would be more accurate to say that the themes of separation, liminality, and reincorporation—or enclosure, metamorphosis, and emergence—that describe the state of the coven as community, occur and reoccur in various stages of the ritual, and change or shift according to perspective as we progress through the ritual performance of initiation. If we were to try to graph this series of shifting transformations, such a graph would certainly not be a straight line. Groupings of interweaving and shifting circles that change according to perspective would perhaps be more to the point.

AND BACK AGAIN   One final circular movement is worth mentioning before leaving this section—the return to the house by the initiates. This marks the return of the initiates to the mundane world, a final reincorporation in its own way of the community of Witches into the larger community of humanity. In this way, the entire movement of the ritual performance of initiation finds its completion in the return of the practitioners to the safe and warm environment of the house, where the sharing of food and laughter seal and affirm the sense of community created by ritual.

With and Through the Body-in-Practice

As in the dedication ceremony, the body in the initiation rite becomes foregrounded as an active participant in the ritual. In initiation—as in dedication—the body is an *actor*, a *doer*, and a *performer* of the rite. More importantly, initiation is the means by which the natural body is ritually transformed into the *body-in-practice*. The initiation ceremony effects this transformation by ritually unmaking the natural body and then remaking it as the body-in-practice. This is accomplished in large part through a Dedicant's symbolic death, his blindfolding, his journey around the outside of the Circle, and his encounters with the elements.

Let's begin with the moment of Brian's symbolic death—a sure sign that he is about to be unmade in some important fashion. In Wiccan initiation ritual, the transformation of person is keyed to the transformation of space; both processes begin with the use of the sword. In Circle casting, the Witches use the sword—a tool representing the element of fire—to separate the sacred space from its ordinary location. In initiation, the Witch who personifies Death wields the sword in a symbolic "death blow" that separates the Dedicant from his ordinary life. This separation from the ordinary marks both space and person as a site of transformation.

The transformation processes of both space and person are mutually interdependent and dynamically related. The transformation of mundane or ordinary space into sacred ritual space depends upon the actions of initiated and skillful Witches in casting and consecrating the magic Circle. The transformation of person depends upon the presence of the Circle's elemental Guardians who perform the actions necessary to change the Dedicant into a new Witch and Priest. Just as the Witches invoke each element and direction to purify and consecrate the Circle, so, too, do the Guardians of the four directions employ their elemental powers to purify and consecrate the Dedicant.

Transforming space, the Witches banish all negativity and invoke the blessing of the elemental Guardians into the Circle. Transforming person, the Witches banish Brian's old ways of perceiving reality through the purification of his bodily senses, which are themselves keyed to the directions and elements of the Circle.

Immediately after the deathblow, Brian is blindfolded and partially bound. While this can readily be perceived as a statement of power differential between the Witches and the candidate for initiation, what is often missed is the ritual unmaking of our cultural dependence on "visualism" in the production of knowledge. Describing the problem with vision and visualism, anthropologist Johannes Fabian calls for a return to materialism, the body, and embodiment in our epistemology.

> Vision requires distance from its objects; the eye maintains its "purity" as long as it is not in close contact with "foreign objects." Visualism, by instituting *distance* as that which enables us to know, and purity or immateriality as that which characterizes true knowledge, *aimed to remove all the other senses and thereby the body* from knowledge production (this incidentally, is also a context in which the gender question needs to be raised). Visualism, nonetheless, needed some kind of materialization which it found in signs, symbols, and representation. If it is true, as we have said, that the question of ethnographic objectivity has been displaced by a shift of emphasis in critical thought from production to representation, then our response should be to *explore again body and embodiment* as involved in objectification and the grounding of objectivity. It is in epistemology more than in, say, economics or even aesthetics, that we need to maintain, or rehabilitate, a materialist position. What is at stake here is whether we can give to intersubjectivity a *more concrete, palpable meaning* than that of an abstract "condition." (italics mine)[8]

In other words, Brian is blindfolded in order to compel him to rely upon his other senses more fully—to rely upon his *body*—in grasping the transformation he is undertaking. In so doing, the purification by the elements takes on a more concrete, palpable meaning, rather than an abstract or metaphorical one. The death and transformation, the unmaking and remaking of a newly purified and blessed Brian as Priest, is made real by his engagement with and through his *body-in-practice*.

Brian will cultivate through the body-in-practice what anthropologist Thomas Csordas calls "somatic modes of attention," defined as "culturally elaborated ways of attending to and with one's body in surroundings that include the embodied presence of others."[9] In this case, the "embodied presence of others" encompasses not only the Witches in the Circle, but also those entities invoked or otherwise called into the Circle—including the Gods, who are *made manifest* in and through the bodies-in-practice of the Priests and Priestesses invoking Them.

In other words, when the Goddess is invoked by Lauren, She *becomes present* with and through Lauren's body-in-practice. It is at once both Lauren *and* the Goddess Who signal that the invocation is complete. Brian will learn not only to become increasingly aware of or attentive to the elements, to the spirits and Guardians, to the Gods, and to Nature-as-person, but he will also learn to sense and engage them through his body-in-practice. Csordas helps us grasp the significance of somatic modes of attention:

Because attention implies both sensory engagement and an object, we must emphasize that our working definition refers both to attending "with" and attending "to" the body. To a certain extent it *must* be both. To attend to a bodily sensation is not to attend to the body as an isolated object, but to attend to the body's situation in the world. The sensation engages something in the world because the body is "always already in the world." Attention *to* a bodily sensation can thus become a mode of attending to the intersubjective milieu that give rise to that sensation. Thus, one is paying attention *with* one's body. Attending with one's eyes is really part of this same phenomenon, but we less often conceptualize visual attention as a "turning toward" than as a disembodied, beam-like gaze. We tend to think of it as a cognitive function rather than as a bodily engagement. A notion of somatic mode of attention broadens the field in which we can look for phenomena of perception and attention, and suggests that attending to one's body can tell us something about the world and others who surround us.[10]

Attending to what is perceived by the *body-in-practice* tells Brian something about the concrete reality of those who inhabit the intersubjective field of the consecrated Circle. The somatic modes of attention cultivated by the *body-in-practice* represent a significant achievement in the realm of individual practice—one that ideally continues to develop long after the initiation ceremony is over.

Power Dynamics within the Rite

A necessary part of any analysis of initiation ritual is the way in which community and power are negotiated throughout the ceremony. Here, at least, we might expect to discover a fairly straightforward balance of power weighted in the favor of the initiates. And so we do—for the most part. Let's review some of the ways in which the Witches clearly exercise power and control over the Dedicant who is asking for initiation—in this case, Brian.

First, of course, is the point at which Brian asks for initiation. Clearly, the Witches hold the power at this moment—they can say no. They further demonstrate this power by gathering together to grill him over his understanding of the Craft, his motivations for wanting to be clergy, his personal habits, and so forth. This is a rather serious and daunting experience, somewhat mitigated later on by the new sets of activities and new feelings of closeness that Brian, as a candidate for initiation, will experience with the initiates. Shopping for athames, pouring over sources for names, sharing stories of how and where different Witches got their names—all of this makes for positive, supportive, and friendly interaction between the Dedicant and initiates.

On the actual day of initiation, the ritual kidding that takes place with Brian upon his arrival at Lauren's home simultaneously deflates and inflates anxiety levels. The broad hints about ordeals to come are delivered with a smile and a wink, but also just enough ambiguity to make him nervous—and intentionally so, especially by me. Brian does not know it at the time, but his ambiguous feelings and the uncertainty that he has about me in particular, as the Witch least known to him, are about to reach their peak in my performance as Death, the Challenger at the Circle's edge. I use my position of ambiguity consciously and deliberately to increase the effectiveness of my performance as Death, and to establish the *power of the presence* of Death in the Circle at the critical moment of the challenge.

Brian's removal from the scenes of activity to the edge of the pond is simultaneously designed to immerse him in his own solitude, his "apartness" from us, and also to immerse and make him open to the presence of Nature-as-person all around him. In some sense, Brian is already empowered in communion with Nature-as-person, but his power is unavailable to him; it cannot be actualized until his body-in-practice is engaged in the unmaking and remaking of initiation. Additionally, the fact that he can almost, but not quite, hear the Circle being cast is both a statement about his standing in the community within the Circle and a statement about his power—he is not allowed to participate in the casting with the others.

The series of ordeals and physical actions that begin with Brian's being led to the Circle's edge most definitely establish him at a lower level of power compared to the initiates. He is symbolically killed—perhaps the ultimate ritualization of vulnerability and loss of power—and then ritually unmade in his journey around the outside of the Circle. At every quarter of the Circle, Brian is denied access and ordered to pass on. Even after Brian is reborn into the Circle, he still stands blinded and bound, at the mercy of the Gods, the Guardians, and the Witches who continue to test him by giving him further instructions to love Nature, to allow no one to suffer by his hands, and to swear yet another oath on the sword.

How are we to understand the power dynamics expressed through ritual action? We might expect a fairly straightforward understanding of the initiation ritual as an exercise of "power over" the candidate,[11] rather than an example of "power with" or "power from within."[12] One scholar has suggested that the "hierarchical, power-over styles" of traditional Wiccan ritual are the result of people who come from the more "ceremonial" and "hierarchical" traditional Christian religions and who have an "abusive family background."[13] It is true that serious abuses of ritual power and authority do occur, and not only among traditional Wiccans. Yet a superficial reading of the initiation process as a simple case of power over the student fails completely to take into account participants' understandings of either the embodied nature of ritual praxis or the development of an intimate community.

EMBODIED PRACTICE AND THE LICENSE TO WITCH   First, let's address the embodied nature of ritual praxis. Brian's initial powerlessness at the beginning of the initiation ritual must be compared and contrasted with his experiences at the end of the series of ordeals. Brian is finally remade and transformed by his rebirth into the Circle. As a Priest and a Witch, he is restored to some semblance of power and is even given gifts by the Guardians of the Watchtowers as signs of his total transformation and empowerment. Brian may now be shown the secrets of the Craft, which only initiates know, and, from that moment on, may participate in any activity of the Circle *according to his level of experience and practice.*

This, too, is embodied in the performance of the rite. At the point at which Brian passes the final test, he is restored to sight and released from his bonds. However, there is still some limit to his empowerment. As in the Rite of Dedication, Brian must kneel to swear the oath; when he rises, he can do so *only with the help* of two of the Priestesses. This signifies that even after being reborn and fully admitted into the Circle of initiates, and even after being restored to power, the balance of power is still not equal. Brian must continue, at least for now, to depend upon the other Witches to help him stand on his own feet, perhaps much as a child must depend on its parents and older brothers and sisters for guidance. In other words, initiation is only the *beginning* of establishing a religious praxis.

Let's again use the analogy of the student driver in order to penetrate what is occurring at this point in the learning process. The driving instructor exercises power over the student, from the first class to the final test, unless the student chooses not to continue with the instruction. The two are not equal in their ability to drive the car.

Initiation is analogous to the moment at which the drivers' education student successfully passes his test and receives his license to drive a car. For the student driver, the real learning is only just beginning. This learning comes with time spent behind the wheel of the car, engaged in the embodied praxis of driving—strengthening and sharpening his skills, learning how to drive under different weather and road conditions, learning how to drive different kinds of vehicles in different circumstances, deepening his proficiency—until he becomes a fully competent and expert driver.

Our newly initiated Witch is like our newly licensed driver—he has just received his "license to Witch." Brian is not an "expert" yet; he will need many more years of practice and experience in order to advance to the next stage, which, in the tradition that the Merry Circle practice, is elevation to the second degree.

Again, the analogy of learning how to drive a car has an advantage over learning how to be a Witch—driving a car is easily understood as an embodied practice. We can readily ascertain that the student driver and his instructor do not share in the same level of experience. Moreover, we not only think it is a sensible idea for the student driver to attend classes, practice with an expert driver, and pass ordeals given by stern looking uniformed state officials, we have also actually ritualized the process by making it part of the legal requirements of driving.

The student's transformation from non-driver to competent driver to expert driver is not a metaphorical process in which the instructor is merely asserting his social and psychological power over the student in the ritual of drivers' education, but one that evokes *real* change and requires the acquisition of *real* skills.

In the context of the analogy of learning how to drive a car, the relationship of power-with or power-from-within between driving student and driving instructor exists as a goal; it is an achievement, the end result of years of practice on the part of the student. So, too, with Wiccan ritual praxis. In other words, power-with and power-from-within are ideals to be reached through disciplined communal praxis, not something bestowed upon us by democratic decree. Like the body-in-practice, they must be cultivated and acquired through work and discipline.

INTIMACY'S SECRETS   Second, in order to uncover the significance of the coven as an intimate community, let's consider some puzzling questions: How does Brian know not to *really* be scared when I swing the sword at his neck? How does he know that we will not do anything to really hurt him during the ordeal around the outside of the Circle when he is made fairly helpless by being bound and blindfolded?

Of course, one way to understand how Brian copes with his situation is to assume that he understands that the challenge is only metaphorical. He is in no real danger because "everyone knows" the challenge and the death stroke are simply meant to be symbolic. The tension in the ritual's mock ordeal between "real and not real," "scary but not scary,"[14] exists only on the metaphorical plane, and the power that the Witches are exercising over Brian is meant to be understood as an empty social gesture that merely puts Brian in his (lower) place.

This is a tempting way to understand the puzzle of how Brian knows not to really be scared, but it does not satisfy me completely. My physical, embodied experiences as an initiate and an initiator tell me that there is another dimension to unlocking this puzzle. While the symbolic and metaphorical dimensions no doubt exist, it is also necessary to look carefully at the bodied and performed dimensions of his experience—the experiential reality of the rite as embodied. By the rather admittedly odd constructions of those two phrases—experiential reality and embodied—I mean to point our attention to what is going on with the whole person, the body-in-practice at the moment of Brian's challenge and death. The word "witch" still has negative connotations in popular culture, and everyone at the Circle, including Brian, is fully aware of this.[15] This knowledge forms an additional dimension, another layer of context and meaning for the experience that he is about to undergo.

Put yourself in Brian's place. Here you are, at night, at a remote spot in the country, about to join a coven of Witches, and you come face to face with a large, very stern looking woman—not well known to you—who is robed in black and holding a very large sword that is subsequently raised to your chest. The woman is not friendly. In fact, the woman delivers a challenge and raises her sword in threat.

Let's pause for a moment, and ask whether Brian really understands this ordeal as only metaphorical. I can assure you that he does not, just as I did not when I was initiated. In fact, in order for a successful ritual initiation to occur, Death *must* be personified in the body of the Challenger, Death *must* be made present in the voice of the Challenger, and Death *must* certainly be made "real" with the swing of the sword that separates the Dedicant from his ordinary life and begins the process of rebirth. Rather than understanding this ordeal as a symbolic Death, perhaps it might be more fruitful to think of it as a *performed* Death in order to more fully get to the level of reality that is known with the body-in-practice during the actual performed rite.

I fear that I haven't yet solved the puzzle of Brian's trust, and have, in fact, only made it worse. Perhaps the following is a clue to its solution: Brian brings to the Circle two magic passwords that he must give to pass the challenge—"perfect love" and "perfect trust." Witches in my lineage understand these passwords as pregnant with power—as words of *magic*—rather than as pretty sentiments. As expressions of power, of magic, the passwords are thought to sustain the Dedicant through the travails of even death itself, their power being completed by the third password, which is not a word, but an action that completes the movement of rebirth into the Circle.

But whom or what does Brian have *perfect* love for and *perfect* trust in? What makes these two passwords "magic" words? There are several possible answers.

One answer could be that Brian is supposed to have perfect love for and perfect trust in the Witches in the coven. Certainly, the Witches and the Dedicant must have already established a close working relationship that is built at least somewhat on trust in order even to get to the stage of asking for initiation. But *perfect* love and *perfect* trust seem unlikely. And then we would have a lengthy scholarly discussion about how this assumption of perfect love and perfect trust is fraught with psychological peril, is clearly the demanding and unrealistic expectations of people who come from the more "ceremonial" and "hierarchical" traditional Christian religions and who have an "abusive family background."

Another answer could be that Brian is supposed to have perfect love for and perfect trust in the Gods, and that this is what makes the passwords magical. This would be quickly dismissed by scholars who don't see the Gods as having anything but the most illusory reality for Their worshippers—just another case of hallucination, neurosis, oppression, or other misrecognition.

We could simply ask Brian. But the chances are good that Brian would be hard pressed to tell us why he wasn't really scared, and where the magic of the passwords comes from.

So what *is* the right answer to these questions?

Perhaps it's a "secret."

This suggestion is not meant in any way to be flippant. Rather, I am using secret in the sense of "esoteric," one of the primary characteristics of intimate knowledge. Noting that this characteristic of intimacy is "perhaps the most difficult to grasp,"[16] Kasulis explains the way in which intimate knowledge is dark and esoteric:

> By saying intimacy is "dark" I mean that the foundation or ground of intimate knowledge is not obvious even to those involved in the intimate locus. How I know my car needs fuel differs from him I know my child is worried about something. . . . Perhaps I just sense that my son is "not his usual self." If you ask me what this means, I may not be able to specify the precise behavior that is atypical. If I am relatively intelligent, sensitive, and articulate, I may be able to do so after thoughtful reflection. But the significant point is that the basis of my judgment only becomes clear to me after thinking about the judgment I have already made. . . . [T]he ground is dark— at least until I later shed the self-conscious light of reflection on it.
>
> The term "esoteric" adds another dimension to the darkness. . . . As intimacy is frequently reduced to sexuality in common parlance, the esoteric has often been reduced to black magic, the occult, mystic experiences, even chicanery. I use the word to refer specifically to the context in which a nonpublic, but objective, insight is available only to members of a certain group who have undergone special training. . . . In our sense, then, the esoteric is not necessarily secretive or exclusive. It is open to everyone who has entered the intimate circle. How does one do that? By undergoing the appropriate praxis.[17]

In other words, Brian will have to reflect thoughtfully on his experience at the Circle's edge in order to fully articulate why he was not really scared. But he still may have some difficulty expressing exactly how he knew what he knew—*especially if his initiation was successful.* Using the experiences of a hypothetical football star named Eddie, Kasulis explains the dilemma:

> The content of his intimate knowledge . . . cannot be adequately described discursively in a step-by-step logical manner. Wishing a full discursive account, we must settle for an account of the praxis used to initiate him into the intimate locus. . . . All we can do is explain the practical experience—perhaps the praxis guided by a master— that brought us to this intimate, esoteric knowledge. Indeed, if a completely satisfactory discursive account of the intimate content itself could be given, this would prove that the initiation was bogus— that the insight could have been communicated plainly even to someone who has not undergone the praxis. Why should Eddie even

bother to go to practice if everything he needs to know can be found in a playbook?[18]

In other words, both Brian's esoteric knowledge and the magic of the passwords are actually rooted in the shift from an integrity to an intimacy orientation that is made manifest through the transformation of the relationship between the Dedicant and the Witches into an intimate community. Intimacy and integrity entail two different rhetorical or communicative strategies that are relevant to the changes in relationship that the Dedicant and Witches experience throughout the entire initiatory process. Essentially, the overarching initiation process represents a shift in communicative or rhetorical styles from ones of integrity to ones of intimacy.

According to Kasulis, integrity entails a relationship and a communicative style that is both public and objective, is not based on shared experiences, is independent, and contains no affective or somatic components. This is the relationship and communicative style that the teaching Witch and her student begin with during the very first introductory class or lecture.

Intimacy entails a relationship and a communicative style that is both private and objective, is based on shared experiences, is interdependent, and contains an affective and somatic component.[19] At some point in the middle of the introductory series of classes, the student and the Witch begin to build a relationship and communicative style that is more intimate, that includes some hints of somatic practice and shared experiences.

From the moment that the student embarks upon a serious study of the Craft and becomes a Dedicant, he is engaged in an intensive process of paradigm shift from integrity to intimacy, a shift that will affect how he thinks about and experiences the world and the self. Communication between the Dedicant and the Witches becomes increasingly dark, based on a growing number of shared experiences, and constantly builds on the somatic, and therefore esoteric, knowledge gained through interdependent forms of religious praxis. The Witches and the Dedicant have constructed an intimate community.

Brian brings to the Circle the magic words that will get him through the ordeals, words that derive their power from the context of an established intimacy. By this point in the learning process, Brian simply *knows* that the sword will not kill him; he *knows* that the Witches will not hurt him. This knowledge is private, but it is not subjective. Brian does not merely feel that the Witches will not harm him; he *knows*.

Such knowledge is not merely metaphorical but arises out of the context of intimate community. It is embedded in his body, in the interdependent sets of practices that he has performed with the members of the coven in Circle after Circle. What seems to be simply a case of the Witches having total power over Brian must also be understood in the context of the intimate community. In other words, the tension of the ordeal lies not on the metaphorical plane but in the embodied presence of Death versus the trust intimated by the community. Brian is indeed made vulnerable, but that vulnerability is mitigated or countered by the embedded certainty of perfect love and perfect trust, the magic passwords that enable him to safely pass through the ordeals of initiation, through the very gates of Death itself to ultimate transformation.

Death and the Descent of the Goddess

The myth of "The Descent of the Goddess" comes at a time in the ritual when Brian has just completed his ordeals and has emerged triumphant and transformed as a Priest and a Witch. The new Priest, still very much aglow with his new experiences, is told that he will now be read a myth, a sacred story. He must pay special attention to the story, as it contains meanings that will become clear upon reflection and experience. The very presentation and performance of the story mark it as something important, as it stands out from the more relaxed ritual context of the sharing of wine and cakes. Before Brian hears the story, he is instructed to make connections between the events in the story and the events of his initiation. As a new Witch, Brian must learn to see in the story's events the pattern and the key to his own experience of initiation. This is even clearer in the full and exact wording of the text, which I cannot provide.

The performance of the myth at this point in the ritual is not merely to impress similarity of the experience upon the new Witch, but ultimately to promote *identification* with the Goddess, who has undergone a similar journey, a cosmic transformation, a transformation through Death, a change in status, bestowing in Her, in Lincoln's words, "a defined place in the universe, and a place of importance and dignity."[20] It is significant to note here that both female *and* male initiates are presented with the same text in the same way. Not only does the descent of the Goddess to the Underworld provide a model of cosmic transformation for women, but it does so for *men* as well.

Let's consider for a moment the extent to which Death is emphasized and understood throughout the entire initiation ceremony. From the moment of the challenge at the gateway to initiation, Death is immediately foregrounded in the very first experiences of the new Priest; His transformative power is manifested in the ritual and impressed upon Brian as a teaching of central importance. Initiation is quite literally *performed* as a transformative process of symbolic death and rebirth for the Wiccan practitioner. In order to begin a life as a Priest of the Craft, Brian must first die—leaving behind his old life and old ways of perceiving with the natural body to learn new ways of perceiving with the body-in-practice.

Death clears the way for the birth of a new being—one who has met all challenges with perfect love and perfect trust, who has passed through the ordeals of initiation, and who is now ready to begin a new life with a new name. Death is performed as a transformative process *in relation* to life, a process of change more fully understood nonlinearly—death and birth in a never ending circle, death understood as an ending only so that a new beginning can occur, which, in its turn, will also fulfill its journey to an end and another new beginning.

The "Myth of the Descent of the Goddess" thus derives its religious meaning from its embodied performance during the initiation ritual. The narrative as transformation is grasped not as a metaphor, but again is realized and embodied through the transformation of the body-in-practice. For Brian, his personal transformation from Dedicant to Priest is intimately and somatically keyed to the transformation of the myth from just a story to something that expresses and embodies one of the most powerful and transformative experiences of his life.

Coming Full Circle—Again

There is one final part of the ceremony that I wish to address briefly before making my concluding remarks—the "cool down" time that occurs in Lauren's kitchen immediately after the ritual is over and all of the Witches have returned to the mundane world of the house. All the Witches engage in an extensive grilling of Brian about his experiences. In a way, I suspect that this final act expresses a kind of circular completeness, as it takes us back to where we began—questioning Brian.

Brian's inquisition serves many other purposes besides establishing a neat pattern of circularity, however. Every one of the Witches gets a chance to show her interest in Brian's reaction to the ritual, and he gets the opportunity to give them important feedback on their performances. This gives the Witches an opportunity to see if the ordeals had their intended effect. It also makes Brian begin the process of reflection about the rite itself, making him think about these and other questions that will eventually enable him to sort out the threads of the experience. In this respect, the final ordeal of writing a paper on his initiatory experiences becomes an explicit reminder that the lessons are just beginning.

The time that is spent telling old war stories—telling stories about old initiations, especially ones which weren't so well planned—helps to give Brian something to compare to, and makes the experience of his own initiation something extra special and wonderful. Of course, it also implies that his fellow Witches have their collective acts together—which might be seen as self-serving if done in a negative or self-righteous fashion. As Witches, sharing our own deeply personal experiences of initiation is also a way to deepen and solidify the close sense of community and sense of bonding we all feel with one another.

After the rite is over, this moment of final closure, this final circular movement, enables the Witches to warmly welcome their new Priest and make him feel like a deeply valued and important part of the Merry Circle—our place of intimate community, of embodied practice, and a place of perfect love and perfect trust.

7

Concluding Remarks

At the end of this book, I feel it appropriate to assess reflexivity as a non-traditional methodology for religious studies scholarship. What do we lose and what do we gain in the reflexive mirror? Lost is the innocence, the purity of objectivity. Gained is the intimation of a rich and complex intersection of person and perspective with the subject of study. While purity is an admirable goal, it is not, I think, a realistic one. But there is much to gain by honest examination of the "situatedness" of all knowledge in human experiences and perspectives.

This situatedness is admittedly difficult to unpack. Simply categorizing me as both a scholar and practitioner does not quite capture the range of perspectives found in either dimension. Certainly multiple experiences and perspectives blend and weave together to create my voice throughout this book. It is difficult, in fact, to separate them: Scholar, philosopher, Priestess, feminist, folklorist, theologian—and, at their base, that skeptical blue-collar Appalachian Hungarian-Pagan-Serbian girl blowing kisses at the Moon.

I wear a lot of hats. I suspect that you do, too.

Certainly, one of those hats—no doubt, a large and colorful one—belongs to a Priestess, and one of my goals in this book is to provide information about what I feel are understudied aspects of Wicca, since so many of my generation of Witches practiced in silence and secrecy. Our voices, our experiences, and our practices seem to be largely missing from discourse in the academy. How would our voices change the conversation? How would our practices and experiences change the ways we perceive and understand not only the Craft, but other religious practices as well?

And while I cannot speak for anyone but myself, I anticipate that offering a close description and analysis of even one kind of ritual practice from a specific coven might get the conversation going in some new and profitable directions.

One of the things I want to alter is a perception so often held by my students that Wicca—or Witchcraft, since I use the terms interchangeably—is a women-only religion that worships the Goddess exclusively. Witchcraft has long existed, if not from the dawn of time, at least well before the Women's Spirituality Movement discovered it.

The Witchcraft that I was introduced to contained Priests and Priestesses who worshipped Gods and Goddesses. As such, it presents us with an opportunity to study a Western religious tradition that has both Goddesses and Gods, and that at least potentially provides equal access to the sacred for both women and men. Perhaps this will contribute to future theological reflection about how women and men can share power and authority collectively, enabling us to imagine new forms of leadership within a religious community.

But stemming as it does from a time before widespread feminist discovery and influence, the Craft (in my experience) also reminds us that a religion is not feminist heaven simply because it has Goddesses. Feminist suspicion, which is also part of my Priestess hat, cautions us to be more critical of the roles female images of deity play. Do the Goddesses merely reinforce roles and attitudes that favor the patriarchy? Or are they truly challenging us to rethink the ways in which we perceive the sacred and ourselves as women and men? How might our religious roles and practices reflect not only the diversity of human experiences of the sacred, but the range of human expressions of gender and sexuality as well?

In my book, I show that religious practices change, even on a very small, very local level. I also reveal that Witches disagree with one another. That's not a secret among Witches, but it might surprise some scholars who assume that insiders are alike. Both contestation and change demonstrate that Wicca, like other religions, is not monolithic. An enormous number of voices are engaged in discussion—agreement, argument, negotiation, discord, harmony—across a wide spectrum of beliefs and practices. Witchcraft is not "one kind of thing."

An example: Although I discovered the Craft in college, not every Witch is a college student who gets her material from dusty folklore manuals in libraries through "cultural poaching"—a description of the religion I once actually heard at a folklore conference. I have also come across academics who confidently assert that Witchcraft is a mostly urban, coastal phenomenon. In that case, the Merry Circle illustrates that covens include all types of people: conservatives, midwesterners, blue-collar workers, residents of small towns, nonacademics, older persons, even a few people without tattoos and spiky hair—the kind of regular folk who typically do not make it into academic studies that deliberately emphasize the exotic.

Not that all academic studies do. But there are enough badly done ones that are so culturally stereotyped that they add little to an understanding of the diversity and complexity of this religious practice. Perhaps my work will contribute in some small way to making Witchcraft, a religion that has been both badly maligned and historically marginalized, better understood as a positive religious path—one that is as deserving of respect, analysis, and criticism as any other religion in the world.

As you can see, the reflexive impulse has by now become deeply ingrained. I cannot consider my religious practice without also wondering about its implications for new models and ways of doing scholarship about religion. Nor can I evaluate scholarship on and theories about religion without reflecting on the actual religious practices and experiences of its practitioners for comparison.

I suppose that was how I got into this project in the first place. As a scholar, I intended from the outset to use Wiccan initiation ritual as material to think with. I reasoned that by examining one kind of initiation done by a single religious community, we might be able to uncover some of the ways initiation rituals in particular, and rituals more generally, are constructed and made meaningful to their participants. And by focusing on the religious practices of a single community—at the level of individuals-practicing—we might also avoid some of the essentialized and decontextualized discourses about religion and ritual that we encounter so often in our studies.

Initially, I was certain that Wiccan initiation ritual would fit the tripartite rites of passage model I had learned at university. But when I compared it to an actual practice of a ritual initiation, the model simply didn't fit. It was time to challenge what had become normative ideas about rites of passage, those "set analyses" that seem to function as paradigms, dominating and even determining what we see when we look at ritual.

Using Wiccan initiation ritual to think with, we are able to discover upon closer inspection that what is commonly understood as an isolated ritual moment with a simple unilinear directional movement is actually embedded in a long and multidirectional process of increasingly somatic learning and practice, the shift in orientation from what I identify as integrity to intimacy, and the complex formation of an intimate community.

A reflexive methodology uncovers significant emic insights that are otherwise not available to scholarly examination, including the range of perspectives and experiences embodied throughout different stages of the initiation process. The familiar tripartite themes of separation, liminality, and reincorporation (or enclosure, metamorphosis, and emergence) may occur and reoccur in various stages of the ritual, but they change or shift according to perspective as we progress through the heavily circular movements of the ritual performance of initiation.

In fact, initiation offers shifting sets of multidimensional, multidirectional, and multispatial experiences to its participants, depending on their role at any particular moment in the performance of the rite. Capturing the shifting roles and perspectives of the participants allows us to see there is no single or uniform understanding of initiation. It also permits us to see that, for participants, understanding of the ceremony will probably change in time, as each takes on different roles and new perspectives that were not experienced before.

At the level of individuals-practicing, the same ritual is truly *never* the same ritual.

By exploring the experiences of individuals-practicing, we also discover the critical importance of intimacy both in the cultivation of what I term the body-in-practice and the development of the coven as a site of community. Within an intimacy framework, ritual itself—in particular, the embodied nature of Wiccan ritual praxis—becomes a form of pedagogy, a learning process that cultivates within the body-in-practice those somatic modes of attention that are necessary for successful ritual performance and that provide the psychophysical context for creativity to work effectively in ritual.

An intimacy model of learning also sheds light on the dark mysteries of the occult, revealing that the esoteric secrets of religion are often hidden in plain sight, in the body itself, and not in obscure books of spells or incantations. The dark ways of knowing, the arcane wisdom of the ancients, are perhaps things that can only be learned by and through the body—in more mundane terms, practices that are fully as mysterious as learning how to swim, ride a bicycle, or drive a car.

Using Witchcraft to think with, we may want to examine other religious traditions in terms of practices that are done with the body. Moving at least this far away from text gives us more insight into how people live and perform their religions and takes us away from the reified atmosphere of disembodied official religion that—I have on good authority—doesn't actually exist in religions as they are lived.

When we move from texts to individuals-practicing, we also gain insights into how communities are constructed. In Wicca, we glimpse shifting balances of power within the overarching learning process, seeing moments when that balance of power seems fairly equal between student and teacher, and other moments in which it is not. In the initiation rite itself, we uncover dimensions to the Witches' power over the candidate in addition to those typically constructed along social and metaphorical lines—dimensions that depend on understanding initiation as both a learning process and an embodied praxis, and that depend on understanding the Wiccan community as a paradigm shift from integrity to intimacy.

Finally, framing the Wiccan community within an intimacy orientation also illuminates the presence of Nature-as-person, a significant extension of what is usually considered "community" within those analyses that are traditionally grounded in etic perspectives. Intimacy allows us to understand the reality of Wiccan practice, the embodied presence of Nature-as-person, and the manifest presence of the Gods within a properly cast Circle. It enables us to understand the way in which the Circle itself forms an intersubjective field in which the Gods and those persons who have developed the body-in-practice may mutually engage one another in shared subjectivity.

In short, it helps us to "capture magick."

At the end of this book, I am amazed at how much more there is to be said about even this single Wiccan initiation ritual. Standing at that Circle's edge so long ago, I could never have dreamed where life's journeys would take me. This particular journey has been one of discovery and revelation for me, uncovering things about my practice as a scholar and about my practice of my religion that I would not otherwise have learned.

I hope that this book challenges some of the ways that we approach religious rituals in general and raises new questions that we might fruitfully explore together.

May our journeys continue ever onward.

Epilogue

She Changes Everything She Touches

"She Changes Everything She Touches" is a refrain from a popular Wiccan chant. Time and the Goddess do indeed bring change, and many changes have come to the Merry Circle. The Merry Circle no longer exists as a single practicing group. Because some of its members either have already relocated or will relocate so far from one another geographically, it is unlikely that they—that *we*—will ever all practice in the same Circle again in this lifetime. It is for that reason that this project has taken a bittersweet turn for me as it ends. In some respects, I must admit that I am almost reluctant to let it go—it makes the end of the Merry Circle that much more real.

The four of us High Priestesses—who I consider the heart of our group—met once more before the relocation (Dot now lives in the far west, and I have moved farther into the middle of the country). Our final Circle together, though informal, was powerful and deeply moving—laughter shared through tears of sadness and parting. Somehow it has given me the strength to go on, to complete this project, this turning of the wheel, and to make an ending so that a new beginning may occur. Although our time together in this life has likely come to an end, I have every expectation that someday we will meet and know one another and practice together once more.

As we Witches say, 'tis the "Silver Promise."

Lauren, Dot, and Sandy: *Merry meet, merry part, and merry meet again.* So mote it be.

Notes

1. The musician Walter Carlos may be more familiar to today's music listeners as Wendy Carlos.

2. Witches use the term "circle" in various ways. It may mean the actual blessed and consecrated ritual space; a rite or ceremony that is being held, as in "Are you coming to the Circle?"; or the coven itself, as in "She's part of my Circle." When Circle is used in any of these three ways, it will be capitalized in this work. The polysemous, but interrelated, use of central religious terms is a common phenomenon in religious traditions. See the discussion of mantra in esoteric Buddhism and "Body of Christ" in Kasulis (1992) "Philosophy as Metapraxis."

3. See, for example, the impressive and diverse collection of articles addressing this issue in McCutcheon (1999) *The Insider/Outsider Problem in the Study of Religion*. In the "General Introduction" to the volume, McCutcheon calls the insider/outsider problem "one of the most important issues in the study of human behavior and institutions," a problem "that must be faced by all scholars of the human condition" (1–2).

4. For an extensive and passionate discussion of the perils of crossing boundaries, including the boundary between insider and outsider, see Gross (1998) *Soaring and Settling*, especially chapter 4, "Passion and Peril: Transgressing Boundaries as a Feminist Buddhist Scholar-Practitioner" (34–48). Gross informs us that not only is it perilous to be an insider in the Academy, but it is also possible to be considered the "wrong kind" of insider, for example, a "white Buddhist" rather than an Asian.

5. See Clifford and Marcus (1986) *Writing Culture*.

6. Although my experience was closer to the "invisible gender," De-

bora Kodish (1987) "Absent Gender, Silent Encounter" sheds some interesting light on the phenomenon of women as the "silent gender" who are "magically brought to voice" (perhaps brought into sight?) by the attention of the folklorist.

7. See, for example, "Heraclitus" (87–106) and "Parmenides" (107–26) in Robinson (1968) *An Introduction to Early Greek Philosophy*.

8. Throughout this work, I will be using the word praxis to mean a traditional system of related practices forming a self-disciplinary process that involves the whole person—body, mind, and spirit. This disciplinary process is repeated as a way of integrating the self and transforming the way one acts in and thinks about the world. I think that it is important to emphasize, especially in the context of the way that I use religious praxis, that the body is as much involved in transformation as is the mind or spirit.

9. For example, see Clifford and Marcus (1986) *Writing Culture*; Bruner and Turner (1986) *The Anthropology of Experience*; and Fabian (1971) "History, Language and Anthropology," (1983) *Time and the Other*, and (1994) "Ethnographic Objectivity Revisited."

10. See Lawless (1993) *Holy Women, Wholly Women*; O'Connor (1995) *Healing Traditions*; Goodman (1988b) *How About Demons?*; Jackson (1989) *Paths Toward a Clearing*; and Gold and Raheja (1994) *Listen to the Heron's Words*; to name a few.

11. For instance, Segal (1983) "In Defense of Reductionism."

12. Diane Goldstein (1995) suggests in "The Secularization of Religious Ethnography" that it is the subject of our study—religion itself— that throws off our ethnography:

> As ethnographers, we describe cultural groups and practices, hopefully with an eye toward at least trying to understand notions of significance and meaning for the people we study. But . . . in the church, at prayer meetings, at religious ceremonies, we become frightened scientists hiding behind complex theories, narrow definitions, and sometimes even older notions of an irrational-but-quaint peasantry clinging to remnants of primitive thought and behavior. We don't do this in our other ethnographic works, only in those which involve belief issues, only in those which present a threat to our own safe worldview. (25)

13. Hufford (1995) "The Scholarly Voice and the Personal Voice," 68.

14. See, for example, Smart (1973) *The Science of Religion*.

15. Hufford (1995) "Introduction" in *Reflexivity and the Study of Belief*, 6. For a debate on skepticism and neutrality, see Hufford (1987) "Traditions of Disbelief"; Simpson (1988) "Is Neutralism Possible?"; Goldstein (1989) "Belief and Disbelief"; and Hufford (1990) "Rational Skepticism."

16. Hufford (1995) "The Scholarly Voice and the Personal Voice," 68–69.

17. Hufford (1995) "The Scholarly Voice and the Personal Voice," 69.

18. Goldstein (1995) "The Secularization of Religious Ethnography," 25.

19. For example, Kuipers (1990) *Power in Performance*.

20. What "feels real" is a term coined by folklorist Margaret Mills (1993) "Feminist Theory and the Study of Folklore." Mills, like Hufford, addresses the dangers inherent in an extreme postmodern abandonment of notions of objectivity in favor of life as "mere literary reflection." Her point is that the pain and suffering of oppression entails *real* consequences for *real* people, not just another literary construct. The "experience of being the object of stereotyping and marginalization yields a potent reminder of the *concrete consequences* of essentialist ideas, however *socially constructed* we see them to be" (185, italics mine). Getting at what "feels real" is an important step of placing the focus of our attention back in the world of real people, in the context of the study of religion, getting at the level of what I call "individuals-practicing."

21. Driver (1991) *The Magic of Ritual*, 166–67.

22. In her paper, the Pagan drew on two mythic themes in particular: the "Golden Age of the Goddess" and the "Burning Times." The Golden Age of the Goddess describes a prehistoric age in which women and "the" Goddess reigned supreme because of their mysterious fertile wombs, until the coming of the evil male invaders who brought war and devastation to the peaceful Goddess people. This hypothesis has a large body of scholarship (pro and con) connected with it and also presents scholars with an interesting puzzle on how to read material artifacts or understand material culture in ways that might shed light on prehistoric religious life—none of which was even remotely considered in the paper. The Burning Times theme refers to the Inquisition, in which nine million European witches (mostly women) were allegedly tortured and killed. Both of these themes are prime candidates for an exploration of how myth and rhetoric are used by religious communities, here specifically feminist communities, to construct a narrative of protest. Again, no attempt was made by the student to explore these potentially fascinating and fruitful lines of scholarly inquiry.

23. In his 1997 article "Intimations of Religious Experience and Interreligious Truth," philosopher of religion Thomas P. Kasulis emphasizes the importance of beginning analysis with a critical investigation of the experiences of particular religious communities in all their rich complexity, reminding us "not to let the categories of analysis impoverish the nature of the experience." And if the experiences do not fit our categories, he advises us to adjust the theory before assuming that "there is something wrong or philosophically suspicious" with the experiences (39).

He also reminds us that religion "has an intrinsically social or communal dimension" with shared meanings and assumptions, and to avoid analyzing a "particular religious utterance without first asking who the audience of that utterance is and what practices and assumptions the audience and speaker might share" (39).

24. Scholar of religions Nancy Falk addresses her own experiences as a commuter across multiple boundaries in her 1997 article "Crossovers and Cross-ups: A Cautionary Tale":

> I find it far less helpful to think of myself as insider or outsider than as a perpetual commuter across multiple boundaries. For more than thirty years I have shuttled mentally, and sometimes physically, between India and the United States—born and bred and mostly residing and working in the latter, but constantly steeping myself in experiences—my own and other scholars'—of the former. I have traversed for nearly as long the boundary between two academic disciplines: History of Religions, the discipline of my appointment and academic training, and Women's Studies, which one might call my discipline of existential commitment. Finally, with a life divided for more than two decades between the roles of mom, wife, scholar, and teacher, I move day to day across a kind of experiential boundary between the preoccupations of a very ordinary middle class housewife and the concerns of the academy. (2)

Commuting across such multiple and diverse boundaries is certainly challenging, and may at times even be disorienting, producing the feeling of "having no true psychic home" (2). Falk notes that the benefits derived from commuting between such multiple realms nevertheless far outweigh the costs:

> Crossing between two cultures has allowed me to mediate between them professionally, interpreting India to students and scholars in the U.S. (and sometimes vice versa). As Miriam Peskowitz has also described in this issue, crossing between Women's Studies and History of Religions has brought me my most important critical insights into both disciplines. And crossing between the world of moms and the world of the academy has helped me connect with students and aid them in making their own crossovers to my disciplines and to India. (2)

I suspect that many of us are, like Falk, commuters across the boundaries of the multiple worlds in which we live.

25. Hufford (1995) "Introduction" in *Reflexivity and the Study of Belief*, 2.

26. Hufford (1995) "Introduction" in *Reflexivity and the Study of Belief*, 2.

27. Hufford (1995) "Introduction" in *Reflexivity and the Study of Belief*, 2–3.

28. Hufford (1995) "The Scholarly Voice and the Personal Voice," 60.

29. See Kasulis (1992) "Philosophy as Metapraxis."

30. Too often scholarly discourse about religion takes place on a de-contextualized level far removed from the worlds of believers and practitioners. My term "individuals-practicing" is an attempt to move the locus of our studies from the literary—the realm of texts and "fictions"—to the practical—the realm of individual experiences and practices of religion.

31. Mary Hufford (1995) "Context," 531–32.

32. Goldstein (1995) "The Secularization of Religious Ethnography," 25.

33. Titon (1995) "Text," 436–37.

34. Limon and Young (1986) "Frontiers, Settlements and Developments in Folklore Studies, 1972–1985," 445.

35. Babcock (1988) "At Home, No Women are Storytellers," 373.

36. See, for example, Falk and Gross (1989) *Unspoken Worlds*; Goldstein (1995) "The Secularization of Religious Ethnography"; and Gross (1996) *Feminism and Religion*.

CHAPTER 2

1. For the purposes of this book, I will make no distinctions between the terms Wicca, Witchcraft, the Craft, or The Old Religion, and will use the terms Wiccan and Witch completely interchangeably.

2. Lauren continued to keep in touch with Sam after we left his group and started our own coven. Some years later, Sam performed the second degree or "elevation rite" on Lauren, who passed it on to others of us— myself included—interested in obtaining closure to our experiences of being in Sam's group. As we had done with so many other rituals, Lauren and I later modified the second degree ceremony and other materials that we subsequently inherited from Sam for use in our group.

3. I use the term "contemporary Pagan" or simply "Pagan" to refer to modern worshippers of nature religions as opposed those of classical antiquity. For more specific information about the larger world of contemporary Pagan practices, please refer to the several books and articles on contemporary Paganism listed in the bibliography, many of which contain quite extensive bibliographies of their own.

4. For information on prominent Pagans, see Adler (1979) *Drawing Down the Moon*; Harvey and Hardman (1995) *Paganism Today*; and Hopman and Bond (2002, 1996) *Being a Pagan*.

5. Hutton (1999) *The Triumph of the Moon*.

6. Carpenter (1996) "Practitioners of Paganism and Wiccan Spirituality."

7. Pearson, Roberts, and Samuel (1998) *Nature Religion Today*.

8. Rabinovitch (1996) "Spells of Transformation."

9. See Jorgensen and Russell (1999) "American Neopaganism"; Kirk-

patrick, Rainey, and Rubi (1986) "An Empirical Study of Wiccan Religion"; and Carpenter and Fox (1992) "Pagan Spirit Gathering 1991."

10. For information about the larger Western mythological and magical tradition, sometimes called the "Western Mystery Tradition," see especially Matthews and Matthews (1985) *The Western Way*.

11. Adler (1979) *Drawing Down the Moon*, 389.

12. See, for example, Farrar and Farrar (1981) *Eight Sabbats for Witches*; or Campanelli (1992) *Ancient Ways*.

13. This was an issue in Craft circles at least as early as 1975, when Morning Glory Zell, a prominent Pagan Priestess, wrote "Mother Hertha spare us from Jahweh in drag!" in *Green Egg* 8.72 (August 1, 1975): 43.

14. This observation grew out of reflection on a paper given by Nancy Falk at the 1988 Midwest American Academy of Religion conference in Terre Haute, Ind. She was making a distinction between two kinds of women's roles in India: nuns are generally valued by society, but perceived as having very little power; yoginis are generally perceived as powerful, but are not openly valued by the culture, which may fear or even scorn them.

15. For a particularly thought-provoking feminist critique of the Goddess, see the special section on Neopaganism in the 1989 spring issue of the *Journal of Feminist Studies in Religion*, specifically the articles by Weaver, Hackett, Eilberg-Schwartz, and the response by Adler.

16. See Bado-Fralick (1990) "Stirring the Cauldron" for a discussion about the impact of feminism on the practice of the Craft.

17. An argument and precedent for this kind of study has been well established by Falk and Gross (1989), Gross (1996), Erndl (1993), and Gold and Raheja (1994).

18. See Barbara Myerhoff (1982) "Rites of Passage: Process and Paradox," 131, on the significance of created secular ritual.

19. Aidan Kelly, both a scholar of religions and a Wiccan practitioner, maintains that Gardner literally created the Craft and that all Witches must necessarily trace their practices back to him. His book *Crafting the Art of Magic* (1991) is infamous in Craft circles not only for challenging the ancient origins of the Craft, but—as some see it—for misrepresenting Gardnerian practices and attacking its founder's sex life.

Kelly's wild speculation about Gardner's sex life is mostly a distraction from the more serious flaws and leaps of logic in the book. While this is not the place to fully critique Kelly's work, it may serve to situate the nature of the controversy within a scholarly context. Kelly makes some initially promising moves, demonstrating a sense of reflexivity and stressing that all religion is a dynamic, creative, ongoing process. Despite this initial thrust toward a more fruitful way of understanding the dynamic nature of religious tradition, he quickly becomes bogged down in a textbound search for origins, and actually employs a narrow and static view of tradition throughout his analysis. This becomes an absolute fixation on the written word—if it isn't written down, it isn't a tradition—completely ignoring the issues of orality and folk custom, as well as ritual praxis. This, along with a category mistake that conflates ritual and written text, ignores the dimension of ritual as dynamic, creative, and even spontaneous performance.

20. Jonathan Z. Smith (1988) "Religion and Religious Studies: No Difference at All." Quotation from reprinted selections in *Theory and Method in the Study of Religion,* edited by Carl Olson, 27.

21. Primiano (1995) "Vernacular Religion," 38–39.

22. Primiano (1995) "Vernacular Religion," 46.

23. Thomas P. Kasulis, personal communication.

24. Patrick B. Mullen, personal communication, for the phrase "dynamic tradition." See Handler and Linnekin (1984) "Tradition, Genuine or Spurious" for a discussion of tradition as something that is always interpreted in the present. See also Zimmerman (1985) "Tradition and Change in a Ritual Feast: The Serbian Krsna Slava in America" for a discussion of ritual as a continuously changing process that participants adapt and reevaluate according to shifting circumstances.

25. See, for example, Kmietowicz (1976) *Ancient Slavs* and (1982) *Slavic Mythical Beliefs*; and Zimmerman (1985) "Tradition and Change in a Ritual Feast: The Serbian Krsna Slava in America" and (1986) *Serbian Folk Poetry.*

CHAPTER 3

1. For a discussion of power, sacrality, and group dynamics within our coven during the early years of its formation, see Bado-Fralick (1989) "Changing the Face of the Sacred."

2. According to the tradition of our parent coven, initiations can be said to fail for a number of reasons, most of them having to do with how successfully the new initiate takes to further interaction with and instruction from the full coven. We initiated three women at about the same time—two of them "didn't take." One left to pursue a boyfriend almost immediately after receiving her initiation; the other left for a different spiritual practice. The third, Sandy, is still an active Witch within the Merry Circle's tradition. It's probably fair to say that Lauren and I became more cautious about initiations after our experience with the first two students.

3. Covens may break up for a wide variety of serious reasons, such as differences in theology or practice. However, groups are even more likely to split up for a variety of perfectly mundane reasons: a job in a new city, graduation, personal dislike of someone's new spouse or partner, limitations on time as a result of marriage or having children, and so forth.

4. See especially Isaac Bonewits (1996) "The Druid Revival in Modern America." Bonewits has been a Druid priest for over twenty-five years and traces the flourishing of Druidry in America to the creation of the

Reformed Druids of North America (RDNA) in 1963. He states that most American Druids trace themselves back to the RDNA via his group *A'r nDrai'ocht Fe'in*: A Druid Fellowship, or ADF. The coveners who now explore Druidry are members of ADF.

5. A few of the members of our group who are ethnically Slavic have noted similarities between old Slavic practices—such as customs connected with honoring the dead or foodways in which special seasonal breads are baked and shared—and those that have come to be classed among Wiccans as "Celtic." While this reassures some of us who are Slavic that we are "really" following practices that have a basis in our own ethnic ancestry, it raises questions about the fluid and constructed nature of national identities. It also enables us to inquire about what kinds of similarities in customs and religious practices one might expect to find between cultures that share roots in an agriculturally based calendar.

6. See Bado-Fralick (2002) "Mapping the Wiccan Ritual Landscape."

7. Information on the creation and use of ritual tools can be found in many books on the Craft. See especially Farrar and Farrar (1981) *Eight Sabbats for Witches* and (1984) *The Witches' Way*; or Valiente (1987) *Witchcraft for Tomorrow* and (1989) *The Rebirth of Witchcraft*.

CHAPTER 4

1. For example, see Turner (1969) *The Ritual Process* or (1987) "Betwixt and Between."

2. These actions or special activities provide a frame for interpretation within the ritual process, much as Barbara Babcock's metanarrative markers function to "call attention to the problems and processes of narration as an act and provide a frame for interpretation." Babcock (1977) "The Story in the Story," 73.

3. See Patton (1997) "Insider, Outsider, and Gender Identities in the Religion Classroom," 1. In her article, Patton puts it well: "[Categories such as insider and outsider] are less like categories and more like provisional descriptions of particular moments in the learning process. As such, the spatial metaphors of insider and outsider are content-less in and of themselves, and exist only in relationship to what is being counted as 'in' and what is being counted as 'out.'"

4. Ironically, cases of religious discrimination can sometimes increase precisely *because* the public is more aware of Witches in their communities. Representative Bob Barr's "recent discovery" of Witches in the military is a good case in point. The military has legally recognized the Craft as a religion since the mid-seventies, even including it in their official chaplain's handbook. On May 11, 1999, the newspaper *Austin-American Statesman* ran a favorable story, complete with photographs, on a Spring Equinox ritual at Fort Hood. The story was picked up by other newspapers throughout the country and internationally.

Although the article generated a great deal of positive press for the Wiccan religion, Representative Barr responded by launching an attack against the religious freedom enjoyed by military Witches for over twenty years. He led with a press release ridiculing the Wiccan religion and demanding an end to Wiccan religious services on military installations. Barr has followed his media attack with a series of legislative moves designed to outlaw the practice of the Craft by military personnel. To date, his attacks have been unsuccessful, but they are continuing. The fall 1999 issue of *Circle Magazine* (formerly *Circle Network News*), a publication of Circle Sanctuary, includes an extensive article about Barr's attempts to garner support to successfully pass anti-Wiccan legislation, as well as responses made by the Pagan community working in cooperation with other religious leaders and the resulting media coverage (*Circle Magazine* 73 [Fall 1999]: 42–49).

5. Since its founding in 1974, Circle has been making people aware of religious freedom issues through ongoing columns in its newsletter and magazine and through special mailings. In 1988, Circle founded The Lady Liberty League (LLL) in response to a growing number of calls about religious freedom, and maintains a Web page that informs its readers about breaking news events and updates on previous cases of discrimination or religious conflict. CoG and the now defunct *Green Egg*, a publication of the Church of All Worlds, have also been instrumental in educating the public about Pagan paths, educating Pagans about their legal rights, and organizing a legal response to the challenges of discrimination when intolerant portions of the public strike out against "alternative" religions. For example, a 1999 *Green Egg* issue (Volume 31, Number 129) was entirely devoted to Pagans, the law, and religious freedom.

Sometimes cases of religious discrimination occur alongside examples of religious tolerance. For example, a Wiccan shop owner in Catskill, New York, was harassed by one local church congregation but welcomed by another in the same town (*Circle Network News* 60 [Fall 1998]: 50). Occasionally the issue is censorship rather than discrimination, such as when a Wisconsin high school that blocked access to Witchcraft sites on the Internet to a student researching world religions (*Circle Network News* 60 [Fall 1998]: 50). Although this particular situation was resolved, the problem of Internet software remains an issue pending federal legislation to require Internet filters on pornography and "other controversial sites" such as Witchcraft.

6. Glossy, professional magazines such as *Circle Magazine*, *PanGaia*, and the exciting, new *Teen Witch* ("not your mother's broomstick") are available in mainstream bookstores. Less expensive, in-house newsletters such as *Isian News* and *The Unicorn* are available to a list of subscribers.

7. See Kasulis (1997) "Intimations of Religious Experience."

8. Today, organizations such as Cherry Hill Seminary in Vermont employ a number of qualified teachers, mentors, and counselors for Pagan ministries.

9. As Kasulis (1993c) demonstrates in his paper "Hypocrisy in the Self-Understanding of Religions."

10. Yuasa (1987) *The Body: Toward an Eastern Mind-Body Theory*, 207.

11. Witches and other contemporary Pagans sometimes spell "magick" with a "k" to distinguish religious magic from mundane magic such as card tricks and other sleight of hand.

12. Yuasa (1987) *The Body: Toward an Eastern Mind-Body Theory*, 85.

13. Kasulis (1987) "Editor's Introduction" in Yuasa *The Body: Toward an Eastern Mind-Body Theory*, 3.

14. For example: Buckland (1978) *The Magick of Chant-o-Matics*; Manning (1972) *Helping Yourself with White Witchcraft*; and Morrison (1971) *Modern Witch's Spellbook*.

15. Buckland (1978) *The Magick of Chant-o-Matics*, 3.

16. See especially Budapest (1989) *The Holy Book of Women's Mysteries*; Stein (1987) *The Women's Spirituality Book* and (1991) *The Goddess Celebrates*; and Morgan (1970) *Sisterhood Is Powerful*.

17. For a discussion of the "rules of the road" and "getting behind the wheel," see Bado-Fralick (1995a) "The Dynamics of Ritual, Part I. The Rules of the Road" and (1995b) "The Dynamics of Ritual, Part II. Training Wheels."

18. Yuasa (1987) *The Body: Toward an Eastern Mind-Body Theory*, 5.

19. Yuasa (1987) *The Body: Toward an Eastern Mind-Body Theory*, 5.

20. Yuasa (1987) *The Body: Toward an Eastern Mind-Body Theory*, 6.

CHAPTER 5

1. For much the same reasoning as followed by my parent coven, the Witches in the Merry Circle do not formally dedicate anyone who is under the age of eighteen into the Craft.

2. See Kasulis (2002) *Intimacy or Integrity*, 24–25, and especially chapter 2, "What is Intimacy?", and chapter 3, "What is Integrity?"

3. Kasulis (2002) *Intimacy or Integrity*, extrapolated from chapters 2 and 3.

4. Kasulis (2002) *Intimacy or Integrity*, 24.

5. Kasulis (2002) *Intimacy or Integrity*, 37.

6. Kasulis (2002) *Intimacy or Integrity*, from chapter 3.

7. For a discussion of the way in which the world becomes "personal," see Driver (1991) *The Magic of Ritual*. A thought-provoking analysis of "Reality is a person" comes from eighth-century Japanese philosopher Kukai, founder of Shingon Buddhism. Drawing upon the classical Indian definition of person as mandala (thought), mantra (word), and mudra (deed), Kukai's two interrelated concepts of *hosshin seppo* and *sokushin jobutsu* articulate Dainichi (the Cosmos) as radiating thought, word, and deed, with which we can resonate in intimate bodily praxis. See especially Hakeda (1972) *Kukai* and Kasulis (1995) "Reality as Embodiment."

8. For a discussion of power dynamics within a particular Circle as they are connected to the development of practice, see Bado-Fralick (1989) "Changing the Face of the Sacred." Starhawk (1987) *Truth or Dare* also presents us with a provocative distinction between "power over," "power with," and "power from within" as different modes of power dynamics.

9. Turner (1969) *The Ritual Process*, 95.

10. Lincoln (1981) *Emerging from the Chrysalis*, 103.

11. See Csordas (1993) "Somatic Modes of Attention."

12. Yuasa (1987) *The Body: Toward an Eastern Mind-Body Theory*, 5.

13. Yuasa (1987) *The Body: Toward an Eastern Mind-Body Theory*, 6.

CHAPTER 6

1. Kasulis (2002) *Intimacy or Integrity*.

2. Although the process of finding a Craft name is often filled with anxiety, there are moments of great hilarity as well. I recall in particular when a Dedicant named Frank was talking with other Dedicants about naming practices in the coven. Considering myself thoroughly American in this regard, I ventured the opinion that there was far too much pomposity and pretense of nobility in naming oneself Lord or Lady Such-and-Such—as was the habit of far too many covens. We all got on to a discussion of what constitutes appropriate and inappropriate names, and we agreed that Frank managed to win the prize for most "revolting" name. He informed us that his Craft name was going to be "Lord Farfull," inspired by the dog at the end of the old Nestle's Quick commercials. While this evoked a lot of laughter at the time, I was worried in the back of my mind that he just might take this name upon his actual initiation. Thankfully, he did not, and the Merry Circle has never had a Lord Farfull on its coven rosters. It took me a long time to forget this. Unfortunately, Frank reminded me of it one day when we were talking about the initiation process over the phone. Sigh. Now I'll have to work at forgetting this all over again.

3. Variations on the myth of the Descent of the Goddess can be found in several books on Wicca, including Starhawk (1979) *The Spiral Dance*; Farrar and Farrar (1981) *Eight Sabbats for Witches* and (1984) *The Witches' Way*; and Valiente (1987, 1978) *Witchcraft for Tomorrow* and (1989) *The Rebirth of Witchcraft*. This variant is quite close to the one we use in our Circle.

4. See Bado-Fralick (2002) "Mapping the Wiccan Ritual Landscape."

5. Mary Hufford (1995) "Context," 532.

6. This particular ordering of space should not imply a vertical hierarchy in which "up" is more closely associated with "sacred." In my own home many years later, my coven cast its Circles in the basement, because that was where we had sufficient room.

7. See Csordas (1993) "Somatic Modes of Attention"; Daniel (1984)

"The Pulse as an Icon"; Merleau-Ponty (1962) *Phenomenology of Perception*; Schutz (1970) *On Phenomenology and Social Relation*; and Schwartz-Salant (1987) "The Dead Self."

8. Fabian (1994) "Ethnographic Objectivity," 98–99.

9. Csordas (1993) "Somatic Modes of Attention,"138.

10. Csordas (1993) "Somatic Modes of Attention," 138–39.

11. Starhawk (1987) *Truth or Dare* and Parkin (1992) "Ritual as Spatial Direction and Bodily Division."

12. Starhawk (1987) *Truth or Dare.*

13. Rabinovitch (1996) "Spells of Transformation."

14. Ellis (1981) "The Camp Mock-Ordeal."

15. Bauman (1971) "Differential Identity."

16. Kasulis (2002) *Intimacy or Integrity,* 47.

17. Kasulis (2002) *Intimacy or Integrity,* 47–48.

18. Kasulis (2002) *Intimacy or Integrity,* 50.

19. Kasulis (2002) *Intimacy or Integrity,* see especially 24–25 on the differences between intimacy and integrity.

20. Lincoln (1981) *Emerging from the Chrysalis,* 105.

Selected Bibliography

Adler, Margot. 1989. "A Response." Special section on Neopaganism, *Journal of Feminist Studies in Religion* 5.1 (Spring): 97–100.

———. 1979. *Drawing Down the Moon: Witches, Druids, Goddess-Worshippers, and Other Pagans in America Today*. New York: Viking Press.

Anonymous. 1978. *A Book of Pagan Rituals*. New York: Samuel Weiser.

d'Aquili, Eugene G., and Charles D. Laughlin, Jr. 1979. "The Neurobiology of Myth and Ritual." In *The Spectrum of Ritual: A Biogenetic Structural Analysis*, ed. d'Aquili, Laughlin, and McManus, pp. 153–64, 168–82. Reprinted in *Readings in Ritual Studies*, ed. Grimes, pp. 132–45.

d'Aquili, Eugene G., Charles D. Laughlin, Jr., and John McManus, eds. 1979. *The Spectrum of Ritual: A Biogenetic Structural Analysis*. New York: Columbia University Press.

Babcock, Barbara. 1988. "At Home, No Women are Storytellers: Potteries, Stories, and Politics in Cochiti Pueblo." *Journal of the Southwest* 30:357–71.

———. 1978. *The Reversible World*. Ithaca, N.Y.: Cornell University Press.

———. 1977. "The Story in the Story: Metanarration in Folk Narrative." In *Verbal Art as Performance*, ed. Bauman, pp. 61–80.

Bado-Fralick, Nikki. 2002. "Mapping the Wiccan Ritual Landscape: Circles of Transformation." *Folklore Forum* 33.1/2:45–65.

———. 1999. "Spinning in the Moonlight: Women's Rites of Transformation." Unpublished paper given at the American Academy of Religions Conference, Boston, Massachusetts.

———. 1998. "A Turning on the Wheel of Life: Wiccan Rites of Death." *Folklore Forum* 29.1:3–22.

———. 1995a. "The Dynamics of Ritual, Part I. The Rules of the Road: Shifting into Gear." *Mezlim* 6.1:24–26.

———. 1995b. "The Dynamics of Ritual, Part II. Training Wheels." *Mezlim* 6.3:42–44.

———. 1990. "Stirring the Cauldron: The Impact of the Women's Movement on the Old Religion." Unpublished paper given at the American Academy of Religions Conference, New Orleans, La.

———. 1989. "Changing the Face of the Sacred: Women Who Walk the Path of the Goddess." *Explorations* 8.1:5–14. Reprinted in *Mezlim* 2.3 (1991): 24–29.

Barthes, Roland. 1957. *Mythologies.* Paris: Editions du Seuil.

Bauman, Richard, ed. 1977. *Verbal Art as Performance.* Prospect Heights, Ill.: Waveland Press.

———. 1971. "Differential Identity." In *Toward New Perspectives in Folklore,* ed. Paredes and Bauman. Special issue of the *Journal of American Folklore* 84:31–41.

Bell, Catherine. 1992. *Ritual Theory, Ritual Practice.* Oxford: Oxford University Press.

Bethe, Monica and Karen Brazell. 1995 [1990]. "The Practice of Noh Theatre." In *By Means of Performance,* ed. Schechner and Appel, pp. 167–93.

Bonewits, Isaac. 1996. "The Druid Revival in Modern America." In *The Druid Renaissance: The Voice of Druidry Today,* ed. Philip Carr-Gomm, pp. 73–88. London: Thorsons Press.

Bourdieu, Pierre. 1977. *Outline of a Theory of Practice.* Trans. Richard Nice. Cambridge: Cambridge University Press.

Briggs, Charles, and Amy Shuman, eds. 1993. *Theorizing Folklore: Toward New Perspectives on the Politics of Culture.* Special issue of *Western Folklore* 52:109–400.

Brown, Karen McCarthy. 1991. *Mama Lola: A Vodou Priestess in Brooklyn.* Berkeley: University of California Press.

Bruner, Edward M., and Victor Turner, eds. 1986. *The Anthropology of Experience.* Urbana and Chicago: University of Illinois Press.

Buckland, Raymond. 1978. *The Magick of Chant-o-Matics.* West Nyack, N.Y.: Parker.

———. 1971. *Witchcraft from the Inside.* St. Paul, Minn.: Llewellyn.

Budapest, Zsuzsanna E. 1989. *The Holy Book of Women's Mysteries.* Oakland, Calif.: Wingbow. Expanded and revised version of *The Feminist Book of Lights and Shadows.* Venice, Calif.: Luna, 1976.

———. 1979. "Self-Blessing Ritual." In *Womanspirit Rising,* ed. Christ and Plaskow, p. 271.

Bynum, Caroline W. 1984. "Women's Stories, Women's Symbols: A Critique of Victor Turner's Theory of Liminality." In *Anthropology and the Study of Religion,* ed. Robert L. Moore and Frank E. Reynolds, pp. 105–25. Chicago: Center for the Scientific Study of Religion. Reprinted in *Readings in Ritual Studies*, ed. Grimes, pp. 71–85.

Campanelli, Pauline. 1995. *Rites of Passage: The Pagan Wheel of Life.* St. Paul, Minn.: Llewellyn.

———. 1992. *Ancient Ways: Reclaiming Pagan Traditions.* St. Paul, Minn.: Llewellyn.

Carpenter, Dennis. 1996. "Practitioners of Paganism and Wiccan Spirituality in Contemporary Society: A Review of the Literature." In *Magical Religion and Modern Witchcraft*, ed. Lewis, pp. 373–406.

Carpenter, Dennis, and Selena Fox. 1992. "Pagan Spirit Gathering 1991 Tribal Survey Results." *Circle Network News* 45 (Summer): 20.

Christ, Carol P. 1997. *Rebirth of the Goddess: Finding Meaning in Feminist Spirituality.* Reading, Mass.: Addison-Wesley.

———. 1995. *Odyssey with the Goddess: A Spiritual Quest in Crete.* New York: Continuum.

———. 1989. "Embodied Thinking: Reflections on Feminist Theological Method." *Journal of Feminist Studies in Religion* 5.1 (Spring): 7–15.

———. 1987a. *Laughter of Aphrodite: Reflections on a Journey to the Goddess.* San Francisco: Harper & Row.

———. 1987b. "Toward a Paradigm Shift in the Academy and in Religious Studies." In *The Impact of Feminist Research in the Academy*, ed. Christie Farnham, pp. 53–76. Bloomington: Indiana University Press.

Christ, Carol P., and Judith Plaskow, eds. 1979. *Womanspirit Rising: A Feminist Reader in Religion.* San Francisco: Harper.

Circle Magazine. 1999. (73: Fall). Special Issue.

Circle Network News. 1998. (60: Fall). Special Issue.

Clifford, James, and George Marcus, eds. 1986. *Writing Culture: The Poetics and Politics of Ethnography.* Berkeley: University of California Press.

Clifton, Chas S., ed. 1994. *Witchcraft Today, Book Three: Witchcraft and Shamanism.* St. Paul, Minn.: Llewellyn.

———, ed. 1993. *Witchcraft Today, Book Two: Modern Rites of Passage.* St. Paul, Minn.: Llewellyn.

de Coppet, Daniel, ed. 1992. *Understanding Rituals.* London: Routledge.

Crowley, Vivianne. 1989. *Wicca: The Old Religion in the New Age.* Northamptonshire, England: Aquarian.

Csikszentmihalyi, Mihaly. 1990. *Flow: The Psychology of Optimal Experience.* New York: Harper and Row.

Csordas, Thomas, ed. 1997a [1994]. *Embodiment and Experience: The Existential Ground of Culture and Self.* Cambridge: Cambridge University Press.

———. 1997b [1994]. *The Sacred Self: A Cultural Phenomenology of Charismatic Healing.* Berkeley: University of California Press.

———. 1993. "Somatic Modes of Attention." *Cultural Anthropology* 8: 135–56. Reprinted as chapter 9 of *Body/Meaning/Healing.* New York: Palgrave Macmillan, 2002.

Daly, Mary. 1973. *Beyond God the Father: Toward a Philosophy of Women's Liberation.* Boston: Beacon.

———. 1968. *The Church and the Second Sex.* Boston: Beacon.

Daniel, E. Valentine. 1984. "The Pulse as an Icon in Siddha Medicine." *Contributions to Asian Studies* 18:115–26.

Dilthey, W. 1976. *Selected Writings,* ed. and trans. by H. P. Rickman. Cambridge: Cambridge University Press.

Drew, A. J. 1999. *Wicca for Men: A Handbook for Male Pagans Seeking a Spiritual Path.* Secaucus, N.J.: Citadel.

Drewel, Margaret Thompson. 1992. *Yoruba Ritual: Performers, Play, Agency.* Bloomington: Indiana University Press.

Driver, Tom F. 1991. *The Magic of Ritual.* San Francisco: Harper.

Dundes, Alan. 1980. "A Psychoanalytic Study of the Bullroarer." In *Interpreting Folklore,* by Alan Dundes, pp. 177–98. Bloomington: Indiana University Press. Originally published in *Man* (n.s.) 11 (1976): 220–38 by the Royal Anthropological Society.

Eilberg-Schwartz, Howard. 1989. "Witches of the West: Neopaganism and Goddess Worship as Enlightenment Religions." Special Section on Neopaganism in the *Journal of Feminist Studies in Religion* 5.1 (Spring): 65–95.

Eisler, Riane. 1987. *The Chalice and the Blade: Our History, Our Future.* San Francisco: Harper & Row.

Ekman, Paul, Wallace Friesen, and Phebe Ellsworth. 1972. *Emotion in the Human Face.* New York: Pergamon.

Eliade, Mircea. 1969. *The Quest: History and Meaning in Religion.* Chicago: University of Chicago Press.

———. 1964. *Shamanism: Archaic Techniques of Ecstasy.* New York: Pantheon.

———. 1963. *Myth and Reality.* Trans. by Willard Trask. New York: Harper and Row.

———. 1958. *Rites and Symbols of Initiation: The Mysteries of Birth and Rebirth.* Trans. Willard Trask. New York: Harper & Row.

Eller, Cynthia. 1995. *Living in the Lap of the Goddess: The Feminist Spirituality Movement in America.* Boston: Beacon.

Ellis, Bill. 1981. "The Camp Mock-Ordeal: Theater as Life." *Journal of American Folklore* 94.374 (October–December): 486–505.

Emerson, V. F. 1972. "Can Belief Systems Influence Neurophysiology? Some Implications of Research on Meditation." *Newsletter Review,* the R.M. Bucke Memorial Society 5:20–32.

Erikson, Erik H. 1968. "The Development of Ritualization." In *The Religious Situation,* ed. Donald R. Cutler, pp. 711–33. Boston: Beacon. Reprinted in *Readings in Ritual Studies,* ed. Grimes, pp. 201–11.

Erndl, Kathleen. 1993. *Victory to the Mother: The Hindu Goddess of Northwest India in Myth, Ritual, and Symbol.* New York: Oxford University Press.

Evanchuk, Roberta J. 1996. *When the Curtain Goes Up, the Gods Come*

Down: Aspects of Performance in Public Ceremonies of Orisha Worship. UCLA dissertation. Ann Arbor: UMI Dissertation Services.

Fabian, Johannes. 1994. "Ethnographic Objectivity Revisited: From Rigor to Vigor." In *Rethinking Objectivity*, ed. Allan Megill, pp. 81–108. Durham: Duke University Press.

———. 1983. *Time and the Other: How Anthropology Makes Its Object*. New York: Columbia University Press.

———. 1971. "History, Language and Anthropology." *Philosophy of the Social Sciences* 1:19–47.

Falk, Nancy A. 1997. "Crossovers and Cross-ups: A Cautionary Tale." *Religious Studies Newsletter* 12.4 (November): 2.

———. 1993. "Shakti Ascending: Hindu Women, Politics, and Religious Leadership during the Nineteenth and Twentieth Centuries." In *Religion in Modern India* (third edition), ed. Robert Baird, pp. 298–334. Columbia, Mo.: South Asia Publications.

———. 1988. "Value v. Power: A Women's Dilemma." Unpublished manuscript. Delivered at the Midwest American Academy of Religion, Terre Haute, Ind.

———. 1987. "Feminine Sacrality." *The Encyclopedia of Religion* 5:302–12. New York: Macmillan.

———. 1973. "Wilderness and Kingship in Ancient South Asia." *History of Religion* 13.1 (August): 1–15.

Falk, Nancy A., and Rita M. Gross. 1989. *Unspoken Worlds: Women's Religious Lives*. Belmont, Calif.: Wadsworth.

Farrar, Janet, and Stewart Farrar. 1987. *The Life and Times of a Modern Witch*. Custer, Wash.: Phoenix.

———. 1984. *The Witches' Way: Principles, Rituals, and Beliefs of Modern Witchcraft*. London: Robert Hale.

———. 1981. *Eight Sabbats for Witches*. London: Robert Hale.

———. 1971. *What Witches Do: The Modern Coven Revealed*. New York: Coward, McCann, and Geoghegan.

Farrar, Janet, Stewart Farrar, and Gavin Bone. 1998. *Discovering Witchcraft: A Journey through the Elements*. Video produced by Sothis Films.

———. 1995. *The Pagan Path*. Custer, Wash.: Phoenix.

Feintuch, Burt, ed. 1995. *Common Ground: Keywords for the Study of Expressive Culture*. Special issue of *Journal of American Folklore* 108: 391–549.

Flores-Pena, Ysamur. 1998. *"The Tongue Is the Whip of the Body": Identity and Appropriation through Narrative in Lucumi Religious Culture*. UCLA dissertation. Ann Arbor: UMI Dissertation Services.

Gadon, Elinor W. 1989. *The Once and Future Goddess: A Symbol for Our Time*. San Francisco: Harper & Row.

Gardner, Gerald B. 1971 [1954]. *Witchcraft Today*. New York: Citadel Press.

———. 1959. *The Meaning of Witchcraft*. New York: Magickal Childe.

———. 1949. *High Magick's Aid*. Published under the pen name of Scire. London: Michael Houghton.

Gawr, Rhuddlwm. 1986 [1985]. *The Way: A Discovery of the Grail of Immortality, Welsh Witchcraft and the Old Religion*. Athens, Ga.: Camelot.

Geertz, Clifford. 1988. *Works and Lives: The Anthropologist as Author*. Stanford, Calif.: Stanford University.

———. 1983. *Local Knowledge: Further Essays in Interpretive Anthropology*. New York: Basic.

———. 1973. *The Interpretation of Cultures*. New York: Basic.

Gennep, Arnold van. 1960 [1909]. *The Rites of Passage*. Trans. by Monika B. Vizedom and Gabrielle L. Caffee. Chicago: University of Chicago Press.

Gimbutas, Marija. 1989. *The Language of the Goddess*. San Francisco: Harper and Row.

———. 1982 [1974]. *The Goddesses and Gods of Old Europe: Myths and Cult Images*. Berkeley: University of California Press.

Glass, Justine. 1965. *Witchcraft, the Sixth Sense—and Us*. London: Neville Spearman.

Goffman, Erving. 1974. *Frame Analysis: An Essay on the Organization of Experience*. New York: Harper Colophon.

———. 1959. *The Presentation of Self in Everyday Life*. New York: Anchor.

Gold, Ann Grodzins. 1992. *A Carnival of Parting: The Tales of King Bharthari and King Gopi Chand as Sung and Told by Madhu Natisar Nath of Ghatiyali, Rajasthan*. Berkeley: University of California Press.

———. 1987. *Fruitful Journeys: The Ways of Rajasthani Pilgrims*. Berkeley: University of California Press.

Gold, Ann Grodzins, and Gloria Raheja. 1994. *Listen to the Heron's Words: Reimagining Gender and Kinship in North India*. Berkeley: University of California Press.

Goldenberg, Naomi R. 1990. *Returning Words to Flesh: Feminism, Psychoanalysis, and the Resurrection of the Body*. Boston: Beacon.

———. 1979. *Changing of the Gods: Feminism and the End of Traditional Religions*. Boston: Beacon.

Goldstein, Diane E. 1995. "The Secularization of Religious Ethnography and Narrative Competence in a Discourse of Faith." In *Reflexivity and the Study of Belief*, ed. Hufford. Special issue of *Western Folklore* 54.1:223–36.

———. 1989. "Belief and Disbelief: Is Neutralism Really the Issue?: A Response." *Talking Folklore* 1.6:64–66.

Goodman, Felicitas D. 1994. "Shamans, Witches, and the Rediscovery of Trance Postures." In *Witchcraft Today, Book Three*, ed. Clifton, pp. 15–34.

———. 1990. *Where the Spirits Ride the Wind: Trance Journeys and Other Ecstatic Experiences.* Bloomington: Indiana University Press.

———. 1988a. *Ecstasy, Ritual, and Alternate Reality: Religion in a Pluralistic World.* Bloomington: Indiana University Press.

———. 1988b. *How About Demons? Possession and Exorcism in the Modern World.* Bloomington: Indiana University Press.

Green Egg. 1999. (31.129). Special Issue.

Grimes, Ronald L., ed. 1996. *Readings in Ritual Studies.* Englewood Cliffs, N.J.: Prentice Hall.

———. 1995 [1982]. *Beginnings in Ritual Studies* (revised edition). Columbia: University of South Carolina Press. See especially "Interpreting Ritual in the Field," pp. 5–23; "Mapping the Field of Ritual," pp. 24–39; "Jerzy Grotowski's "Poor Theater," pp. 164–76; and "Jerzy Grotowski's Theater of Sources," pp. 177–88.

Gross, Rita M. 1998. *Soaring and Settling: Buddhist Perspectives on Contemporary Social and Religious Issues.* New York: Continuum.

———. 1996. *Feminism and Religion: An Introduction.* Boston: Beacon.

———. 1993. *Buddhism after Patriarchy: A Feminist History, Analysis, and Reconstruction of Buddhism.* Albany, N.Y.: SUNY Press.

———, ed. 1977. *Beyond Androcentrism: New Essays on Women and Religion.* Missoula, Mont.: Scholars.

Grosz, Elizabeth. 1994. *Volatile Bodies: Towards a Corporeal Feminism.* Bloomington: Indiana University Press.

Grotowski, Jerzy. 1968. *Towards a Poor Theatre.* New York: Clarion.

Hackett, Jo Ann. 1989. "Can a Sexist Model Liberate Us? Ancient Near Eastern 'Fertility' Goddesses." Special section on Neopaganism in the *Journal of Feminist Studies in Religion* 5.1 (Spring): 65–76.

Hakeda, Yoshito S. 1972. *Kukai: Major Works.* Translated, with an account of his life and a study of his thought, by Hakeda. New York: Columbia University Press.

Handler, Richard, and Jocelyn Linnekin. 1984. "Tradition, Genuine or Spurious." *Journal of American Folklore* 97:273–90.

Haraway, Donna. 1992. "The Promises of Monsters: A Regenerative Politics for Inappropriate/d Others." In *Cultural Studies*, ed. Lawrence Grossberg, et al., pp. 295–337. New York: Routledge.

Harrow, Judy. 1999. *Wicca Covens: How to Start and Organize Your Own.* Secaucus, N.J.: Citadel.

Harvey, Graham, and Charlotte Hardman. 1995. *Paganism Today: Wiccans, Druids, the Goddess and Ancient Earth Traditions for the Twenty-First Century.* London: Thorsons.

Hick, John. 1997. "Religious Pluralism." In *A Companion to Philosophy of Religion*, ed. Philip L. Quinn and Charles Taliaferro, pp. 607–14. Cambridge, Mass.: Blackwell.

———. 1990. "Religious Faith as Experiencing-as." In *Classical and Contemporary Readings in the Philosophy of Religion*, ed. John Hick, pp. 406–18. Englewood Cliffs, N.J.: Prentice Hall.

Hopman, Ellen Evert, and Lawrence Bond. 1996. *People of the Earth: The New Pagans Speak Out.* Rochester, Vt.: Destiny. Reprinted in 2000 by the same press with the title *Being a Pagan.*

Hufford, David. 1996. "Beings without Bodies." In *Out of the Ordinary: Folklore of the Supernatural,* ed. Walker, pp. 11–45.

———. 1995. "The Scholarly Voice and the Personal Voice: Reflexivity in Belief Studies." In *Reflexivity and the Study of Belief,* ed. Hufford. Special Issue of *Western Folklore* 54.1:57–76. See also his "Introduction," pp. 1–11.

———, ed. 1995. *Reflexivity and the Study of Belief.* Special issue of *Western Folklore* 54.1.

———. 1990. "Rational Skepticism and the Possibility of Unbiased Folk Belief Scholarship." *Talking Folklore* 1.9:19–31.

———. 1987 [1982]. "Traditions of Disbelief." *Talking Folklore* 1.3:19–29. Originally printed in *New York Folklore Quarterly* 1982, 8.3/4: 47–56.

Hufford, Mary. 1995. "Context." In *Common Ground: Keywords for the Study of Expressive Culture,* ed. Feintuch. Special issue of *Journal of American Folklore* 108:528–49.

Huson, Paul. 1970. *Mastering Witchcraft: A Practical Guide for Witches, Warlocks, and Covens.* London: Rupert Hart-Davis.

Hutton, Ronald. 1999. *The Triumph of the Moon: A History of Modern Pagan Witchcraft.* Oxford: Oxford University Press.

———. 1997. *The Stations of the Sun: A History of the Ritual Year in Britain.* Oxford: Oxford University Press.

Jackson, Michael. 1998. *Minima Ethnographica: Intersubjectivity and the Anthropological Project.* Chicago: University of Chicago Press.

———. 1989. *Paths toward a Clearing: Radical Empiricism and Ethnographic Inquiry.* Bloomington: Indiana University Press.

James, William. 1985 [1902]. *The Varieties of Religious Experience: A Study in Human Nature.* New York, London: Penguin.

———. 1976. *Essays in Radical Empiricism.* Cambridge: Harvard University Press.

Jennings, Ted. 1982. "On Ritual Knowledge." *Journal of Religion* 62.2: 111–27. Reprinted in *Readings in Ritual Studies,* ed. Grimes, pp. 324–34.

Jones, Prudence, and Nigel Pennick. 1997 [1995]. *A History of Pagan Europe.* London and New York: Routledge.

Jorgensen, Danny L., and Scott E. Russell. 1999. "American Neopaganism: The Participants' Social Identities." *Journal for the Scientific Study of Religion* 38.3:325–38.

Kapchan, Deborah. 1995. "Performance." In *Common Ground: Keywords for the Study of Expressive Culture,* ed. Feintuch. Special issue of *Journal of American Folklore* 108:479–508.

———. 1994. "Moroccan Female Performers Defining the Social Body." *Journal of American Folklore* 107:82–105.

Kartzer, David. 1988. *Ritual, Politics, and Power.* New Haven: Yale University Press.

Kasulis, Thomas P. 2002. *Intimacy or Integrity: Philosophy and Cultural Difference.* The 1998 Gilbert Ryle Lectures. Honolulu: University of Hawaii Press.

———. 1997. "Intimations of Religious Experience and Interreligious Truth." In *The Recovery of Philosophy in America: Essays in Honor of John E. Smith,* ed. T. P. Kasulis and R. C. Neville, pp. 39–58. Albany, N.Y.: SUNY Press.

———. 1995. "Reality as Embodiment: An Analysis of Kukai's *Sokushinjobutsu* and *Hosshin Seppo.*" In *Religious Reflections on the Human Body,* ed. Law, pp. 166–85.

———. 1993a. "Introduction." In *Self as Body in Asian Theory and Practice,* ed. Kasulis, Ames, and Dissanayake, pp. xi–xxii.

———. 1993b. "The Body—Japanese Style." In *Self as Body in Asian Theory and Practice,* ed. Kasulis, Ames, and Dissanayake, pp. 299–319.

———. 1993c. "Hypocrisy in the Self-Understanding of Religions." In *Inter-religious Models and Criteria,* ed. James Kellenberger, pp. 151–65. New York: St. Martin's.

———. 1992. "Philosophy as Metapraxis." In *Discourse and Practice,* ed. Frank Reynolds and David Tracy, pp. 169–96. Albany, N.Y.: SUNY Press.

———. 1990. "Kukai: Philosophizing in the Archaic." In *Myth and Philosophy,* ed. Frank Reynolds and D. Tracy, pp. 131–50. Albany, N.Y.: SUNY Press.

———. 1987. "Editor's Introduction." In *The Body: Toward an Eastern Mind-Body Theory,* by Yuasa, pp. 1–15.

Kasulis, Thomas, with Roger Ames, and Wimal Dissanayake, eds. 1993. *Self as Body in Asian Theory and Practice.* Albany, N.Y.: SUNY Press.

Kelly, Aidan A. 1991. *Crafting the Art of Magic, Book I: A History of Modern Witchcraft, 1939–1964.* St. Paul, Minn.: Llewellyn.

Kirkpatrick, R. G., R. Rainey, and K. Rubi. 1986. "An Empirical Study of Wiccan Religion in Postindustrial Society." *Free Inquiry in Creative Sociology* 14.1:33–38.

Kmietowicz, Frank A. 1982. *Slavic Mythical Beliefs.* Windsor, Ontario: Author.

———. 1976. *Ancient Slavs.* Stevens Point, Wisc.: Worzalla.

Kodish, Debora. 1993. "On Coming of Age in the Sixties." In *Theorizing Folklore: Toward New Perspectives on the Politics of Culture,* ed. Briggs and Shuman. Special issue of *Western Folklore* 52:193–208.

———. 1987. "Absent Gender, Silent Encounter." *Journal of American Folklore* 100:573–78.

Kuipers, Joel C. 1990. *Power in Performance: The Creation of Textual Authority in Weyewa Ritual Speech.* Philadelphia: University of Pennsylvania Press.

Laderman, Carol, and Marina Roseman, eds. 1996. *The Performance of Healing*. New York: Routledge.

Langer, Susanne K. 1993 [1942] *Philosophy in a New Key: A Study in the Symbolism of Reason, Rite, and Art*. Cambridge, Mass.: Harvard University Press.

Law, Jane Marie, ed. 1995. *Religious Reflections on the Human Body*. Bloomington: Indiana University Press.

Lawless, Elaine J. 1993. *Holy Women, Wholly Women: Sharing Ministries of Wholeness through Life Stories and Reciprocal Ethnography*. Philadelphia: University of Pennsylvania Press.

Leek, Sybil. 1973. *Diary of a Witch*. New York: Signet.

Leland, Charles G. 1998 [1899]. *Aradia or the Gospel of the Witches*. A new translation by Mario Pazzaglini and Dina Passaglini, with additional material by Chas S. Clifton, Robert Mathiesen, and Robert E. Chartowich. Forward by Stewart Farrar. Blaine, Wash.: Phoenix.

Lethbridge, T. C. 1972 [1962]. *Witches: Investigating an Ancient Religion*. Secaucus, N.J.: Citadel.

Lewis, Gilbert. 1980. *Day of Shining Red: An Essay on Understanding Ritual*. Cambridge: Cambridge University Press.

Lewis, James R., ed. 1996. *Magical Religion and Modern Witchcraft*. Albany, N.Y.: SUNY Press.

Liddell, E. W., and Michael Howard. 1994. *The Pickingill Papers: George Pickingill and the Origins of Modern Wicca*. Berks, England: Capall Bann.

Limon, Jose, and Jane Young. 1986. "Frontiers, Settlements and Developments in Folklore Studies, 1972–1985." *Annual Review of Anthropology* 15: 437–60.

Lincoln, Bruce. 1981. *Emerging from the Chrysalis: Studies in Rituals of Women's Initiation*. Cambridge, Mass.: Harvard University Press.

Luhrmann, T. M. 1990. *Persuasions of the Witch's Craft*. Cambridge, Mass.: Harvard University Press.

Mahdi, Louise C., Steven Foster, and Meredith Little. 1987. *Betwixt and Between: Patterns of Masculine and Feminine Initiation*. La Salle, Ill.: Open Court.

Magliocco, Sabina. 1996. "Ritual Is My Chosen Art Form: The Creation of Ritual as Folk Art Among Contemporary Pagans." In *Magical Religion and Modern Witchcraft*, ed. Lewis, pp. 93–120.

Manning, Al G. 1972. *Helping Yourself with White Witchcraft*. West Nyack, N.Y.: Parker.

Matthews, Caitlin. 1989. *The Elements of the Goddess*. Longmead: Element.

Matthews, John, and Caitlin Matthews. 1985. *The Western Way: A Practical Guide to the Western Mystery Tradition* (2 vols.). London: Arkana.

McCutcheon, Russell T. 1999. *The Insider/Outsider Problem in the Study of Religion: A Reader*. London and New York: Cassell.

McFague, Sallie. 1990. "Toward a Metaphorical Theology." In *Classical and Contemporary Readings in the Philosophy of Religion,* ed. John Hick, pp. 433–63. Englewood Cliffs, N.J.: Prentice Hall.

Merleau-Ponty, Maurice. 1964. *The Primacy of Perception and Other Essays,* ed. James M. Edie. Evanston, Ill.: Northwestern University Studies in Phenomenology and Existential Philosophy series.

———. 1962. *Phenomenology of Perception.* Trans. C. Smith London: Routledge.

Miles, Margaret R. 1990. *Practicing Christianity: Critical Perspectives for an Embodied Spirituality.* New York: Crossroad.

Mills, Margaret. 1993. "Feminist Theory and the Study of Folklore: A Twenty-year Trajectory toward Theory." In *Theorizing Folklore: Toward New Perspectives on the Politics of Culture,* ed. Briggs and Shuman. Special issue of *Western Folklore* 52:173–92.

Moore, Sally F., and Barbara G. Myerhoff, eds. 1977. *Secular Ritual.* Assen, The Netherlands: Van Gorcum and Co. B.V.

Morgan, Robin. 1970. *Sisterhood Is Powerful: An Anthology of Writings from the Women's Liberation Movement.* New York: Vintage.

Morris, Brian. 1987. *Anthropological Studies of Religion.* Cambridge: Cambridge University Press.

Morrison, Sarah Lyddon. 1971. *Modern Witch's Spellbook: Everything You Need to Know to Cast Spells, Work Charms and Love Magic, and Achieve What You Want in Life through Occult Powers.* Secaucus, N.J.: Citadel.

Motz, Lotte. 1997. *The Faces of the Goddess.* Oxford: Oxford University Press.

Mullen, Patrick B. 2000. "Belief and the American Folk." *Journal of American Folklore* 113:119–43.

———. 1988 [1978]. *I Heard the Old Fishermen Say: Folklore of the Texas Gulf Coast.* Logan: Utah State University Press.

Murphy, Joseph M. 1994. *Working the Spirit: Ceremonies of the African Diaspora.* Boston: Beacon.

Murray, Margaret. 1970 [1931]. *The God of the Witches.* Oxford: Oxford University Press.

———. 1962 [1921]. *The Witch Cult in Western Europe: A Study in Anthropology.* Oxford: Oxford University Press.

Myerhoff, Barbara G. 1982. "Rites of Passage: Process and Paradox." In *Celebration: Studies in Festivity and Ritual,* ed. Victor Turner, pp. 109–35. Washington, D.C.: Smithsonian Institution Press.

Narayan, Kirin. 1989. *Storytellers, Saints, and Scoundrels: Folk Narrative in Hindu Religious Teaching.* Philadelphia: University of Pennsylvania Press.

Nevadomsky, Joseph, with Norma Rosen. 1988. "The Initiation of a Priestess." *Drama Review, a Journal of Performance Studies* 32.2 (T118) Summer: 186–207.

Obeyesekere, Gananath. 1981. *Medusa's Hair: An Essay on Personal*

Symbols and Religious Experience. Chicago: University of Chicago Press.

O'Connor, Bonnie Blair. 1995. *Healing Traditions: Alternative Medicine and the Health Professions.* Philadelphia: University of Pennsylvania Press.

Olson, Carl, ed. 1983. *The Book of the Goddess Past and Present.* New York: Crossroad.

Orion, Loretta. 1995. *Never Again the Burning Times: Paganism Revived.* Prospect Heights, Ill.: Waveland.

Pagels, Elaine. 1981. *The Gnostic Gospels.* New York: Vintage.

Paredes, Americo, and Richard Bauman, eds. 1971. *Toward New Perspectives in Folklore.* Special issue of the *Journal of American Folklore* 84.

Parkin, David. 1992. "Ritual as Spatial Direction and Bodily Division." In *Understanding Rituals,* ed. de Coppet, pp. 11–25.

Patai, Raphael. 1967. *The Hebrew Goddess.* New York: Avon.

Patton, Laurie L. 1997. "Insider, Outsider, and Gender Identities in the Religion Classroom." *Religious Studies Newsletter* 12.4 (November): 1.

Pearson, Joanne, Richard H. Roberts, and Geoffrey Samuel, eds. 1998. *Nature Religion Today: Paganism in the Modern World.* Edinburgh: Edinburgh University Press.

Plaskow, Judith. 1991. *Standing Again at Sinai: Judaism from a Feminist Perspective.* San Francisco: Harper.

Plaskow, Judith, and Carol P. Christ, eds. 1989. *Weaving the Visions: New Patterns in Feminist Spirituality.* San Francisco: Harper & Row.

Polyani, Michael. 1959. *Personal Knowledge.* Chicago: University of Chicago Press.

Primiano, Leonard. 1995. "Vernacular Religion and the Search for Method in Religious Folklife." In *Reflexivity and the Study of Belief,* ed. Hufford. Special issue of *Western Folklore* 54.1:37–56.

Rabinovitch, Shelley Tsivia. 1996. "Spells of Transformation: Categorizing Modern Neo-Pagan Witches." In *Magical Religion and Modern Witchcraft,* ed. Lewis, pp. 75–92.

Raphael, Melissa. 1996. *Thealogy and Embodiment: The Post-Patriarchal Reconstruction of Female Sacrality.* Sheffield: Sheffield Academic Press.

Rappaport, Roy A. 1999. *Ritual and Religion in the Making of Humanity.* Cambridge: Cambridge University Press.

Robinson, John Mansley. 1968. *An Introduction to Early Greek Philosophy.* Boston: Houghton Mifflin.

Ruether, Rosemary R. 1992. *Gaia and God: An Ecofeminist Theology of Earth Healing.* San Francisco: Harper.

———. 1983. *Sexism and God Talk: Toward a Feminist Theology.* Boston: Beacon.

———. 1975. *New Woman, New Earth: Sexist Ideologies and Human Liberation.* Seabury.

Sax, William S. 1991. *Mountain Goddess: Gender and Politics in A Himalayan Pilgrimage.* Oxford University Press.

Schechner, Richard. 1995 [1990]. "Magnitudes of Performance." In *By Means of Performance,* ed. Schechner and Appel, pp. 19–49.

———. 1985. *Between Theater and Anthropology.* See especially "Points of Contact between Anthropological and Theatrical Thought," pp. 3–33. Philadelphia: University of Pennsylvania Press.

Schechner, Richard, and Willa Appel, eds. 1995 [1990]. *By Means of Performance: Intercultural Studies of Theatre and Ritual.* See especially "Introduction," pp. 1–7. Cambridge: Cambridge University Press.

Schutz, Alfred. 1970. *On Phenomenology and Social Relation,* ed. Helmut R. Wagner. Chicago: University of Chicago Press.

Schwartz-Salant, Nathan. 1987. "The Dead Self in Borderline Personality Disorders." In *Pathologies of the Modern Self,* ed. David M. Levin, pp. 114–62. New York: New York University Press.

Segal, Robert. 1983. "In Defense of Reductionism." *Journal of the American Academy of Religion* 51.1:97–124.

Simpson, Jacqueline. 1988. "Is Neutralism Possible?" *Talking Folklore* 1.4: 12–16.

Sjoo, Monica, and Barbara Mor. 1975. *The Great Cosmic Mother: Rediscovering the Religion of the Earth.* San Francisco: Harper & Row.

Smart, Ninian. 1986. *Concept and Empathy: Essays in the Study of Religion,* ed. Donald Wiebe. New York: New York University Press.

———. 1973. *The Science of Religion and the Sociology of Knowledge: Some Methodological Questions.* Princeton: Princeton University Press.

Smith, Jonathan Z. 1988. "Religion and Religious Studies: No Difference at All." *Soundings* 71.2–3:231–44. Selections reprinted in *Theory and Method in the Study of Religion: A Selection of Critical Readings,* ed. Carl Olson, pp. 25–29. Belmont, California: Wadsworth, 2003.

———. 1978. *Map Is Not Territory: Studies in the History of Religions.* Leiden: Brill.

Smith, Wilfred Cantwell. 1982. "Religious Diversity and Mutual Understanding" In *Religious Diversity,* by Wilfred C. Smith, ed. Willard G. Oxtoby. New York: Crossroad.

Spretnak, Charlene, ed. 1982. *The Politics of Women's Spirituality: Essays on the Rise of Spiritual Power within the Feminist Movement.* Garden City, N.Y.: Anchor.

———. 1978. *Lost Goddesses of Early Greece: A Collection of Pre-Hellenic Myths.* Boston: Beacon.

Starhawk [Miriam Simos]. 1987. *Truth or Dare: Encounters with Power, Authority, and Mystery.* San Francisco: Harper & Row.

———. 1979. *The Spiral Dance: A Rebirth of the Ancient Religion of the Great Goddess.* San Francisco: Harper & Row.

Stein, Diane, ed. 1991. *The Goddess Celebrates: An Anthology of Women's Rituals.* Freedom, Calif.: Crossing.

————. 1987. *The Women's Spirituality Book.* St. Paul, Minn.: Llewellyn.

Stewart, David, ed. 1998 [1980]. *Exploring the Philosophy of Religion.* Englewood Cliffs, N.J.: Prentice-Hall.

Stewart, R. J. 1985. *The Underworld Initiation.* Wellingborough: Aquarian.

Stone, Merlin. 1979. *Ancient Mirrors of Womanhood: Our Goddess and Heroine Heritage.* Vol. I & II. New York: New Sibylline.

————. 1976. *When God Was a Woman.* New York: Dial.

Tambiah, Stanley J. 1990. *Magic, Science, Religion, and the Scope of Rationality.* Cambridge: Cambridge University Press.

Titon, Jeff. 1995. "Text." In *Common Ground: Keywords for the Study of Expressive Culture,* ed. Feintuch, Burt. Special issue of *Journal of American Folklore* 108:432–48.

Turner, Edith, with William Blodgett, Singleton Kahona, and Fideli Benwa. 1992. *Experiencing Ritual: A New Interpretation of African Healing.* Philadelphia: University of Pennsylvania Press.

Turner, Victor. 1995 [1990]. "Are There Universals of Performance in Myth, Ritual, and Drama?" In *By Means of Performance: Intercultural Studies of Theatre and Ritual,* ed. Schechner, Richard, and Appel, pp. 8–18.

————. 1987 [1967]. "Betwixt and Between: The Liminal Period in Rites of Passage." In *Betwixt and Between: Patterns of Masculine and Feminine Initiation,* ed. Mahdi, Foster, and Little, pp. 3–19.

————. 1982. *From Ritual to Theater.* New York: Performing Arts Journal Press.

————. 1974. *Dramas, Fields and Metaphors: Symbolic Action in Human Society.* Ithaca, N.Y.: Cornell University Press.

————. 1969. *The Ritual Process: Structure and Anti-Structure.* Ithaca, N.Y.: Cornell University Press.

————. 1968. *The Drums of Affliction.* Oxford: Clarendon.

Valiente, Doreen. 1989. *The Rebirth of Witchcraft.* London: Robert Hale.

————. 1987 [1978]. *Witchcraft for Tomorrow.* Custer, Wash.: Phoenix.

Walker, Barbara, ed. 1996. *Out of the Ordinary: Folklore of the Supernatural.* Logan: Utah State University Press.

Warner, Marina. 1983. *Alone of All Her Sex: The Myth and the Cult of the Virgin Mary.* New York: Vintage Press.

Weaver, Mary Jo. 1989. "Who Is the Goddess and Where Does She Get Us?" Special section on Neopaganism in the *Journal of Feminist Studies in Religion* 5.1 (Spring): 47–64.

Weber, Max. 1993 [1922]. *The Sociology of Religion.* Trans. by Ephraim Fischoff. Boston: Beacon.

Weckman, George. 1970. "Understanding Initiation." *History of Religions,* Vol. 10.1 (August): 62–79. Chicago: University of Chicago Press.

Wilson, William A. 1995. "Folklore, a Mirror for What? Reflections of a

Mormon Folklorist." In *Reflexivity and the Study of Belief*, ed. Hufford. Special issue of *Western Folklore* 54.1:13–21.

Wittgenstein, Ludwig. 1979. *Remarks on Frazer's Golden Bough*, ed. Rush Rhees. Doncaster: Brynmill.

———. 1972. *Lectures and Conversations on Aesthetics, Psychology, and Religious Belief*, ed. Cyril Barrett, compiled from notes taken by Yorick Smythies, Rush Rhees, and James Taylor. Berkeley: University of California Press.

———. 1958. *Philosophical Investigations*, trans. G.E.M. Anscombe. New York: Macmillan.

Wolford, Lisa. 1996. *Grotowski's Objective Drama Research*. Oxford: University of Mississippi Press.

Wolkstein, Diane, and S. N. Kramer. 1985. *Inanna, Queen of Heaven and Earth: Her Stories and Hymns*. Bloomington: Indiana University Press.

Yoder, Don, ed. 1974. *Symposium on Folk Religion*. Special issue of *Western Folklore* 33.1.

Young, Frank W. 1965. *Initiation Ceremonies: A Cross Cultural Study of Status Dramatization*. Indianapolis: Bobbs-Merrill.

Yuasa Yasuo. 1993. *The Body, Self-Cultivation, and Ki-Energy*, trans. Shigenori Nagatomo and Monte S. Hull. Albany, N.Y.: SUNY Press.

———. 1987. *The Body: Toward an Eastern Mind-Body Theory*, ed. T. P. Kasulis, trans. by Nagatomo Shigenori and T. P. Kasulis. Albany, N.Y.: SUNY Press.

Zarrilli, Phillip. 1995 [1990]. "What Does It Mean to 'Become the Character': Power, Presence, and Transcendence in Asian In-body Disciplines of Practice." In *By Means of Performance*, ed. Schechner and Appel, pp. 131–48.

Zell, Morning Glory. 1975. *Green Egg*. 8.72:43.

Zimmerman, Zora Devrnja. 1986. *Serbian Folk Poetry*. Columbus, Ohio: Kosovo.

———. 1985. "Tradition and Change in a Ritual Feast: The Serbian Krsna Slava in America." *Great Lakes Review* 11.2:21–36.

Index

Altar, 51, 54
Athame
    choosing the right one, 114–15
    and sword, as representatives of fire,
        50
    uses of, 56, 58, 96, 110
Authority, religious
    and gender, 37, 38, 142
    and text, 40–42, 81, 144, 154–
        55n.19

Babcock, Barbara
    and framing devices for ritual, 19,
        126, 156n.2
    and gender in ritual, 20
Blessing
    in dedication, 95, 103, 104
    five-fold, in initiation, 120
Body
    as actor and learner, 78–80, 103, 107–
        8, 129
    in dedication, 102–4, 107–10
    and relation to body-in-practice, 80,
        108, 129
    respect for, 79–80, 104
    See also Body-in-practice
Body-in-practice
    as an achieved state, 80, 107–10, 129–
        31

    as context for creative ritualizing, 81–
        83
    and esoteric knowledge, 108–10, 134–
        38, 144
    and intimacy with Nature-as-
        Person, 125–26, 128, 132
    in performance of Death, 134–39
    somatic modes of attention and, 127,
        130–31, 144
    and transformation of myth, 138–39
Bodymind practice
    breath control, example of, 79, 109–
        10
    driving as, 65, 77–79, 82, 107–10,
        144
    failure in, 73–76, 110
    and training the spirit, 78–80
    See also Driving
Boundary, as problematic, 64
Bright and dark consciousness, 82, 109–
        10
    aspects of integrity and intimacy,
        92, 136–37, 144
    See also Intimacy

Cakes and wine, 58, 106
Calling Down Ceremonies, 44–46
Chalice, 50, 58
    as representative of water, 51

Circle
    as between the worlds, 126–28
    casting or construction as ritual
        space, 49, 54–58, 159n.6
    deconstruction or unmaking, 61, 106
    as intersubjective field, 127, 131,
        144
    as keyed to directions, elements,
        tools, 50
    as liminal space, 126, 128
    as multivalent term, 149n.2
    as transforming process, 126–31
Coven leadership
    avoidance behavior, 69–74
    implications of failure in, 72–76
    levels of skill, 69, 70, 72, 73
Craft name, 55, 114, 159n.2
Culture of disbelief, 7, 9

Death
    as challenge(r), 119, 132, 134–39
    in "Descent of the Goddess" myth,
        121–22, 138–39
    as transformative ritual practice,
        127, 129, 138–39
Dedication, Rite of, 87–111
    analysis of, 96–111
    body in, 102–4, 107–10
    cakes and wine ceremony in, 96,
        106
    in context of intimacy, 92–94
    description of, 94–96
    formal intention required, 88–89, 91
    location of, 97–98
    and Nature-as-Person, 97–98, 103
    no single understanding of, 89–90
    nudity in, 95, 98–101, 102–3
    oath of, 95–96, 105–6
    power dynamics of, 89, 98–102
    as ritual blessing, 95, 103, 104
    role of Goddess in, 104–5
    as screening process, 87–91
    and shift in modes of instruction,
        106–11
    timing of, 96–97
Deities, in Wicca, 35–38
    invocation of, 44–46, 58, 117–18,
        130–31
    as present and alive in the world,
        36, 127, 130

and problem of "Jahweh-in-Drag,"
    36–38
as times for practice, 35–36, 96–97,
    105
See also Goddess; Moon
Dichotomous thinking
    avoiding trap of, 9–14
    and binary absolutes, 5–6, 16, 41
    framed as insider/outsider, 4–7
    inadequacy of, 5–6, 9
Discrimination, religious, 27, 66, 156–
    57n.4, 157n.5
Driver, Tom, 8, 158n.7
Driving
    as bodymind practice, 65, 77–79, 82,
        107–10, 144
    and consequences of failure, 74–75
    as esoteric, 144
    as metaphor for initiation process,
        65, 94, 110
    power dynamics of, 101–2, 133–34
    shift from bright to dark
        consciousness, 109

Elements
    invocation of, 49, 56–57, 117
    represented in Circle, 50
    as purification and transformation,
        120, 129
    symbolized by the pentagram, 49
Elevation, to second degree, 31, 44,
    133, 153n.2
Embodied practice, 137, 139
    religion as, 79–83, 133–34, 144
    See also Bodymind practice; Driving
Esoteric knowledge, 92, 108–10, 136–
    38, 144. See also Intimacy
Ethnicity, and religious practices, 42,
    47, 156n.5

Failure
    in bodymind practice, 73–76, 110
    in coven leadership, 72–76
    in initiation, 155n.2
Feminist Witchcraft, 36–38, 142
Festival movement, Pagan, 31, 32, 66

Gardner, Gerald, 40, 154–55n.19
Gender, 20, 149–50n.6
    composition in the Merry Circle, 47

and ritual nudity, 100
as a theological problem, 44–46
Gennep, Arnold van
rites of passage model, 63, 92–93,
125, 128, 143
Goddess
in dedication, 104–5
and descent myth, in initiation, 121–
22, 138–39
men's identification with, 105, 138
and monotheism, 36–38
as Moon, 35, 96–97, 105
Golden Age of the Goddess, 151n.22
Goldstein, Diane, 8, 19
Grounding and centering, 84–85, 117
Guardians of the Watchtowers, 57, 117–
20

Hiving off, 46, 71, 155n.3
Hufford, David, 7, 13
Hufford, Mary, 19, 126

Individuals-practicing, 41, 144, 151n.20
defined, 153n.30
Initiation, Rite of 113–39
analysis of, 124–39
author's, 26–31
blessing in, 120
and body-in-practice, 129–31
and death, 119, 129, 132, 134–39
"Descent of the Goddess" myth in,
121–22, 138–39
description of, 115–23
failure of, 155n.2
and formal intention, 113
Guardians of the Watchtowers in,
117–20
inadequacy of linear model, 63–64,
92–93, 125, 127–28
and intimacy, 92–93, 134–38
invocation of Deities, 117–18, 130–
31
joking in, 116, 125, 132
as learning process, 63–65, 93, 126,
137, 144
liminality in, 125, 126, 128, 143
and Nature-as-Person, 125–26, 128,
130, 132, 144
oath of, 120, 132, 133
and passwords, 119, 120, 135–38

power dynamics in, 131–38
as shift from integrity to intimacy,
137, 143–44
and somatic modes of attention, 127,
130–31, 144
spatiality and movement in, 124–29
timing and location of, 115, 124,
126
Insider/outsider
avoiding trap of, 9–14
commuting between, 13, 152n.24
insider scholarship as pleading, 7
problem in religious studies, 4–5,
149nn.3–4
as provisional descriptions in
initiation process, 64, 156n.3
and woman as silent gender or
invisible insider, 5, 149–50n.6
See also Dichotomous thinking
Insider pleading, 5, 6–7, 9, 11
Integrity
defined, 92
and paradigm shift to intimacy, 137,
143–44
Intimacy
and coven as community, 91–94, 98,
101, 107
as dark or esoteric, 92, 108–10, 136–
38, 144
defined, 92
with Nature-as-Person, 97–98, 125–
26, 128
and paradigm shift from integrity,
137, 143–44
and power, 101–2, 132, 134–38
as somatic learning, 107–10, 134–38

"Jahweh-in-Drag," 36–38
Joking, ritual, 118, 119, 121
as deliberate framing strategy, 116,
125, 132

Kasulis, Thomas P., 41, 69, 80, 82
and importance of experience,
151n.23
on intimacy and integrity as ways
of relating, 92, 137
on intimacy as esoteric, 136
Kelly, Aidan, 154–55n.19

Kodish, Deborah
    on woman as silent gender, 5, 149–
        50n.6

Language game, 9–13, 64–65
Learning process, 63–65, 76–77, 93
    as Dedicant, 96–97, 101–11
    role of teacher in, 68–76
    somatic nature of, 65, 78–80, 104,
        106–11, 126, 137, 144
    See also Driving
Liminality
    in Circle, 126, 128
    clothing and, 102–3
    in placement at pond, 125
    reflected in ritual teasing and
        silence, 125
    repeating cycles of, 128
Lincoln, Bruce, 102–3, 125, 127, 138

Magic(k), 8, 34, 73, 80, 81, 158n.11
    as intimate knowledge, 135–38, 144
Merry Circle
    composition of, 47
    creation of, 43–46
    elements of ritual in, 48–61
    elevation to second degree and, 44,
        153n.2
    ethnicity and religious practices of,
        47, 156n.5
    gender and, 44–46, 47
    and hiving off, 46, 71, 155n.3
    public outreach and, 66–68
Methodologies used in this work, 17–
    21
Moon
    cycles keyed to events, 35, 96–97,
        105, 124
    identified with Virgin Mary, 24, 27
    men's identification with, 105
    as Triple Goddess, 35, 96–97, 105

Nature-as-Person, 158n.7
    in dedication, 97–98, 103
    in initiation, 125–26, 128, 130, 132,
        144
    member of spiritual community, 34,
        115
Nudity, ritual, 55, 95, 98–104

Oath
    of dedication, 95–96, 105–6
    of initiation, 120, 132, 133

Pagan, contemporary, 32, 33, 153n.3
Parent coven
    author's initiation into, 26–31
    confidentiality and secrecy in, 27–
        29, 30–31
    dissolution of, 31–32, 71, 72
    elevation from, 31, 44, 153n.2
    and problem of gender roles, 44–46
Passwords, 119, 120, 135–38
Pentacle, as representative of earth, 50,
    51
Pentagram, 49–50
Philosophy, 14–21
Power
    dynamics in dedication, 89, 98–102
    dynamics in initiation, 131–8
    as a theological problem, 44–46
Praxis, defined, 150n.8

Reductionism, 5–9
    and secularization of religions, 8,
        150n.12
Reflexivity
    assessment of, 141–43
    within the culture of disbelief, 7
    as methodology, 13–15
    religious, author's, 23–32
    scholarly, author's, 14–21
Religion
    as dynamic tradition, 41–42,
        155n.24
    misnaming as official and folk, 41
    as somatic or embodied practice, 78–
        80
Religious upbringing, author's, 23–26
Ritual
    as deliberately constructed, 39, 80–
        83
    as embodied and gendered process,
        20
    and experiential reality, 61, 134–38
    as pedagogy, 84–85, 104, 106–11,
        144
    space, 48–49, 54–58, 129, 159n.6
    tools, 50–51

See also Dedication, Rite of;
    Initiation, Rite of
Robe, 93–94, 105–6

Sam. See Parent coven
Skyclad. See Nudity, ritual
Somatic
    knowledge and intimacy, 92, 137
    learning in religious praxis, 65, 78–
        80, 104
    modes of attention, 127, 130–31,
        144
    practices as a paradigm shift, 78–83,
        107–10, 137, 139, 143
    See also Driving
Space
    neutral, in teaching 76–77
    ritual, 48–49, 54–58, 129, 159n.6
    See also Circle
Subjectivity, shared, 127, 130–31
Sword, 50
    and challenge at initiation, 119, 129,
        134, 135, 137
    in Circle casting, 56, 129
    in oaths, 95–96, 106, 120, 132

Text. See Authority, religious
Tradition, as dynamic, 40–42, 155n.24
Tripartite models of rites of passage
    inadequacy of, 63–64, 92–93, 127–28
    shifting of, 92, 125, 143
Triple Goddess, 35, 96–97, 105
Turner, Victor, 102, 125

Van Gennep, Arnold. See Gennep,
    Arnold van
Virgin Mary, as the Moon, 24, 27

Wand, as representative of air, 50
Wheel of the Year, defined, 34
White-handled knife, 50, 51
Wicca, Witchcraft
    confidentiality of members in, 27–
        28, 68
    as distinct from Satanism, 32, 49–50
    as distinct practices, 32
    diversity of, 32–34
    overview of, 33–42
    and public outreach, 66–69, 156–
        57n.4
    and religious discrimination, 27, 66,
        156–57n.4, 157n.5
    structure and organization of, 38–
        39
    as terms used interchangeably in
        this book, 26, 32, 153n.1
    as Western Mystery Tradition, 33–
        34
    women's roles in, 37–38, 154n.14
    See also Feminist Witchcraft
Wittgenstein, Ludwig. See Language
    game

Yuasa Yasuo
    and bodymind practice, 73, 80, 82
    and bright and dark consciousness,
        109, 110